P9-AFZ-863

The Hinckley Guide to
Yacht Care

THE HINCKLEY GUIDE TO
Yacht Care

How to Keep Your Boat the Hinckley Way

HENRY R. HINCKLEY III

INTERNATIONAL MARINE
CAMDEN, MAINE

International Marine/
Ragged Mountain Press
A Division of The **McGraw-Hill** Companies

2   4   6   8   10   9   7   5   3   1

Library of Congress Cataloging-in-Publication Data

Hinckley, Henry R.
    The Hinckley guide to yacht care : how to keep your boat the
Hinckley way / Henry R. Hinckley III
        p.   cm.
    Includes index.
    ISBN 0-07-028997-2 (acid-free paper)
    1. Yachts—Maintenance and repair.   I. Title.
VM331.H56   1997
623.8'2023—dc21   97–15960
                                                                      CIP

Questions regarding the content of this book should be addressed to:
International Marine
P.O. Box 220
Camden, ME 04843

Questions regarding the ordering of this book should be addressed to:
The McGraw-Hill Companies
Customer Service Department
P.O. Box 547
Blacklick, OH 43004
Retail customers: 1-800-262-4729
Bookstores: 1-800-722-4726

The Hinckley Guide to Yacht Care is printed on acid-free paper
and is set in 10 point Electra, with old style numbers.

Prepress and color by 4-Colour Imports, Ltd.
Printed by R.R. Donnelley and Sons, Crawfordsville, IN
Design by Dan Kirchoff
Production by Dan Kirchoff and Mary Ann Hensel
All illustrations by Jim Sollers
All black-and-white photography by David Westphal unless otherwise noted
Edited by Jonathan Eaton; Kathryn Mallien; Jon Cheston; Nancy Hauswald
Principal color photography by Neil Rabinowitz
unless otherwise noted.

DEDICATION

*This book is dedicated to Henry R. Hinckley II,
my father, founder of Henry R. Hinckley & Company*

Contents

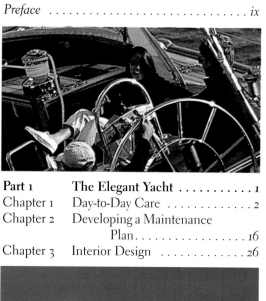

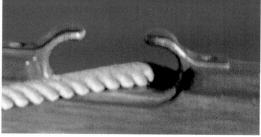

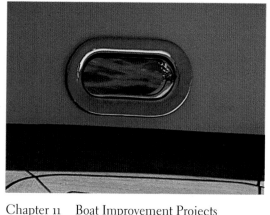

Acknowledgments

This book could not have been completed without the help of many people. As this is the first project of this scope that I have ever tried, the number of folks who were besieged with questions and requests is no doubt extraordinarily high. I wish to thank all these people for their help.

The people at the Hinckley Company have been of immeasurable help and have given freely of their time and talents. Rig Reese and Marnie Wright helped set up the project and provide access to the Hinckley photo library. My brother, Hinckley President Bob Hinckley, and Chairman Shep McKenney put me in touch with the people who had the information I needed.

Also within the company, John Pratt, the assistant service manager; Patrick Lucey, paint supervisor for service; Garnet Johnson, head of the sewing department; and Henry Wilensky-Lanford, head of electronics, along with many others, freely shared ideas, experience, and time.

Greg Smith and others in my small organization reviewed and edited several chapters.

Hinckley customers are always the best sources for ideas on upgrading boats. Many have passed on their experiences to me and I've included them in this book as sidebars. I regret that I was only able to use a few of the many terrific ideas they shared.

I had no idea how much time and work it would take to write this book when Jon Eaton of International Marine looked at my early manuscript and said it would fly. Since that time, I have tested his patience and challenged his editing skills. He has been supportive throughout the project, even as I stumbled.

I owe thanks to my daughter, Julia, who read the articles I had pulled together and suggested I talk to someone about publishing the work. As I recall, she said, "I didn't fall asleep when I read it as I expected to." Wonderful people, daughters.

Marla Major joined me and helped with both editing and ideas. She also gently nudged me to keep things moving.

David Westphal, a longtime friend who has worked with me in the past building boats, has incredible photographic talent. Filmmaking is his love, but he was persuaded to shoot the bulk of still photography seen here. He also selected the work of others to complete the visual parts of the book.

Finally, a host of others who work for the many companies contacted for information gave freely of their expertise. They, too, deserve a heartfelt thank you.

Preface

Yacht maintenance has always fascinated me. I have been involved with yacht care pretty much all my life. Even when I held honest jobs—that is, jobs outside the marine industry—I stayed in touch with friends who had boats and old customers and acquaintances who shared my interests. The subject always turns to boats, and this book has grown from that interest.

This book is for boatowners who wish to perform more maintenance chores on their boats, as well as those who wish only to know more about what goes into maintaining a boat. It is not, by any means, a complete treatise on all aspects of boat maintenance. It is targeted primarily to the owner (or potential owner) of power- or sailboats in the 20- to 50-foot range.

Throughout the book, I share tips on day-to-day care, as well as thoughts on interior design and decoration. In addition, I discuss varnish and paint work, fiberglass techniques, the basics of mechanical and electrical systems, and rigging. For do-it-yourself boatowners, I've included a few upgrade and improvement projects.

Some of the information is presented in a step-by-step format; some is in a narrative style. All of it aims to help you be an informed consumer.

Some boaters learn how to perform certain basic maintenance chores because they like to maintain the beauty of their vessels. Others learn because the cost of having a boatyard do all their maintenance is prohibitively high. For everyone, getting behind on maintenance means unnecessary added expense and, frequently, the hassle of having to replace gear. It also means decreased value in what may well be one of your most valuable assets.

I have been involved in the marine industry for more than thirty years and have seen the costs of maintaining a boat rise tremendously. During that time, equipment has become more sophisticated on the one hand, yet easier to maintain on the other. And increased taxes on waterfront property, environmental costs, and escalating labor rates have added to the hourly rate at boatyards. My point? Almost every boater needs to be an informed participant and consumer when it comes to yacht care.

But beyond the cost element, becoming more familiar with your boat's maintenance needs brings peace of mind. You know that you will be able to handle most problems that arise. Have you ever seen a boat towed in to a yard with an overheated engine because someone hadn't cleaned the strainers regularly? (Overheating, of course, may lead to cracks in the block or burned gaskets, both of which may mean the end of the engine.) Or how about the boater in the next slip who hasn't checked out the through-hulls and hoses lately? Want to go offshore on that boat? And then there is the owner who, because of the cost, tries to squeeze a few extra weeks from the brightwork. A few weeks become a month or so, and "suddenly" the varnish is lifting and needs to be wooded. This means a lot more work, cost, and lost boating time.

Experienced cruisers know the importance of

preventive maintenance. They look for problems before they become serious. They tear down seemingly perfect equipment just to check it over and regrease or oil it.

Without question, maintenance requirements vary greatly from boat to boat because of variations in size and design. But all boats require maintenance. If you keep your boat shipshape, you will save money and enjoy your boating time more. This book will help you do so.

Today, The Hinckley Company builds yachts that roam all around the world. The quality of these yachts is renowned; so is the service. Parts and information are dispensed from the yard in Southwest Harbor, Maine, to all corners of the globe. Hinckley customers expect to receive the highest level of service, and indeed, they do.

It takes more than desire to provide such a high level of performance and to provide it quickly. The people who work at The Hinckley Company must have a thorough knowledge of a broad range of subjects. These folks are curious about all things nautical and have a deep-seated desire to be the best.

One Hinckley customer once told me that, without people, a company is nothing but a pile of paper. For my money, The Hinckley Company has the best: the folks from the coast of Maine. Any boat will benefit from the treatment bestowed by The Hinckley Company on the boats built by or kept with them. The idea behind this book is that there is an audience of boaters out there who would like to know how.

I hope you glean some useful ideas from the information presented here and enjoy the images of boatbuilding at its finest.

(opposite page) Taking care of a yacht requires some dockside time. Whether yours is a powerboat or sailboat, knowing that it is well maintained and in top operating condition will bring you peace of mind.

PART 1

The Elegant Yacht

CHAPTER 1

Day-to-Day Care

Day-to-day care is the cornerstone of boat maintenance, and for many boatowners, puttering around the boat is relaxing. They and others get great pleasure from seeing a boat that has been well cared for.

Your boat is one of the largest investments you are likely to make. Therefore, it behooves you to take some time on a regular basis to wash, ventilate, and generally maintain your boat—if not for the joy of messing about in boats, then for financial reasons. This chapter is an overview of basic maintenance procedures you should regularly perform. Although many of these suggestions may be obvious, they still warrant a brief discussion. Some of the more complex areas of boat maintenance, such as engine and fiberglass care, are expanded upon in whole chapters.

Washing Down

On any boat—fiberglass, metal, or wood—the sun, accrued grime, and acid rain deposits combine to cause the surface finishes to fade. In addition, saltwater boaters need to protect their boats from the effects of salt. If a boat's surfaces are protected and pollutants are not allowed to accumulate too long, these damaging materials are easily removed by washing. Left unprotected and unwashed, painted and varnished surfaces will lose their gloss, anodized aluminum will fade, and covering materials such as canvas and vinyl will deteriorate faster.

When you come in from a day on the water, check for any dirt, soot, or salt on the deck and take the time to wash down. You will be the best judge of whether you need to use just fresh water or an appropriate boat soap. If the boat is clean except for salt accumulation, just rinse off the salt. Then use a chamois to wipe off as much excess water as possible (The Absorber, a synthetic chamois, is an excellent choice). At the least, wipe the brightwork and glass to prevent water spots.

When using soap, stick with one of the many biodegradable products on the market (see sidebar, page 3). It pays to protect the environment, and these cleaners are "boat friendly" also.

The Hinckley dock crew use Sudbury Boat Zoap and Star brite Boat Wash In A Bottle for general washdown. For molded nonskid areas, they often use Star brite Nonskid Deck Cleaner.

If possible, avoid using abrasive cleaners except for the toughest stains. The abrasive materials will actually remove a bit of the surface. When they are necessary, use them sparingly and be sure to rinse the surface liberally with water when done. Consider stain removal products such as Y-10 and other cleaners that have little or no abrasive properties, yet are able to remove most of the stains that the gentler boat soaps do not. These products also require substantial rinsing when complete, and be careful—unrinsed residue may damage varnish and paint surfaces. Read instructions carefully.

If a gelcoat surface has been scrubbed clean and the wax has been removed, rewax the area. 3M "One Step" Fiberglass Cleaner and Wax is finding favor at Hinckley as an excellent wax for both hull and deck use with gelcoat surfaces. Keep wax off nonskid areas to avoid slippery footing. Chapter 8 provides more detailed information on surface protection.

Some boaters face restrictions on the use of fresh water. A rainy day then becomes a blessing, and it is helpful to wipe down after a rain storm. If rain is in short supply, wipe surfaces before salt water evaporates and leaves a salt film; this is better than no attention at all. A bucket of fresh water will also help.

When water restrictions are in effect, covering part or most of the boat (see "Using Covers," page 5) becomes more important. Obviously, covers will not completely protect surfaces from salt accumulation at sea, but they will minimize the effects of sun and air pollution.

Cleaning Teak Decks

Teak decks are a beautiful addition to most boats, but caring for them is a concern for many owners as it can be time consuming. The trick, as with so much day-to-day care, is to not let the maintenance get ahead of you. There are three levels of cleaning for teak decks: normal day-to-day washing; cleaning with a special teak cleaner; and using two-part teak cleaners and bleaching products. If none of these produces an acceptable look, consider sanding the deck. Let's look briefly at each of these options.

Cleaning a teak deck periodically with a soft brush and a mild soap such as Sudbury Boat Zoap or Star brite Boat Wash In A Bottle, along with the regular washdown, will usually do a good job of maintaining it. Use the brush cautiously, though, because overenthusiastic scrubbing will abrade the softer fiber in the wood surface. Contrary to usual inclination, you should brush across the grain, not with it. For more intense cleaning, 3M Scotch Brite white or gray scrubbing pads or Gerson Scuff-Rite nylon abrasive pads work well. Remember to keep the deck wet while cleaning and lightly brush the surface during rinsing to help ensure complete soap removal. The process is much the same as the washdown procedure.

For teak decks that need more cleaning to remove the dirt and oil buildup, you will need to use a teak cleaner. I've had good luck with these two: BoatLIFE Teak Brite Teak Cleaner and Star brite Sea Safe Biodegradable Teak Cleaner. First, rinse the deck with lots of water; teak cleaners typically contain some mild bleaching properties as well as abrasives, both of which can be harmful to painted and varnished surfaces.

Unless a deck has a significant accumulation of oil and dirt, teak cleaners such as these should do the job. If you're looking for a generic approach, trisodium phosphate (TSP) works well and is readily available from paint and hardware stores. Mix this saltlike material with warm water and apply evenly over the wet deck. Let it stand for a few minutes before washing it off with lots of fresh

What is Biodegradable?

Ask major suppliers about currently available boat soaps and you will hear a wide range of definitions of what is "biodegradable." Some claims seem to assume that because water is the universal solvent, darn near everything will biodegrade over time. The prudent solution is to avoid cleaning products with phosphates, solvents, strong acids, or alkalis whenever possible.

water. Be sure to rinse off the whole boat, because TSP will affect other surfaces as well.

If the teak is badly stained and will not respond to teak cleaner, you'll have to try the commercial two-part wood cleaner/bleach products such as Snappy Teak-Nu and Travaco Te-Ka Teak Wood Cleaner. These products contain caustic (part A) and acid (part B) components. It is highly recommended that you use twice as much part B as part A; it is imperative to neutralize the action of part A so as not to leave black spots in the wood and etching on other surfaces.

Apply these products carefully, with proper boat and personal protection. Wear boots, gloves, and glasses at the least. An old pair of foul-weather pants is great. To protect the boat, tape off the surrounding area and, if possible, cover any brightwork and topsides with plastic sheets— these powerful cleaners will do a job on both.

1. Wet the wood and surrounding area completely.

2. Apply part A with a brush, being careful to spread it evenly. Allow it to set; it will turn black as dirt and oil are lifted from the wood.

3. Apply a second coat of part A to further clean the grain.

4. Scrape off the excess goo from the surface with a plastic or wood scraper. Keep a heavy-duty plastic bag handy for this purpose. This step is not essential, but it will help part B do its job.

5. Apply part B to the surface to neutralize part A. You may need to do this repeatedly to totally deactivate part A (which is why I suggest above that you buy extra part B). The surface color will improve as part B takes effect.

6. When you are sure that part A has been neutralized, wash the deck, scrubbing gently to remove the excess material. Continue rinsing the deck and hull until you are confident that you have completely removed all traces of the cleaner.

(opposite page) Teak decks are a beautiful addition to a fiberglass yacht and also improve traction on the foredeck for crew. They will, however, require some additional maintenance to keep their rich, golden look.

Although this sounds like a deadly procedure, it need not be if you handle the material carefully and rinse the deck thoroughly.

Sanding a teak deck will bring back the color and texture. Sanding is a last resort, though, because it means removing a layer of wood and possibly lifting plugs in the deck's surface. The decision to sand or not will be influenced by the condition and thickness of the deck. Sanding may be the only reasonable means of removing deep wear from the wood.

Try these teak cleaning procedures in the sequence I have described. Unless the deck has gone a long time without care, the final step should not be needed often. The middle step— cleaning with a teak cleaner—is a good procedure to do annually.

Using Covers

Canvas or vinyl covers are increasingly being used to protect surfaces from the ravages of sun and other elements. Covers on binnacles, winches, and electronics are a familiar sight. Now we also see covers on varnished hatches and toe-rails. I've seen complete boat covers on some boats. Many of these covers are not difficult to

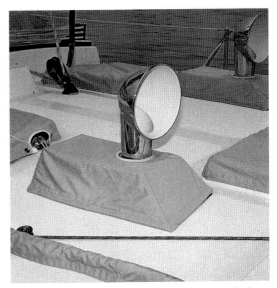

Covers go a long way toward protecting varnished surfaces.

make and can be sewn on a heavy-duty sewing machine.

One important consideration in designing any cover is to incorporate proper fastening. A cover that flaps about in the wind will rapidly deteriorate; one that blows or washes off the surface it is supposed to protect isn't much help. Whenever possible, use snaps, turn posts, and good marine-quality hooks to hold protective covers in place—and don't skimp on the quantity. A cover that is held with elastic or shock cord may not have enough holding power to make it through a good windstorm.

Canvas and Exterior Fabrics

Thorough washing with fresh water is good medicine for all exterior fabrics. Dodgers, cockpit cushions, sailcovers, and sails all benefit from such cleaning. Salt water leaves a residue on fabric that attracts and holds moisture on the surface. Mildew loves a moist environment and, if not cleaned off quickly, may leave a permanent stain.

Sails that are damp with salt water, especially in warm climates, and then stowed, are particularly subject to mildew. If they are bagged or furled when wet, they'll be wearing ugly, dark stains when they are unfurled later. This is especially a problem with the newer Dacron-and-Mylar sailcloth combinations that do not breathe. Whenever possible, rinse sails with fresh water if they have been sprayed with salt water, then dry them thoroughly before putting them away. Fortunately, synthetic sailcloth dries quickly when hung. (See Chapter 21, Sail Care and Maintenance, for more

information on caring for and washing sails.)

The undersides of dodgers and awnings also attract mildew. Products such as Star brite Mildew Stain Remover and Rule Marine Grade Mildew Stain Remover help, but prevention is the best medicine. A hint for taking care of dodger windows: Use Johnson Wax's Pledge. It will help keep them clear and flexible. Try plastic scratch–remover for repairing scratches in the windows.

Cleaning Metallic Deck Hardware

Cleaning chrome and stainless is easier if they are not allowed to deteriorate too far. Stainless, in particular, can be frustrating. It is *not* stain-free. It is simply stain-*less* steel. Surface rust on stainless steel is a real irritant to most new boatowners; it is caused by impurities in the metal and from the forming tools used in its manufacture. Passivation (removing the ferrous material by using acid and a mild electrical current) of the metal will help remove the impurities. This process is most often used when the metal part is manufactured. It is not practical for most owners after the hardware is installed.

The only realistic solution is to polish the metal; in time, the surface rusting will slow. Be forewarned, however—in most cases it does not entirely stop. Waxing the metal after polishing it will help retard the surface deterioration but is not practical on hardware that needs traction to work, such as winches and step pads.

If you are purchasing new stainless steel hardware, look for 316 alloy, the preferred alloy for marine use.

The Beauty of Stainless Steel

In order to cover his scratched and worn windlass, a Hinckley B-40 owner, Bruce Ferretti, replaced his galvanized chain with stainless steel anchor chain; he leaves it wrapped around the windlass. Getting rid of the deck stains from galvanized chain was an added bonus. Replace galvanized shackles and the safety wire on the shackle pins with stainless steel as well, and, as Bruce tells us, "the bow will gleam with super-strong, self-cleaning stainless steel."

Lines, Pendants, and Fenders

The lines on many boats are allowed to degrade to such a horrible state that they are, or should be, an embarrassment to their owners. It takes little time and effort to maintain lines and, if worn out, they are relatively inexpensive to replace compared with the potential cost of damage to the boat.

Although storing wet lines in a locker may be necessary at times, you should avoid doing so whenever possible. Wet lines in a locker are not good for the lines or the locker; trapping moisture below decks is an invitation to rot. Lines that have been soaked in salt water should be rinsed in fresh water and dried before they are stored for any lengthy period to reduce the chance of

Smooth, well-shaped chocks, such as this midrail chock on a Hinckley yacht, are critical to obtaining long life from docking lines.

mildew and rot. Hang the lines on a lifeline or rail to facilitate drying. Anchor lockers are notorious for their moldy, damp atmosphere. Make sure you have plenty of ventilation and draining capabilities in anchor lockers and lazarettes where wet items are sometimes kept.

For years I have washed lines by placing them in a clothes washer with a mild detergent. For tough stains, I used a laundry presoak product such as BIZ. In preparation for this book, I talked with folks at Yale Cordage about caring for lines. They told me that they do not recommend washing lines with any chemicals because they remove the finish of the line, which in turn reduces its strength and performance characteristics. Therefore, I recommend that when absolutely necessary you place a line in a suitable cloth or net bag and wash it in a machine with little or no laundry detergent. The line must be thoroughly rinsed (completely free of chemicals) and dried after this process. Remember, washing is generally not good for the line, so don't do it more often than necessary.

When docking line loops become worn, consider changing the end you use—if the rest of the line is okay and the length allows. Splice a loop in the good end, serve the end adjacent to the old loop, and cut off the damaged loop. If an anchor line is worn in spots, consider cutting out the worn places and using it as a docking line.

Let me reinforce the importance of replacing lines that are suspect. The strength of a line decreases rapidly as individual threads are cut.

Make a practice of checking docklines or mooring lines whenever you are aboard. Well-meaning boaters tying alongside may knock a line out of a chock or improperly retie a line after removing theirs. I remember lectures from my father about passing the looped end of a docking line ashore and taking up the slack aboard the boat. In addition to giving control to the person aboard the boat, this practice kept the coil of extra line off the dock. Also, if someone had to remove the loop for some reason, replacing it at the same tension was no problem. Use springlines and avoid short line leads that can pull out fittings when a large wake rolls past the dock.

Chafe gear is an excellent idea for a boat that is tied for any length of time in one spot, and it's also good insurance for anchor and mooring lines when you are away from the boat and a storm comes up. You can buy commercially available chafe gear or make it yourself from hose or leather. To see the heart-breaking results of inadequate chafe gear, all you have to do is leaf through any boating magazine after hurricane season. Just imagine coming around the last corner to the harbor and seeing your boat high and dry on the beach.

Ample fenders are a must for protecting the topsides. One of my worst fears when I was a boatyard manager was having customers come in, tie up their boats, leave the fenders in what appeared to be a good position, and take off. Then the tide or wind would move them out of position, leaving the topsides exposed to damage from the dock. Take the time to check your

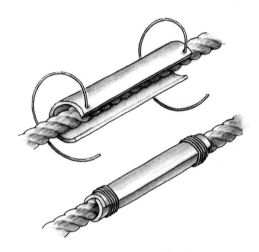

Chafe gear need not be high tech to work well. This style is simply a split hose with lines to secure it in place.

fender arrangement for all likely wind and tide combinations. Some problems can be reduced by a careful job of tying the boat. Whenever possible, tie up so your boat will not press against the dock at any time.

Buy good fenders that can be properly secured. Fenders that are too hard will destroy a paint finish. Your dock may require the use of other docking aids, such as fender boards.

If your topsides are painted, consider buying fender covers to protect the topsides from fender wear—but keep the covers clean! Using terry cloth fender covers is a great idea because they can be easily washed, which will keep them doing their job well. Fenders are always picking up tar and grime from pilings and other docks. I have found that wiping the fenders with corrosion preventive sprays, such as CRC or WD-40, does a good job of removing this type of mess from most plastic fenders and dockside gear. Automotive tar removers will also work.

One final bit of advice: Occasionally move or retie your boat to minimize fender abrasion.

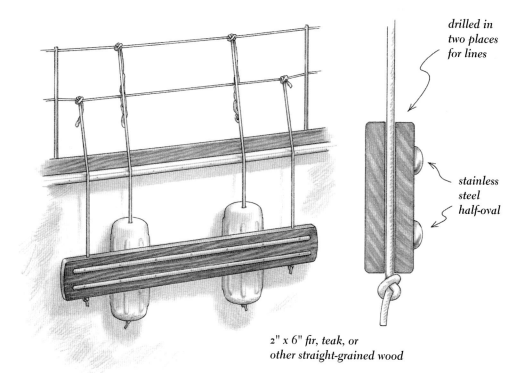

*drilled in
two places
for lines*

*stainless
steel
half-oval*

2" x 6" *fir, teak, or
other straight-grained wood*

*You can make or purchase terry cloth covers. They
reduce the abrasion of fenders on topside paint and
can be easily removed and washed.*

*If you tie alongside pilings, a fender board, along
with a couple of large fenders, provides good protection from chafe.*

Ventilating the Interior

Proper ventilation is of great importance in a
boat. It is critical for crew comfort, maintaining
an odor-free interior, and for the long-term health
of equipment and of the boat itself.

When a boat is in use, its hatches and ports
are open and people move in and out, opening
and closing doors. All this, along with the engine
and blowers, helps ventilate the interior spaces.
An inactive boat, however, may be closed tighter
than a drum. The hull and deck sweat, ports leak,
the engine block condenses, and mold and
mildew start to grow. Moisture in the interior will
swell doors and drawers to the point that they no
longer work. Interior hardware, metal surfaces,
and electronics will start to corrode. The chal-

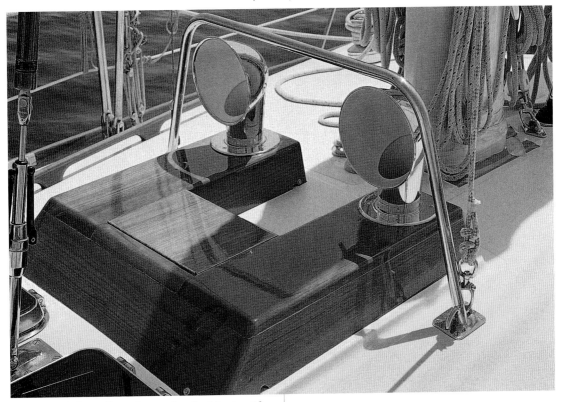

This Dorade box offers other services besides providing air below. Storage in the forward section is handy, and the rail is well placed for crew support near the mast.

lenge for both builder and owner is to minimize this process.

Obviously, in order to maintain a clean-smelling boat, the interior must be clean. Thoroughly scrub locker interiors. Use bilge cleaner under the sole and oil absorbers around engines and generators to remove sources of odor. When the boat interior is clean, it is time to examine how to keep it smelling that way.

Much of what is wrong with many boat ventilation systems is incorporated at the design or manufacturing stage. It is often difficult and costly to install an effective ventilation system in a boat because it must please the eye, not take up excessive interior or deck space, work when the boat is at sea, and, perhaps more importantly, work when the boat is not in use. Dorade ventila-

tors, opening ports, and interior ducting are all important components of an effective ventilation system but add cost to the final product. (See Chapter 11 for more on Dorade vents.)

Different venting problems require different solutions. For example, a boat kept on a mooring has different air collection needs than a boat kept in a slip. Of course, since most boats will see moorings and slips in the course of their lives, a good ventilation system accounts for a variety of air circulation and collection needs.

A boat that is kept on a mooring usually has its bow headed into the wind, and large ventilators placed at strategic locations around the deck will direct air below. Dorade ventilators will do the job nicely while at the same time permitting the passage of a minimum of water.

A typical boat has several vents. Starting in the bow, a cowl vent placed above the chain locker will push air through the forward parts of the boat. If you want to keep chain odor out of the rest of the boat, you may need entrance and exit vents. Additional vents that face forward over the heads, sleeping accommodations, and galley will add to the flow of fresh air.

A ventilation system must also include exit vents or grates of some sort in the after sections of the boat to allow air to escape. On some boats, these will be ventilators with their cowls facing aft. On other boats, grates or slots in companion-way closures or dedicated discharge ventilators will do the trick. Regardless, the exit vents must exceed the volume capacity of the intake vents to prevent pressure buildup within a boat's interior.

You can improve your boat's interior ventilation by opening any doors (and securing them so they will not bang) and, if possible, opening the bilges in a few places. You can even open the engine room door or hatch—if doing so does not create a safety hazard. If they are not already installed, put cabin door hooks on doors to hold them partially open. Consider using louvered vents in solid doors for air passage.

When a boat is tied to a dock, providing air flow becomes more difficult. The same ventilation scheme used on a mooring may work if the prevailing breeze is from the bow or stern of the boat. It would be important to face the cowls forward in the bow and aft in the stern, thus allowing for a draft in either direction. However, steady fore-and-aft breezes can rarely be depended upon. Ideally, the ventilators can turn to accommodate a cross wind, although it is unlikely that someone will be around all the time to turn them. As always, the key is to provide both air intake and discharge.

Where the wind is light or restricted by other boats, solar-powered vents placed around the boat are helpful. They install easily on deck or hatches and require no electrical hookup; the small, low-power fan suffices to keep air moving through the vent. Other low-voltage fan-equipped vents are available, but they require power to operate, which may or may not drain the boat's battery bank. I would hesitate to leave one running unattended for any length of time.

Additional light-air boat ventilation is afforded by fabric wind chutes. These large, cowl-like vents can be attached to hatches and ventilators to increase the air flow. They are often used in forward

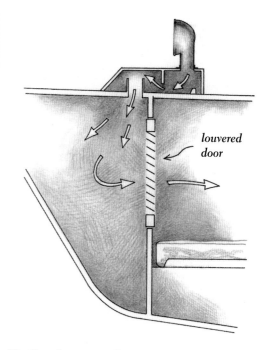

louvered door

The Dorade-type ventilator provides air below through a water-trap system that has been proven over years of offshore use. Louvered locker doors also assist air flow below.

hatches of boats in southern cruising grounds but are occasionally found on boats docked in midlatitude marinas. They should not be left unattended in a boat hatch due to concerns of security and rain, but using a small one to feed a dorade ventilator may be fine in all but a high wind.

Engine room ventilation is a big problem on many boats. Today's diesels require a significant amount of air for combustion, as well as ambient air circulation in the engine room. Inadequate air for combustion is a common diesel problem. The Westerbeke 40NA (37 hp) requires 92 cubic feet per minute (cfm) of air flow. The Yanmar 4LH-TE (110 hp) calls for 339 cfm. Caterpillar, Inc., suggests 2.5 cfm per horsepower for combustion, which works out to 938 cfm for their 375 hp 4208. They also recommend an additional 8 cfm per horsepower for ventilation.

Not many pleasure boats meet these requirements. These are significant numbers and the air

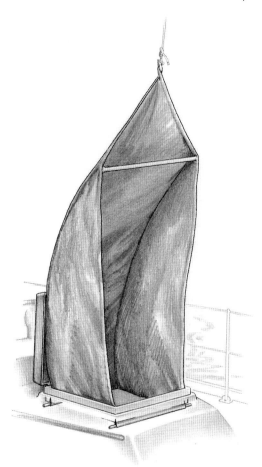

Lightweight-fabric air scoops, such as the Wind Chute, channel air below in light conditions.

supply may not be adequate, particularly if a boat has been repowered. Inadequate air supply will cause combustion problems and, in severe circumstances, will cause an engine to shut down. Consider adding aft cowl or Dorade ventilators to improve air flow into the engine room. If the boat already has hull- or house-side ventilators, you might have to make them larger.

Electronics

I believe electronics that are used often are the least likely to fail when you need them. Moisture is one of the greatest enemies of electronics on board a boat, but damaging effects can be minimized if you turn on the equipment and let it warm up whenever you are aboard—even if you aren't using it. Radar, loran, satnav, GPS, and radios will benefit from being warmed up. If you are alongside the dock and have a shore-power converter, the recharging time will be minimal. If shore power is not available, running the engine or generator will top off the batteries quickly.

Another way to help protect electronics from moisture buildup is to use a moisture barrier spray on the connections at the rear of electronics and on line connections. While you are at it, check the wire connections.

Engine

Even if you are aboard just for a quick visit, check the engine spaces and bilges. If the engine compartment has been closed, give it a chance to air out, and if you are aboard long enough, start the engine and let it warm up.

I cringe when I hear sailors pride themselves on running the engine for only 20 hours per season. Sounds good, but those short runs are not giving the engine a chance to warm up. When the engine runs only for short periods, condensation tends to develop in the engine, creating rust, which gets into the lubricating oil. Whenever possible, run the engine long enough to reach its proper operating temperature. (That may take as long as 20 to 30 minutes if you are idling.)

There is, however, another side of the coin. Diesel engines, particularly those with turbochargers, tend to build up a carbon residue in exhaust components when they are run for extended periods without a load. Therefore, do not let the engine idle for too long. (See Chapter 12, Main Engine Care, for more on engine maintenance.)

Batteries

If you have a battery charger on board, think twice about leaving it on when you are away from the boat. Constantly running a charger may overcharge lead-acid batteries and boil them dry. If you have a refrigeration system or some other equipment that requires leaving the charger on, check the batteries at regular intervals.

Two warning signs with lead-acid batteries are the odor of sulfur and needing additional water in the batteries. Beware of the danger of explosion from the gases that are emitted by overheated batteries. Gel-cell batteries do not typically exhibit these warnings unless the charging rate and/or level is excessive. See Chapter 18 for more on batteries and charging problems.

Protection at the Yard

A common complaint of boatowners is about the wear and tear on their boats around boatyards. Their frustration is often justified. It is my experience that a boatyard may be the worst place to keep a clean boat. In their defense, though, boatyards are learning how to better protect the boats they work on and be more careful in cleaning up their work. Also, it should be said that many customers want their work expedited, so workers are often encouraged to get on and off a boat as fast as possible and are not reminded to take the time for proper job preparation.

Before you take your boat to a boatyard, it's a good idea to do some planning for the work to be done. Many boatowners have canvas runners or pads to make protected passages for workers on their decks, varnished cabin soles, and carpets. The runners and pads are washable and don't take up much room in a locker, so you can keep them aboard all the time.

Even if you do all the work yourself, the protection afforded by runners is worth the effort. When you are lugging gear on or off the boat for a cruise, or when the boat is stored high and dry for the winter, runners can't be beat for keeping grime and grit from being tracked onto the boat's vulnerable surfaces.

I recently tried an alternative to canvas runners that worked well: I bought a few rolls of oil absorption mats. The rolls usually come in lengths of about 100 feet by 18 inches wide, with perforations every foot or so. When I was finished with them, I just tossed them out. You can buy these rolls from an industrial supply house;

I bought mine from the New Pig Corporation (800-468-4647), a catalog sales company that stocks all kinds of waste cleanup supplies.

Another way to keep down the grit that is tracked aboard is to buy "boot" covers for shoes; these inexpensive covers are sold by industrial supply houses and do not take up much precious storage space. Some boaters dedicate a pair of boat shoes for use only on the boat. I have found this a bit of a hassle for a boat that is tied to a dock.

Using a plastic-grass mat is still another way to keep boatyard grit from getting aboard. Although not as effective as removing or covering shoes, these mats do a good job and are common in most yards. They are a must for people who work where there is gravel or sand surrounding the boat. Once

Keep a piece of rug aboard to reduce chafe on cabin soles when working on the interior. Fabric toolboxes and carriers also help prevent chafe and wear.

in a while, you will see one tied to a ladder to ensure that it gets used. And speaking of ladders, do not forget to tie the ladder you are using to a stanchion to prevent an unexpected upset.

If you are leaving your boat at a yard, think carefully about the work that is to be done and try to remove gear that will be in the way of the workers. Although it may not be necessary to remove everything from a boat to store it, it is a great help to have a clear work area for projects. When I go aboard a well-stocked boat to make an estimate of a repair, I sometimes have to increase the labor estimate to allow for moving, storing, and replacing the owner's gear. Most boatyard workers are very conscientious about handling your gear, but no one is likely to handle it as

carefully as you, and no one will know just how you want it stored. If the boat is going to be in the yard for an extended period, unload any foodstuffs and other items that will spoil or, in the north, freeze and break.

A final word about preparing to leave your boat in a yard: Remove liquor and valuables from the boat or store them in a lockable compartment. Problems don't arise often, but it's always better to be safe than sorry.

Although all the ideas expressed in this chapter are basic and most boatowners know or practice them already, that in no way reduces their importance. Practice good boatkeeping skills and see a return on your investment—both in terms of boating pleasure and financial savings.

CHAPTER 2

Developing a Maintenance Plan

Part of keeping an elegant yacht is seeing that things get done on the boat when needed. Even if you wish to have a yard do most of your maintenance, you cannot entirely delegate the responsibility for seeing that all is in order. Although there are many onboard jobs that most boatowners would not want to tackle, it behooves you, at a minimum, to be aware of the boat's service needs and have a basic knowledge of what is required to accomplish most maintenance jobs. The bottom line is: Be an educated consumer.

Do-it-yourselfer or delegator, it is important to protect your investment and ensure your safety and that of your passengers by looking for problems before they become crises. So what do you do? I recommend that you develop a detailed checklist of maintenance projects for your boat. What follows is one way to construct such a list and some suggestions to serve as a starting point.

Developing a Maintenance Chart

Developing and keeping a maintenance chart is an ongoing project because most boatowners add and remove equipment every year. Therefore, your maintenance chart will require updating from time to time. Here are some steps to follow.

Inventory Equipment

Start by taking an inventory of your boat's equipment and listing the obvious maintenance projects. Conduct a stem-to-stern analysis of the mechanical and electrical systems. You may do this in the comfort of your living room, but it is hard to beat doing it aboard your boat. Make the list detailed. For instance, rather than just writing "check bilge pump," write "check the pump, float switch, and foot valve." Each of these subassemblies needs to be inspected, cleaned, and, often, repaired. When it's time to order replacement parts, you'll be happy you've taken the time to list the manufacturer and part number where appropriate.

*(opposite page) **Confidently taking the helm of a well-prepared yacht is the reward for practicing good preventive maintenance.***

Organize the list into sections such as the following:
    engine
    plumbing systems
    electrical/electronic systems
    steering
    rig
    refrigeration/air conditioning

Making a list like this will make it easier to find information, plan a day's work, or figure out which jobs you want to turn over to the yard. Also, quickly reviewing your list will help you avoid overlooking a critical check that might cut short an otherwise perfect cruise.

Refer to Equipment Manuals

No doubt your boat came with manuals for some of the equipment. With luck, these include the engine(s) and generator(s), electronics, pumps, heads, and other equipment. If you are missing any manuals, contact the manufacturer to request them. Manuals often explain the basic maintenance required for your equipment, list information as appropriate on oil, filters, and such, explain adjustment specifications, and give replacement part numbers.

Cosmetic Chores

Not everyone would include cosmetic work in this list, but certainly the work must be done. It is a good idea to divide this list into interior and exterior work. I would break up the list to a fairly high level of detail. For instance, I would separately list the exterior handrails, cockpit trim, and the rubrails because I typically work on a few pieces of brightwork at a time. Don't forget to include the obvious chores such as painting the bottom and waxing the topsides.

Schedule

Start building a schedule of projects and estimate the time required to complete each task. Include service intervals for each item, referring to service manuals for advice on how often tasks need to be performed or relying on your experience. You might want to set up multiple columns: one for the service interval; one for projects you wish to tackle yourself; one for tasks you wish to have done by others; one for the date when the task was last done; and one for the person who performed the work. Obviously, it is possible to get carried away, but you can always modify the chart.

Maintenance Chart Ideas

Here are a few items you may wish to include in your maintenance chart; of course, you'll want to adapt these to meet your own needs. Some of these subject areas are further discussed in other sections of this book. This is a general list and may not cover all equipment on your boat.

Mechanical Systems
Engine
    Cooling System
        Check intake strainer
        Check hoses and clamps
        Test intake seacock handle operation

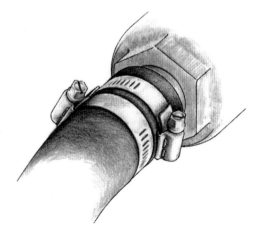

Check all under-the-waterline raw-water hoses for double clamping. Occasionally a fitting that the hose is slid over is not long enough for two clamps. Consider replacing the fitting with a longer one. Also, make sure the two clamps' screw tighteners are not aligned; staggering the clamps as shown here evens the clamping pressure on the hose.

Inspect raw-water impellers
Check coolant levels
Fuel System
    Check fuel filters for dirt and water
    Replace fuel filter elements
    Check for moisture in tanks
    Look for leaks on engine and on fuel
        plumbing
    Test operation on fuel line valves
Lube Oil System
    Check block lube oil
    Change lube oil filter
    Inspect for leaks
    Conduct lube oil analysis
Air Supply/Exhaust
    Check air filter
    Look for intake air restrictions
    Test blower
    Check for blower restrictions
Power Train
    Check transmission oil level

Inspect shaft coupling
Inspect shaft
Inspect stuffing box
Inspect cutlass bearing(s)
Inspect prop(s)
Exhaust System
    Inspect exhaust elbow and vent
    Check hoses and clamps
    Inspect muffler(s)
    Inspect through-hull valves
Miscellaneous
    Check transmission controls
    Check throttle controls
    Inspect engine mounts
    Inspect electrical connections
    Check zincs in heat exchangers

Refrigeration

Check running time against specifications
Check cooling water intake seacock
Check cooling water strainer
Inspect hoses and hose clamps
Look for damaged or corroding coolant
    plumbing
Change dryer (must be done by licensed
    technician)

*An engine's zinc is often overlooked but is
important to the life of the engine's heat exchanger.
As the label suggests, it's a good idea to check
the zinc monthly.*

Recharge gas (must be done by licensed
technician)

Marine Head

Run lubricant through pump/discharge
Check intake seacock/plumbing
Check discharge plumbing: Test valves
Check holding tank and fittings
If a vacuum head: Test vacuum seat in
bowl
If a vacuum head: Check vacuum pump and
accumulator

Electric Bilge Pump

Check foot valve
Check float switch
Check diaphragm or impeller in pump
Check hoses and clamps
Check discharge seacock

Manual Bilge Pump

Check foot valve
Check hoses and clamps
Check diaphragms or impellers
Check discharge seacock

Sump Pump

Check hoses and clamps
Check discharge seacock
Check diaphragm/impellers in pump

Freshwater System

Check pump and diaphragm/impellers
Check hoses and clamps
Inspect and clean tank interiors
Check fill piping
Check hot water tank
Test all valves
Check hand pumps

Steering System

Inspect rudderpost
Inspect quadrant/tiller arm
If cable: Check steering cables for wear and
stretch
Inspect and lube steering sheaves
If hydraulic: Check cylinders and lines

Check rudder and fastenings
Check stuffing box/packing
Emergency tiller: Is it aboard?

Compass

Check compensation
Test for smooth operation

Stove and LPG systems

Check burner operation
Test connections with soapy water
Inspect all valves
Test shutoff valves

Electrical Systems

Batteries

Check electrolyte level
Test specific gravity
Check battery ventilation

Panel

Examine for corrosion and loose wiring
Test breakers

Wiring harness

Conduct visual check

Exterior Light Fixtures

Test bulbs
Check for corrosion and water resistance

Interior Light Fixtures

Test bulbs

Spare Parts Inventory

Check inventory (see Appendix II)

Safety Gear

Check all of the following:
Life jackets
Flares: Are they current?
Bell
Horn(s)
Safety harnesses
Man overboard ring and pole
EPIRB: Are the batteries good?
Life raft: Is the certificate current?
Plugs for through-hulls

Radar reflector
Flashlights
First aid kit

Mast and Rigging

Mast

Inspect step
Check mast collar, wedges, and boot
Inspect mast butt
Make visual check of extrusion
Check tangs
Check masthead
Check cotter pin condition and tape

Standing Rigging

Make visual inspection of wire
Check all terminals for rust and cracks
Inspect turnbuckles
Check cotter pins
Check chainplates for movement and
	leaks

Running Rigging

Inspect for wear

Deck Hardware

Winches and Windlasses

Check for smooth operation
Regrease
Examine winch fasteners and backing
	blocks

Cleats and Tracks

Inspect fasteners and backing blocks
Try car operation

Ports and Hatches

Inspect gaskets
Test locks and hinges

Other Deck Hardware

Inspect fasteners
Check for leaks

Ground Tackle

Check anchor lines
	Check bitter end fastening

Inspect splices and lines for chafe
Check anchor chains and shackles

Docking Gear

Inspect dockline splices
Check fenders

Exterior Cosmetics

Varnish

Handrails
Toerails
Rubrails
Cockpit coamings
Dorade boxes

Paint

Name and hail
Cove
Deck lockers
Boottop
Bottom

Waxing

Topsides
Cabin sides
Cockpit

Interior Cosmetics

Varnish

Cabin sole
Trim

Paint

Lockers
Bilges

Haulout Checklist

Given the cost of hauling the average auxiliary
sail or power yacht, both in terms of time
and money, it is extremely important that
owners use the haulout time to inspect those
parts of their boats that are normally under
water. This section will provide you with some
basic information to help you make the most
of your haulout time. You might want to

use this information to make a haulout check-list similar to the maintenance checklist described earlier.

Bottom Paint and Bumps

During haulout, there are several key areas to inspect. The first is the condition of the bottom paint. If there is growth on the bottom, it's important to see that the growth, or slime, is removed while the bottom is still wet. The methods used may vary somewhat from paint to paint. For instance, a harder bottom paint may be most properly cleaned with a high-pressure wash; however, most ablative paints erode too quickly under such intense pressure.

After the boat has been washed but before it dries, make sure you inspect the bottom for areas of deformation as a result of stress within the hull. These areas typically show quite readily in the mirror-wet finish. Almost all boats have some minor deformation in their bottoms. Checking every time your boat is hauled is more valuable than information gleaned from a one-time snap-shot. (An exception to this, of course, is damage from grounding.)

Blisters

After you have inspected your boat for hull damage, it's time to look even more closely for signs of osmotic blistering on the underbody surface. Typically, the first signs of blistering will be either individual blisters or small areas of blisters that, when first noticed, may be no wider than a dime's diameter. The later and more advanced signs of blistering include the spreading of the smaller blisters and the appearance of larger bubbles that will weep an acidic liquid when punctured.

The time to deal with osmotic blistering is before it happens, in the preventive stage. However, if blisters do appear on your boat, it makes economic sense to deal with the problem seriously and completely, at once. I highly recommend that, at the first signs of osmotic blistering, you contact either a marine surveyor or a competent yard technician to confirm your diagnosis and prescribe proper treatment.

Zincs

Haulout is the ideal time to inspect all of the zincs that are normally underwater, including those in zinc holders and on the shafting, propellers, and rudders. Ensure that enough zinc remains to perform its job (see Chapter 20) and that the zinc is attached so as to permit good electrical contact with the components it is to protect.

Rudder(s)

Grab the rudder with both hands and twist it and pull on it to determine if there is excess motion in its bearings. What is excess motion? This is a difficult question to answer, but most bearings should allow from $5/1000$ to $10/1000$ of an inch clearance, which, in the case of packing glands, can be tightened by the flax packing. Other systems that don't have flax packing may be slightly tighter. The bottom line is, if a rudder has enough wear to allow it to misalign in any of the bearings, it will accelerate wear on the remaining bearing surface, as well as on the rudder itself. Eventually, the rudder will begin to bind.

Additionally, look for any pitting on the rudder surface and wear or pitting on the rudder shaft. Examine any underwater bearings such as gudgeons and pintles; check the condition of their fasteners as well.

Struts

If the propeller shaft is supported by a strut, carefully examine the strut and the heads of the strut fasteners if they are exposed. Pull on the strut to make sure it is securely fastened to the hull; doing so will produce little noticeable movement on even a fairly loose strut on a larger boat because the shaft strength will tend to hold the strut in place. On a smaller boat, however, a loose strut will move significantly.

Shafts

Shafts and shaft bearings should show minimal wear where they contact each other, although you will be able to examine them only at the edges of the bearings. There should be little movement in the shaft when it is pulled from

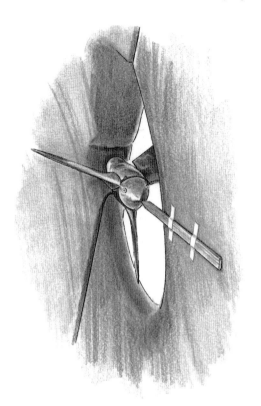

Here is a crude but effective method of checking for shaft runout: Tape a pointed stick to a fixed structure so the point is near the end of the shaft; turn the shaft and watch for wobble.

side to side and, when rotated, the end of the shaft or end of the propeller (whichever is exposed at the back end) should have no run out. This can be checked most easily by propping up a stick with a sharp point close to the end of the shaft and rotating the shaft. Run out will be apparent if the shaft is bent.

Propellers

Thoroughly examine the propeller(s) for damage. Look for signs of metal corrosion, which might indicate an electrolysis problem (corrosion caused by electrical current) or excess cavitation (usually a design or prop selection problem that erodes metal blade tips). Electrolysis and cavitation are very different problems; both deserve

investigation. Discuss them with a qualified marine surveyor or yard worker.

Obvious damage from grounding and smaller dents in the prop blades will cause vibration in the prop and will transmit to the boat unless corrected.

Cleaning a propeller with a synthetic, abrasive disk smoothes the blade surfaces and improves propeller performance. Take care not to change the shape or profile of the blade, which would put the prop out of balance.

Centerboards

Haulout is an excellent time to examine the operation and condition of centerboards. A centerboard can be checked when the boat is being hauled out of the water by a Travelift or crane or when it's being placed back in the water. It is, however, difficult to inspect the full swing of a centerboard when the boat is resting on a cradle, jack stands, or chocks. The centerboard lift mechanisms, cable connections, and pulleys can be checked most readily when the board is in the down position. In some boats this requires removing any cover plates.

You should examine several places on a centerboard. One is the hinge pin. It is difficult to generalize about all centerboards, but the wear of the hinge pin and the condition of the pin mounts are both important items to check. On most Hinckleys the pin is mounted in the lead of the keel casting itself, which acts as a good, solid bearing surface. Also check the cover plates that hold the hinge pins in place. If they are loose, the pin could back out and fall out at sea.

When the board is in the down position, it may be possible to examine the connection of any linkage or cables to the top of the board, a task that might be difficult when the board is in the up position. At the very least, operate the board up and down to ensure that it operates through its full range.

If it is necessary to repaint the centerboard, do so just before the boat is being put back in the water, while it's up in the sling. Although this is not the ideal application for most modern bottom paints, as a practical matter you may have little choice.

Through-Hulls and Transducers

Look carefully at the boat's through-hulls and transducers—they should be free of growth. If you have paddle wheel transducers, spin them to ensure that they are free and that they operate without any chafe or resistance from growth or damage to the impeller.

For depth transducers, leave the surface unpainted or apply a special paint that prevents marine growth and does not reduce the transducer's effectiveness. If you have to clean the transducers, do so very carefully with a soft brush. If that doesn't remove the marine growth, *gently* scrape with either a plastic or wooden wedge, taking care not to gouge the surface of the transducer.

When checking through-hulls, if your boat has a metal through-hull fitting in connection with seacocks that are mounted inside, observe the edges of the through-hulls to be sure that they have not been subject to electrolysis. Typically, electrolysis will show as a discoloration of the metal or porosity in the metal where the less noble elements have eroded. If your boat has no through-hull fittings but has seacocks that are simply bolted to the hull (as they are in many Hinckley boats), make certain that the laminate edges of the hull openings have been carefully covered with resin and that the coating is intact. The coating prevents moisture from seeping into the laminate.

Also examine the condition of the heads of the seacock mounting bolts to ensure that they are in good condition. It's not a bad idea to try to turn the mounting bolts with a screwdriver to check their strength. If they are severely corroded on the inside, turning them may indicate a weakness and prevent a failure at sea.

Intakes

It's important to clean very carefully strainers placed on the outside of the hull as intakes for engine, generators, and pumps. When the bottom is dry and you are touching up the bottom paint, touch up these strainers, too. Be very careful, though, that you don't let any excess paint clog the holes or openings.

External Ballast

On boats with external ballast, especially sailboats, carefully examine the seam between the ballast and the hull for signs of any movement. It is not at all uncommon to see a seam line open up in this area. Normally, such an opening is caused by minute movement of the casting (ballast) rather than the hull. Don't be too alarmed, though—this is often not a serious concern. Movement is most easily observed when the joint between the ballast and hull is filled with a relatively rigid material such as a fiberglass chopping mixture. The seam line can be restored by opening up the seam with a small grinder or chisel and refilling the outer edges with a more flexible material such as 3M #5200 or other appropriate underwater compound.

Packing Glands

Haulout is a good time to replace packing in the rudderport, stern tube, or other through-hull fittings such as axles or centerboards.

Seacocks and Interior Through-hulls

Next, examine the seacocks and through-hulls from inside the hull. Test every seacock to make sure it can be easily turned off. If a seacock doesn't move easily, disassemble it, grease or replace components as necessary, and reinstall before launching. An inoperative seacock will leave an enormous hole in the boat if a hose comes loose or gets torn while at sea. You only need to remove a speed transducer while in the water to get a feeling for the vast amount of water that can rush into a boat if a seacock is not ready to stem the flow.

An additional safety procedure is to tie onto *each* seacock a soft wood plug that will fit into the inside opening of the seacock in the event of a failure. These plugs are now required by most ocean racing authorities and they are a good idea for cruisers—power and sail—as well. Typically, these plugs will also fit in the opening of the hull should the seacock itself become dislodged due to bolt or through-hull failure.

When you are inspecting seacocks, don't neglect to check the mounting bolts for corrosion or damage. Discoloration from electrolysis shows up as light greenish blue on the surface of the metal; in its later stages this discoloration or powder will hide a deterioration of material. As noted earlier, you may also find pitting. The deterioration may be below the surface level of a fitting and therefore extremely difficult to see. A good rule of thumb to remember when examining bolts and fittings: When in doubt, pull it out. There is no substitute for drawing a fitting from the hull, examining it, and if you have the slightest doubt about it, replacing it.

For fittings that are higher in the hull and do not have seacocks attached, or on older boats where below-waterline fittings do not have seacocks, I highly recommend regularly conducting a visual inspection. Of course, you don't have to wait until haulout time to examine both sides of fittings that are above the waterline. Through-hull fittings in sail lockers are in danger of having chains or anchors dropped on them, which often results in fractured or sheared fittings. Although uncommon in my experience, damage such as

this does happen. The results, especially for a sailboat, can be frightening.

Bilges

Cleaning and flushing bilges is another chore that's easier to do when a boat is hauled out. I've occasionally used a steam cleaner to remove oily residue from some bilges. Boats with bilge plugs (a fitting low in the bilge that allows the bilge to drain when the boat is out of the water) are readily drained of this residue. The residue can, of course, be filtered and the oil separated prior to disposal. For boats without bilge plugs it may be necessary to connect the bilge pump discharge to a holding tank or similar container so the oily residue is not dumped into the yard.

It may seem like a lot to do, but most of these suggestions require only a quick visual inspection or a yank on a valve or shaft. Take the time to create lists for planning your work projects. It is so easy to forget something important. Maintenance and hauling checklists don't take long to pull together, and you can fine-tune them while you use them.

CHAPTER 3

Interior Design

Interior design and decoration offer great oppor-
tunities for owners to customize their yachts. In
this chapter, I will examine ideas for interiors
seen on Hinckleys and other yachts. Whether a
boatowner wishes to simply spruce up the interior
a bit or create a whole new decor, there are a surprising number of choices to be made about
color, materials for the sole and bulkheads, trim
styles, and layout. Together, these choices express
the owner's ideas and personality. Not all options,
such as selecting bulkhead materials, are available to everyone, but there are a surprising number of interior elements that can be customized.

I hope the yacht interiors shown in this chapter will provide a starting point for your own
imagination.

Doing It with Color

Probably the easiest way to personalize a yacht is
with color. Accent colors selected for countertops, bunk covers, and throw pillows—as well as
wood colors—need to work together. Although
my tastes tend to be a bit traditional, I have en-
joyed looking at and, in some cases, building
beautifully decorated interiors of many styles.

Some interesting interior choices are presented
in this photographic portfolio for your consideration. Perhaps one will catch your fancy.

One of the most attractive traditional interiors
combines lightly painted bulkheads with contrasting varnished trim for a bright and open feeling. An added benefit of painted bulkheads is that
they are easy to maintain. Dings and scratches
that could be readily fixed in a varnished bulkhead can be faired and repainted with reasonable
ease. The other side of the coin is that painted
wood bulkheads usually require a fair amount of
work to appear smooth. On a varnished bulkhead, particularly one with a satin finish, the
wood grain distracts the eye from small discrepancies; a painted bulkhead will readily show
surface irregularities.

You might consider a painted bulkhead and
varnished trim for an older boat that has a
scratched or stained interior brightwork finish.
Sanding will remove scratches from solid wood

(opposite page) *The detail woodwork on this Hinckley 70-foot sailing yacht shows how decorative wood
can personalize an interior.*

26

(above) This well-laid-out navigation station has the additional benefit of removable instrument panels. Adding or changing instruments later will require only replacing a reasonably small panel.

(below) The inlay in this dinette table provides a nice accent. The top folds out to enlarge the table. This interior shows what can be done with mahogany trim and white bulkheads.

Maple provides a warm feeling and is lighter than most mahogany and teak interiors. Cherry has also become more common in Hinckley yacht interiors.

Story Litchfield

This dinette area's appeal is enhanced by the curved table and soft, comfortable look of the cushions. Note the traditional planking look of the overhead.

corner posts, and, in some cases, if the wood grain has not been cut, steaming dents in the wood with an iron will do the trick. Discolored wood is more difficult to treat. Heavy sanding and bleaching with oxalic acid may work. See Chapter 5 for details.

The damaging effects of age and moisture are more difficult to repair on plywood veneer than on solid trim. Thin surface veneers (often $\frac{1}{42}$ of an inch or thinner) are easily sanded through when trying to remove scratches or moisture-darkened areas. Oversanding the surface veneer will expose the glue and interior woods of the plywood, leaving an unsightly blemish—a reason why you might consider painting a surface that has been varnished.

Painting one bulkhead or cabin does not mean that you have to carry the change through-out the boat. For example, painting only the gal-ley is sometimes a good option. On sailboats where the galley is near the companionway, the wood often gets dinged and cannot be restored to a like-new condition without reveneering. A cabin adjacent to a painted galley is fine left varnished. The corner posts and other trim pro-vide a transition between the two areas.

On many boats, particularly newer ones that use the "painted bulkhead/varnished trim" style, the bulkheads are covered with Formica or another laminate for durability. These lami-nates hold up well over the long haul and can't be beat for ease of cleaning. For that reason, laminates are ideal for us in heads and showers. In most cases, damaged plastic laminates can be replaced with moderate effort.

The roomy after stateroom on this custom 60-foot power yacht uses the space under the berth for easily accessed storage. Note the construction features such as raised panel doors and flush pulls. The owner has chosen light-colored fabrics and carpet to complement the rich, dark mahogany interior.

To remove a laminate that has been attached with contact cement, heat the surface and work the laminate off by pulling gently; you can help it along by using a putty knife. If the laminate doesn't break, the old piece will make a good pattern for the replacement.

Another alternative to painting damaged bulkheads is applying a new layer of wood veneer. For more information, see the section on applying veneers and laminates in Chapter 11.

When applying a paint finish on plywood that has a fine hardwood veneer, occasionally we first seal the wood with a clear wood sealer or varnish to allow for later removal of the paint. If we applied paint on the bare wood, the paint would penetrate the grain and in the future the pigment

would be difficult, if not impossible, to remove, thus restricting refinishing options.

Other coverings find their way into boats to great advantage. Vinyl and other durable wall coverings are used, particularly on power yachts, with wonderful results. The older Hinckley Pilot 35s used carpeting for sheathing the hull in the forward cabin. Carpet also works well as a liner for lockers. The specific product you choose is important, however, because the marine environment is tough on water-absorbing materials.

The Softer Side

Interior fabrics add distinctive personal flavor to a boat. When building or redecorating an interior, some owners hire an interior decorator to help select fabrics. Others undertake the selection themselves—often risking life and marriage! Over the years, some fabric styles have remained constant, but new choices are always entering the market.

Recent developments in interior design in-

Story Litchfield

This traditional power yacht galley uses white countertops to lighten what could be a very dark space.

clude the increased use of Ultrasuede and leather. One hundred percent acrylic fabrics such as Diklon and some of the Sunbrella furniture fabric line are durable and attractive alternatives. Gone are the heavier fabrics of old such as Herculon.

The head of the Hinckley sewing department tells me that the trend in interior boat design is to use acrylic fabrics in sleeping quarters and leather or other exotic fabrics on tufted and over-stuffed cushions in the main cabin or dinette areas. Ultrasuede is used on many boats today because it is so hardy. Years ago I installed Ultrasuede in a SouWester 50 that I ran into again 12 or 13 years later. The new owners told me that the

(right) A fiberglass liner, oval sink, and portlight, combined with a wood countertop, enhance this picnic boat head without reducing its feeling of spaciousness.

Story Litchfield

(above) The cherry interior of a Hinckley Picnic Boat combines the warmth of cherry with white fiberglass and Formica to create a warm and light interior. The curves in the cabin liner and doors add to the beauty of the accommodations.

(below) Wood and fabric work together to provide a unique feel for this yacht's interior. Sculptured trim adds another component to the mix.

Story Litchfield

Mahogany, stainless steel, and white combine to make this galley seem both attractive and efficient. The refrigerator is unusual among sailboats, as its front-loading door loses more cold than would a top-loading unit. The advantage is improved access to stored items.

fabric was original. It was in incredible condition.

Interior boat cushions are no longer just square-sided blocks; contoured and tufted cushions are commonplace. Buttoned cushions, long used on stylish powerboats, are now appearing on sailboats. When the boat is offshore or racing, however, protective covers are often used.

Hinckley is now using foams of two different densities in most of their boats—a high-density foam for sleeping quarters and extra-firm foam for seating areas; the foam is often wrapped in batting for style and comfort. A third type, laminated foam, is also used in some cases to achieve just the right feel.

Curtains are now incorporated into valances with overhead lighting strips. Owners who do not wish to cover beautiful wood often use snaps or Velcro to attach plainer curtain styles for simple porthole covers.

For cockpit cushions, Spongex 1½-inch or 2-inch closed-cell foam is often used and is sometimes laminated for stability. On their 36-foot jet boat, the Picnic Boat, Hinckley uses a material called densified batting for the cockpit cushions. The cushions are often covered with Sunsure mesh fabric. The combination is designed to drain water and dry quickly.

Trim

Some simple yet effective steps to upgrade a boat's interior are to change the trim on counters and bunks, add bookshelves, or change the style of cabinet doors.

Older boats, in particular, often have rather plain trim on their countertops and bureaus. Consider removing the trim, especially if it is nicked or stained, and replacing it with new trim that has some shape. Laminated molding that

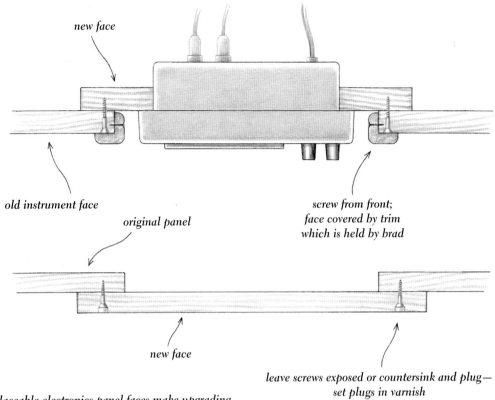

new face

old instrument face

original panel

screw from front;
face covered by trim
which is held by brad

new face

leave screws exposed or countersink and plug—
set plugs in varnish

*Replaceable electronics panel faces make upgrading
equipment easier and neater. Both recessed and
surface-mounted versions work well.*

Replaceable Electronics Cabinetry

With the rapid developments in and decreasing
cost of marine electronics, more and more boatowners are upgrading or adding to their electronic equipment. Too often, though, when
equipment is changed, old cabinet faces are
patched in an effort to hide existing equipment
mounting holes.

Recently I have seen a few boats with electronic locker faces that are specifically designed
to be changed. The lockers have either an easily
removable panel that is cut to fit the current
electronics package, or an ingeniously installed
panel with hidden seams. Both designs let the
boatowner replace the panel with a new one if
needed.

If you have a fixed panel on your boat, you
can modify the face of the electronics locker to
accommodate equipment changes by cutting a
hole in the face and installing a new panel either over or behind the hole. Trim the new face
(if installing the new face over the old) or the
hole (if installing the new face behind the old)
with a matching L-shaped molding that com-
plements other wood in the area. If you
change electronic equipment, the old face
panel can be removed and used as a template
for the new one. Interior partitions and shelves
might need adjusting as well, but they are hidden behind the face and allow for less strin-
gent joinery.

continues right around the corners is one good choice. Solid wood trim with a contoured face and back section has a beautiful look and a comfortable feel. Although trim work requires more effort than some other cosmetic improvements, it's often just the accent an interior needs.

Unfinished bookshelves, mug and glass racks, binocular holders, and other shelving or storage furniture are available from a number of woodworking suppliers and chandleries, usually in teak, mahogany, and ash. These features look great when varnished. Other woods can be ordered with some lead time and at extra expense. Building one of these pieces is an option for the owner who is comfortable with woodworking tools; they are not particularly hard to construct.

Cabinet doors are another likely area for upgrade. Replacing solid plywood doors with louvered or caned doors will improve both ventilation and the boat's appearance.

Keep Looking Around

If you're interested in refurbishing an interior, whether on a new or old boat, study the pictures in this book, cruise a boat show or two, and buy some books on yacht interiors. Your research and thoughtful planning will be well worth it.

PART 2

Varnish and Paint Application

CHAPTER 4

Exterior Brightwork

If you are looking for classic beauty in a yacht exterior, it is hard to beat the look of varnished brightwork. In this chapter I will look at some methods for varnishing and oiling exterior brightwork, consider common problems with these finishes, and offer advice on how to solve them.

There is a lot of controversy about which is the best finishing system for exterior brightwork when considering ease of maintenance, best appearance, durability, and so on. The options include varnishing, oiling, sealing, or, of course, doing nothing. Whatever your preference, your decision about how to finish your exterior brightwork will have a major impact on the maintenance of the boat in the future.

Most people agree that a varnished hatch or rail is prettier than a bare rail, but not everyone wants to spend the time or money to maintain the varnish. Yet, if an owner wishes to keep that new golden look in unvarnished teak, he or she may find it is as much work as varnish to maintain. Therefore, if varnishing or regular oiling take more time than you have or wish to commit, be prepared to live with a bit of gray in your trim.

I must admit that I favor the look of varnish—

not surprising, perhaps, from someone named Hinckley. There is a limit, though, to how much time I wish to spend varnishing.

This chapter discusses the process the Hinckley Company employs for applying and maintaining varnished exterior brightwork and other finishes. Because teak is the predominant exterior marine wood, the discussion will be centered around that wood, but the methods apply to most types of wood used on yacht exteriors.

Materials

Varnishes

A basic varnish is formulated from a mixture of resin and oil, with solvent added to improve its brushing characteristics. Beyond that, marine varnishes typically include dryers and additives. Varnishes vary in the type and amount of these components, with newer varnishes relying more and more on synthetic materials.

Additives are designed to improve a varnish's handling and weathering and include compounds for ultraviolet protection. These materials add considerable life to a varnish coating. Additives may be of several types. Interlux, for example, lists three primary additives:

- one to absorb UV energy;
- another to stabilize the surface of the varnish, inhibiting cracking; and
- a third to reduce oxidation in the varnish.

These and other additives are used in varying degrees in different brands. Some varnishes, such as interior satin finish varnish, contain no ultraviolet additives.

For exterior brightwork, Hinckley uses Epifanes Clear Varnish (a blend of tung oil, phthalic alkyd, and urethane resin) and Stoppani Super Yacht (a Chinese tung oil). The Epifanes is a good, durable building varnish that is also a leader in gloss retention and overall longevity. The Stoppani is used for the final two coats of finish because of its superior gloss retention and durability.

What should you choose? There is a lot of room for user preference. One of the biggest factors in varnish life, if not the biggest, is the thickness of the dry film. This is not just a measure of coats applied, because the thickness of the varnish varies depending on the amount of thinner you use and the number of times you thin it. Further, sanding between coats varies the thickness of the finished coat. Therefore, varnish should be selected based on how much can *smoothly* be applied per coating so that it does not need to be mostly sanded off prior to recoating. This is a function of the varnish, the varnisher, and the environment.

Many varnishers find that two-part polyurethanes, although known for durability, are hard to handle. The mixing and thinning process is tricky, and their handling and drying properties are highly sensitive to temperature and humidity. But once they're on, they provide an outstanding degree of resiliency.

Single-part polyurethanes are more forgiving in use. They tend to be clearer than standard varnishes, which may or may not be seen as an advantage.

More conventional phenolic resin varnishes are closer to what we think of as spar varnish.

These varnishes typically handle well and are used with common thinners. The colors vary between brands, but in general these varnishes tend to be darker than polyurethanes.

Your own experience will be the best guide. Try different types and different manufacturers. If you find one that has good UV protection and handles well so you can apply it in thicker coats than the others, it is probably the one for you.

Thinners

Thinners are used to improve the flow of a varnish during application and for preparation and cleanup. When thinning varnish, adhere to the varnish manufacturer's recommendations for thinners. You may consider other products for cleaning surfaces and equipment. For example, Hinckley uses Pettit 12120 or 12121 thinner as a surface cleaner in preparation for sanding and to remove excess bedding compound and other surface contaminants.

Sandpaper and Sanding Equipment

Sandpaper selection is critical for surface preparation. Grits from 100 through 320 are commonly used. (The higher the number, the finer the grit.) Some varnishers use an even finer grit on final coats; however, Hinckley's varnish personnel do not normally find it necessary. It depends, of course, on the finish condition.

Hinckley uses 220-grit 3M Tri-M-Ite silicon carbide sandpapers to prepare a surface for varnish. It has excellent cutting properties, the surface of the paper is slow to fill, and it is easy to clean for continued use. Heavier-grit papers are used dry, but some varnishers will use a 220-grit or finer wet-or-dry paper.

3M also manufactures hand-sanding blocks that can be used with their adhesive-backed Stikit papers. One style has a flexible foam face to allow for slight contouring of the surface being sanded. Another has a relatively flat, hard face for absolutely flat surfaces. These tools are excellent for flatter surfaces where plain hand sanding is likely to create finger grooves or other unevenness.

Finally, a handy addition to the equipment list is an electric palm sander with an orbital sanding pattern. This tool is recommended for flat surfaces such as hatch covers and bulkhead faces. It should be used with care, because it will cut quickly and may leave unsightly scratches that are difficult to remove.

Tapes

Selecting masking tape is a relatively easy job if varnish work is to be completed indoors. Find a durable tape that will adhere well enough to prohibit "bleeding" or migration of the varnish under the tape. 3M Scotch Brand Fine Line #218 or #233 tapes work well.

If the work is to be completed outdoors, tape

This simple sanding block from 3M uses sticky-back sandpaper and is comfortable to work with.

Sanding flat surfaces can be expedited with a palm sander. However, where there is a thin veneer or inlaid detail as in this coaming, take care to prevent oversanding.

selection is more important. Sun and moisture conspire to permanently adhere tape to a surface. Here Scotch Brand #471 blue or #225 silver are excellent choices. Both will hold for several days and still be easy to remove. In any case, remove masking tape as soon as possible after varnish application.

If you have left tape on too long, 3M General Purpose Adhesive Remover will help remove it. Apply with a rag and let it soak until the adhesive lifts enough to permit scraping or rubbing off the tape.

Brushes

The choice of a varnish brush is a very personal one. Hinckley varnishers mainly use 1½- to 2-inch-wide Omega/Epifanes china bristle brushes for exterior brightwork, as well as the Corona Heritage imitation badger hair brush. The Omega brush has an excellent shape for holding varnish, but it may hold too much for the beginning varnisher. The key is to find a natural bristle brush with fine bristles that will lay the varnish down smoothly, not introduce air into the wet film or leave bristles behind. Another brush Hinckley varnishers recommend is a Torrington #20 artist's brush. This small brush is excellent for working in tight areas.

Foam brushes are coming into favor with varnishers as alternatives to traditional brushes. It was difficult for me to believe that a foam brush could provide as fine a surface as a traditional brush, but I have been impressed with the results I've seen. Foam brushes also offer the boatowner the convenience of tossing them away in lieu of cleaning, which is necessary with expensive bristle brushes. Rebecca Wittman recommends the Jen Poly-foam brushes in her book *Brightwork: The Art of Finishing Wood,* published by International Marine Publishing. I tried them and they work well.

A high-quality natural bristle varnish brush is an expensive tool. If you choose to use one for your varnish work, you should take special care to see that it is well cleaned and cared for. I like to use a paint brush spinner that helps spin out the dust, dirt, and excess thinner when washing my

brushes, both before and after working with them. There are spinners that are used in drills and those that are manually operated. I do not recommend using a drill-type spinner with any flammable liquid such as thinner.

Keep brushes wrapped in a small rag rinsed in thinner and then encased in aluminum foil. The foil keeps the bristles from getting bent or broken and helps keep them soft. Some people use motor oil for a preservative. I understand it works well and washes out fairly easily before the next varnish job.

Paint Pots and Strainers

A supply of untreated paper paint pots of various sizes is important. The one-quart size is a good all-around choice. Some Hinckley varnishers roll the leftover varnish around in the pot when they're done to coat the inside. Then they tilt the pot into another container to drain the excess varnish out and to allow the paper pot to dry. The technique provides a smooth varnish container for future work.

You will obtain a good varnish job only if the varnish is clear of all foreign matter, so paint strainers are important—particularly when using varnish from a can that has been previously opened and partially used. Fine mesh paint strainers (available from any paint supply store) or old nylon stockings work well.

Tack Rags

Hinckley uses Gerson tack rags for most finishes because they contain no beeswax. Red Devil also makes good rags. A good tack rag picks up the dust on the surface without leaving any oily or sticky film behind. Both U.S. Paint and Sterling sell tack rags that are recommended for polyurethane finishes. These rags contain no materials that will react with the polyurethane.

Vacuum Cleaner

A good vacuum cleaner is a must anywhere power is available. Hinckley carefully nurses several Electrolux vacuums for its varnish crew. The perfect unit is small, has lots of power, and is built with a nonscratching case.

Varnishing New Wood

Surface Preparation

The key to a first-class varnish job is preparation. Start by deciding what you are going to varnish; do not attempt to varnish too much at one time. When working alone, I try to break a job down into reasonable pieces. One day I may work on hatches, another day on toerails or rail caps, and so on. This allows me to prepare, clean, and varnish within a reasonable time, and I'm not varnishing late into the day when moisture is likely to flatten the gloss. Look carefully at the job to ensure that stopping points are logical. If there are a number of small parts to be varnished on the deck, select ones to be done at the same time that minimize the chances of stepping on or touching other wet varnish.

I do not leave a lot of sanded and taped surfaces waiting for the next varnish day. This is definitely not a practical approach for a boatyard because they need to be as cost-effective as possible. A boatowner, however, may want to varnish one day and spend the next away from the dock or mooring. If you do not have the luxury of spreading the work out, start the surface preparation early.

The following is a general procedure for preparing bare wood for varnish.

1. Clean the wood. All foreign materials should be removed. Hinckley uses Pettit 12120/12121 thinners for this step. Remove any excess bedding compounds and grease from your hands to prevent sanding the material into the grain. If the teak is weathered, there are a number of teak cleaners on the market that remove a minimum of the wood. See Chapter 6 for information on cleaning teak decks.

2. It is helpful, right at the start, to tape any areas where you are likely to get varnish and where it does not belong, including any painted or gelcoat surfaces adjacent to the brightwork. Handrails, toerails, and accent trim on cabinsides are common areas that require taping.

Tape will also protect the surface from sandpaper scratches or misplaced varnish splatters.

If the tape gets ripped by sanding, replace it before varnishing. If it is scratched away, congratulate yourself on having saved the underlying surface from abrasion.

Remember: If you are outside and leave a poor-quality or mismatched tape on the deck for an extended period, it will be tough to remove. Don't leave any masking tape on longer than absolutely necessary.

3. Sand the surface smooth with a moderate-grit sandpaper. If the wood has aged, you may need to start with 100 or possibly heavier-grit paper to even the grain of the wood. If the wood is new, 120 grit should be sufficient. Use a sanding block wherever possible to improve the flatness of the surface. Orbital sanders may help, but be careful of cutting too much.

Wherever possible, round sharp corners at this stage to improve the life of the new

Careful taping prior to sanding and applying finish is critical to achieve a crisp, professional finish. Fitting tape around hardware, such as stanchion bases, takes time but is worth the effort.

varnish. Varnish does not like to stay on sharp edges. Its tendency to wear off edges is exacerbated by the natural tendency to oversand edges and wear them thin when sanding between coats.

4. Upon achieving a flat surface, sand again with a finer-grit paper to remove the scratches of the previous paper. If you used 120-grit paper to start and sanded carefully, you may be able to shift directly to 220 grit. If 220 does not remove the scratches, try an intermediate paper such as 180 grit. This step is extremely important. Too often, the tendency is to shortcut the sanding. Then, when you apply varnish, the wood grain swells and you will need to sand until all but the varnish in the low areas of the grain is left. Proper sanding before the first coat of varnish will minimize this effect and ultimately speed application.

Apply tape to hardware to protect polished metals from sandpaper scratches or stray varnish. (This tape job could be tighter in the corner.)

5. Clean the work area thoroughly after sanding—a small vacuum cleaner is a great plus. Vacuum the deck all around your work as well as the work itself. If a vacuum (or power) is unavailable, wash the boat carefully to remove all loose dust and dirt. Dry the work area completely.

6. Retape those areas where the masking tape has been abraded.

7. When you are ready to varnish, clean and wipe the surface of the wood with a thinner or other appropriate solvent to again remove dirt and oils. This step is especially important with oily woods such as teak. The oil in teak prohibits varnish from sinking into the grain and developing a good mechanical bond. The best option is to use the thinner recommended by the varnish manufacturer. I have also used acetone to clean bare wood and alcohol to clean prevarnished surfaces. Be sure that all of the washing solvents have evaporated before continuing with the application of varnish.

An orbital sander speeds up the sanding process, but take care to avoid oversanding edges. Hand sanding with a block flattens the surface and is easier to control than a power sander.

8. Use a tack rag on the surface just before you varnish. Lightly rub the surface to remove the final bits of dust and dirt that have collected; pressing too hard on a tack rag leaves a sticky surface that will interfere with smooth varnish application. Frequently refold the tack rag to keep clean fabric exposed.

Application

1. If you use a two-part urethane varnish, mix the two parts in the proportions indicated on the cans and slowly stir the mixture. Some two-part products require the mixture to sit for a few minutes before being applied. Carefully read the manufacturer's directions.

    For a single-part varnish, unless the directions say otherwise, do not stir or shake the varnish; doing so would only introduce air into the mixture, which might show as bubbles in the finished work. Carefully strain the varnish into a clean application pot to remove any solids. This is particularly important with a used can of varnish, which may have skimmed over from exposure to air or been contaminated with dirt or dust.

2. Thin the varnish. The exact amount of thinner necessary will vary with the varnish and the coat. For the first coat, Hinckley cuts the varnish by about fifty percent, allowing it to get deep into the cells of the wood and enhancing the bond. Some companies sell sealers for this purpose. They are thin for penetration and dry quickly. I have always favored using thinned varnish, feeling that a homogeneous film will stand up better.

3. Apply the first coat of varnish. This thinned varnish will go on easily as you get the feel of it, but be careful to avoid splatters.

    When applying varnish, the idea is to avoid introducing air bubbles into the varnish. To that end, when wetting your brush, do not wipe it over the edge of the pot to remove excess varnish. Rather, after you dip it into the varnish, press the brush lightly against the side of the container, first one side of the brush and then the other.

As you apply the varnish to the wood, minimize overbrushing and, as much as possible, brush in a single direction. You should always end up brushing a section of work *toward* the wet edge of the previous area. For example, if you are working from right to left on a handrail, with each new section apply the varnish with strokes going from left to right. Some varnishers make their first strokes from right to left to spread the varnish and then stroke from left to right to draw it out and smooth it over their previous work. If you find you are having to stroke the varnish in an area eight or ten times to get it to spread and flow the way you want, you probably need additional thinner to help it flow. I was taught that the ideal is not to brush an area more than three times, although I find I can stroke an area as much as five times and still get a nice finish.

Work a few feet ahead of yourself with the tack rag if dust is settling on the work.

4. After drying (typically 24 to 48 hours), sand the first coat of varnish with 220-grit sandpaper. Sand lightly and be especially careful of edges. Remove a minimum amount of varnish while sanding off fibers that have been raised and dust that may have collected in the surface.

   If the varnish film has not dried properly, it will tend to fill or "gum up" the sandpaper. The varnish feels rubbery and will rub off rather than abrade.

   The instructions that come with the varnish will tell you the normal drying time before recoating. If you don't wait for the varnish to dry before recoating, you will increase your chances of wrinkling the next coat and reducing the life of the varnish film. My greatest successes with varnished exterior trim have had several days to dry between coats. Varnishing one afternoon and trying to sand the next morning for recoating is pushing the drying process too much with most varnishes.

Before recoating, clean and tack the surface after sanding. Also, replace any damaged masking tape.

5. Apply the second coat of varnish. The procedure is much the same as for the first coat, but use only 25 percent thinner.

6. After allowing the surface to dry, sand it with 220-grit sandpaper and clean as before.

7. Apply the third coat of varnish, thinning only enough for a good flow of varnish from the brush. With too little thinning, the brush will drag. The varnish may handle fine without thinning, but this is unusual where sun and wind create a drying environment. Using too much thinner will cause the varnish to sag and run.

8. Sand with 220-grit paper and clean.

9. Apply the fourth coat of varnish as the third, with just enough thinner for brush control.

10. After four coats of varnish, it is time to prepare the surface for the extra-smooth finish coats. Sand after the fourth coat with 150-grit paper (if necessary) to smooth any grain in the finish. Avoid sanding all the varnish from edges, though in some areas breaking through to wood is likely. The key at this point is to develop a smooth surface.

11. Now the objective is to build film thickness. Apply five to ten coats of minimally thinned varnish. I work with a varnisher who actually leaves the varnish can open to let it thicken a little. It takes experience to handle such a thick coating, but the buildup is better.

    A paint company chemist once told me that, because varnish is clear, even with ultraviolet additives a thickness almost twice that of a pigmented coating is required to last as long in the marine environment.

    These buildup coats should be carefully applied to minimize brush marks. A smooth surface means an improved look and reduces the need to remove material between coats.

12. If you have done your preparation correctly, sanding will now be easier. You may be able to change the sandpaper grit from 220 to 280, 320, or even 400. Hinckley rarely sands finer

than 320 grit, but other varnishers use 400- to 600-grit papers, sometimes wet-sanding. This is particularly true for varnishes that leave a thin, dry film.

You need to work the surface to a smooth finish with the minimum removal of material. It is not uncommon to remove half or more of a varnish layer in trying to smooth the surface, particularly in the initial coats.

If you find you are still breaking through to bare wood after the fifth coat of varnish, stop and give the brightwork a good honest sanding, then touch up the areas of bare wood to help them "catch up" with surrounding areas.

These steps have addressed the process of building up from bare wood or brightwork with bare areas. Obviously, if you have been maintaining the brightwork on your boat, you will not need to do all this work each time. A properly built finish that is well maintained should last years.

Revarnishing

When is it time to revarnish? That depends on many variables, including the weather, the quality of varnish used, the application conditions, the thickness of the varnish film, and its subsequent maintenance. For example, if salt water or airborne pollutants are allowed to dry on the varnish day after day, the brightwork will degrade faster than if it is regularly washed with fresh water. That is why you see the crews of large yachts wiping down brightwork early in the morning. Though innovations are improving the durability of varnish, I have seen no perfect coating yet.

The Hinckley Company maintains a varnish evaluation program to help with their varnish material and application development. They keep test panels of many varnish types on the end of their dock to show which varnishes last longer and when a given coating may fail.

Until the perfect varnish is developed, I suggest revarnishing when the surface starts to lose its gloss or when there is any evidence of breakdown of the film. Signs of breakdown include light or dark spots in the varnish. Underlying wet areas also indicate a problem. Moisture under the film will eventually cause the varnish to lift. The only way to remedy this problem is to remove all the varnish over the wet area.

If you decide to revarnish, keep in mind that uneven wear is common. It pays to give a little extra attention to areas of high wear. An extra

A Better Way to Stow and Protect Your Wooden Boarding Ladder

John and Carol Melchner have owned Jocar, *a Bermuda 40, for twenty years—a lot of time to fine-tune it to their satisfaction. One of their boat improvement projects was designed to reduce the wear and tear on their wooden boarding ladder when it was left unprotected in a locker or on deck. They also wanted to give the ladder better protection when it was stored. Their solution was simple.*

John writes, "We made a gray Sunbrella bag for it and lined the inside with quality cotton bath towels. With the ladder in the bag, it is well protected from dents and scratches. We also designed the bag to have a heavy webbing sewn along the top above the zipper. We put four grommets in the webbing and four jib hanks on the grommets. When we are cruising and using the ladder most days, we attach the bag to the starboard lifeline just aft of the mainmast."

There is much to recommend this arrangement. As John says, "[The ladder] is convenient to use, easy to stow out of the way, and protected from the weather."

coat or two in such places is helpful.

Here is another key to successful varnishing: Timing is everything. It is often assumed that, if a northern boat needs varnish in the fall, it is okay to wait until spring to take care of it. Don't do it. Delay allows troubled areas to spread, and in the spring you will find that the scope of work has increased. Stay ahead of varnish deterioration; doing so will pay big dividends in quality, time, and money.

The procedure for revarnishing is the same as for the last coats of buildup outlined above, except in those areas where extra attention is required.

Repairing Old, Worn, or Cracked Varnish

Depending on the age of brightwork and the care it has received, it may be years after the first coats of varnish have been applied before any major patchwork or repair is needed. When it is required, it is important to deal with the problem area in an appropriate manner. Here are some hints.

1. When brightwork shows light or "dead" varnish in a small area on an otherwise good surface, you can remove the varnish in a small area and blend in fresh varnish over the surrounding area. This kind of problem may be created by a surface being hit with a hard object (such as a winch handle) or by moisture getting under the varnish near a fitting.

2. Remove the varnish in the damaged area only. A Red Devil 1-inch scraper is a good tool for this job. Scrape the area free of damaged varnish (often all of the film) and fair it into the surrounding good film. This faired area should be kept small. For example, for a damaged area of 2 inches in diameter, 1 inch of additional fairing may be enough. Test the area for smoothness by running your hand over it; you should feel minimal variation in the surface.

   For best performance, sharpen the scraper regularly. A 6- or 8-inch mill bastard file will do a fine job.

3. Sand the bare wood and faired area with 100-

grit paper, followed by 120, and finally 220. Each sanding should remove the scratches from the previous grit. The final result should be a fair, smooth surface.

4. Apply several touch-up coats to the area. The first coat should be cut 50 percent, the second 25 percent. The third and fourth coats will need minimal thinning. Be sure to observe proper drying times between coats.

   Sand between coats with 220-grit or finer sandpaper, just to clean up the surface. Remove the minimum amount of varnish.

5. When the patch has been built up to the thickness of the surrounding varnish, sand and varnish the full surface using the techniques described earlier to blend the patch with the whole. If the surface allows, a sanding block is an excellent tool to prepare for this coat.

This toerail exhibits signs of wear on the edges as well as varying stages of dying varnish. The yellowing on the top is apparent, and the light areas on the side indicate the early stages of the varnish letting go of the subsurface.

A bare hand will tend to contour to the dips and not flatten the surface.

It may take some time for the patch color to match the surrounding area, and it is possible the color will not blend in at all. I have seen some experts blend a small amount of color with the varnish to darken it—we use a mixture of burnt umber and black oil paints. It is, of course, important that the tinting material be compatible with the varnish.

When to Strip and Start from Scratch

It is a tough decision to strip a boat with varnished brightwork and start from scratch rebuilding the surface. Any of several conditions might indicate that patching the varnish is not going to work anymore.

- *Crazing.* Crazing will most likely show up after many years in a varnish film that has

The varnish on the side of this teak trim has lifted. When it's repaired, special attention should be paid to keeping the trim sealed tightly to the deck.

what appears to be good thickness. If you see many closely spaced cracks in the varnish, crazing has delivered it to the end of its useful life. When a scraper applied to a small area pulls large sections of varnish from the wood, it is useless to try to cut the old varnish film and patch it.

- *Large areas of moisture damage.* Moisture in such areas as the bottom edges of toerails will both darken the wood and lift the varnish. When the damaged coating is scraped away, the edges will be difficult if not impossible to fair in. Often the stripped area will extend several feet before blending in. In these cases, though it may be possible to patch, the size of the patch will cause the difference in color to stand out.

- *Old, thin varnish.* Varnish that has not been maintained with adequate thickness will lighten in color before it exposes the wood. Large areas of this light (usually pale yellow) varnish show that the whole surface is about to go bare. Building new varnish over old rarely works. The process can be undertaken without stripping, but the color and adhesion are better if the old, thin (and often dead) film

Fasteners have allowed moisture under the varnish around this hinge. Extended exposure caused additional damage in the form of cracks in the top. This is a good example of the need to keep ahead of varnish work.

is removed. Remember: The bond of a new varnish coating can never be stronger than the bond of the underlying film.

To repair these areas, you will have to strip the old varnish, using one of three methods: sanding, heat stripping, or chemical stripping.

Sanding is efficient only in areas where the film is already mostly gone. Overenthusiastic sanding can remove too much wood and remove it unevenly.

Hinckley usually uses heat guns for stripping. The Milwaukee Tool model they use, when moved along uniformly, softens the varnish for removal with a scraper without damaging the surrounding surface. Although taping is still required, the waste material itself will not affect other surfaces.

Chemical strippers such as 5F5 work well, but

they can expose other paint and gelcoat surfaces to damage. When using these strippers, double tape the surface and use masking paper to keep the stripper off surfaces other than the wood. Personal protective gear, such as gloves and safety glasses, is also important.

Apply the stripper with a brush and allow it to stand according to the manufacturer's directions—usually several minutes. Remove the material with a scraper or bronze wool.

When stripping with either heat or chemicals, change the tape at least once during the process.

After stripping, sand the surface with 60- or 80-grit paper, depending on the surface condition, to restore the wood color.

Sand again with 100 grit and proceed as with new wood.

If a fitting or trim piece mounted on a brightwork surface needs rebedding, remove it before revarnishing. Good solid varnish layers running under a fitting will last longer than a varnish edge at the fitting base. Then remount the fitting with adequate bedding or sealant.

Troubleshooting Varnish Problems

The following information is adapted from a troubleshooting guide that comes with the Pettit Paint Company's application instructions. I find it helpful.

Problem: Varnish is wrinkling. It has not cured properly as a result of being applied in too hot an area or it has been recoated before it is ready. In either case, the surface is shrinking faster than the underlying varnish layer or layers.

Cure: Be careful of the time you choose to varnish. If it is too hot but you must continue, use a thinner layer of varnish. If the varnish gums up the sandpaper when preparing for the next coat, stop and allow it to cure further before continuing.

   If you are using a polyurethane varnish on top of another type of varnish, the problem may be in the solvents. Check with your varnish manufacturer. Many varnishes may be used over other types of varnish, but the underlying varnish must have aged at least a couple of months.

Problem: Contaminated, rough, or dirty finish.

Cure: Resand and recoat. When recoating, pay particular attention to the cleanliness of the work area, brushes, pots, and varnish. Use a strainer. Press the brush against the side of container (not the top) when removing excess varnish.

   Work with a tack rag and clean the brush as required if there appears to be additional contamination.

Problem: Poor adhesion, blisters, or lifting or peeling varnish.

Cure: Use extra effort in preparing surface. Remove all old, suspect varnish and sand thoroughly.

   Varnishing in weather that's too cold or wet will also cause these problems. Choose your weather more wisely and ensure that the surface is entirely dry before applying the varnish.

Problem: Dull surface on new work.

Cure: This happens when new varnish has been

When varnish removal is required, careful application of heat and scraping will remove most of the film.

exposed to moisture or cold too soon after application. Select your weather more carefully and/or start varnishing earlier in the day.

Oiled Teak Exteriors

Oiled exterior teak is lovely to look at when it has been recently done. Left unattended for long periods, though, it turns dark and can be quite unsightly. This is why I and many others feel that varnish is not such a bad choice for exterior teak. There are, however, those who still prefer the look and feel of oiled teak.

Materials

Oils used on exterior woods include linseed (usually "boiled") and tung. They are mixed with other materials by manufacturers to provide better handling and longevity, as well as different appearances. Because the life of a "new" oiled finish can be rather short, do not skimp on the cost when purchasing quality teak oil. Hinckley currently uses Sikkens Cetol teak oil or Star brite Premium Golden Teak Oil for exterior applications.

Preparation

Preparing to apply an oil finish is much like preparing to varnish new wood. Review the information on pages 3–5 about cleaning teak and follow the varnish preparation steps (numbers 1 through 8) on page 42–44. One key to successful oil application is having a smooth, clean wood surface. This is true with all finishes and will be repeated again and again in this book. The bottom line is that the surface should be as smooth, clean, and dry for initial oiling as it should be for varnishing.

Application

1. Apply the oil with a bristle brush or foam brush or a lint-free rag. (This is an excellent time to use a foam brush.) Be especially careful of splatters when working with oil; it is thin and easily sprays everywhere. Keep a clean rag handy for immediate cleanup of drips and splatters.

2. Allow the oil to dry and then apply a second coat. Drying time will vary among oils, but it is typically less than one hour in moderate weather. Oils in their natural state want to remain tacky on the surface. Different manufacturers process or blend in additives with the oil to accelerate drying time. Read the directions carefully to guide you in the timing of recoating.

   Basic oiling concludes with this step. Hinckley recommends two coats of oil for a season in Maine. Southern boats will need significantly more because the sun deteriorates the surface faster. If you are striving for a rubbed oil finish, continue with the following steps.

3. Apply the third coat and, while it is still wet, sand the surface with 320- to 400-grit wet-or-dry sandpaper. You may wish to work on a small area to prevent the oil from drying while you are rubbing the finish. If the material be-

comes dry, simply apply more oil. The sandpaper will clog quickly during this process, so turn it over or change it frequently.

4. Wipe off the sanding waste with a clean cloth, working more across the grain than with it to smooth the surface with the paste and to prevent wiping the oil from the grain. Allow the surface to dry for approximately one hour.

5. Apply at least two additional coats using the same process as described in steps 3 and 4. The number of additional coats is subject to the finish you are trying to achieve and the life you wish. Using sandpaper up to 600 grit on final coats will provide a finer finish.

   Remember to properly store oily rags and dispose of them in a safe manner. Hang the rags out to dry or submerse in water. Oily rags have a nasty habit of starting fires in confined lockers.

Bleaching Exterior and Interior Woods

Bleaching the woods commonly used in yacht construction is a frustrating and often less than totally successful endeavor, although it is not a difficult procedure. Bleaching will often change the color of surrounding woods while attacking the stains. Hinckley currently uses Snappy Teak Nu or Travaco Te-Ka two-part cleaners to remove stains from teak. On ash, they are having some success with Klean-Strip, a two-part wood bleach. With mahogany and cherry, however, the success rate is low. In addition to the products already mentioned here, you might try Clorox bleach, oxalic acid, or trisodium phosphate (TSP) on some stains.

It is important to use a neutralizer to stop the bleaching process and to prevent burning the wood with the more potent bleaches. Water will work with most single-part chemicals. Borax, soda ash, and vinegar are often used as neutralizers for milder bleaches such as oxalic acid. A special neutralizer is usually the part B of two-part systems. Hinckley suggests that you purchase and use two times the volume of part

B as part A with products such as Te-Ka.

My experience with mahogany (mostly on interiors) has occasionally produced a bleached surface of a color that, to my eye, looked as bad as the original stain. Experiment and use bleach sparingly. You may need to follow aggressive bleaching of the stain with milder bleaching of the entire piece, to even out colors.

Use bleaches carefully. Wearing boots, gloves, rain gear, and glasses is a good idea when bleaching large exterior areas such as decks.

Bleaching with Two-Part Cleaner/Bleaches

1. Start the bleaching process by carefully covering adjacent or lower surfaces that might be affected by the draining bleach. Paint, varnish, wax, and gelcoat can all be affected by bleach streaks.

2. Rinse the area. It will be necessary to rinse again several times during the bleaching process.

3. Apply the bleach evenly with a brush or fine Scotch-Brite pad. It is important to spread the bleach evenly to prevent streaking of the wood. Immediately wipe up any spills or drips.

4. The surface will turn dark as dirt and oil are lifted. Apply a second coat if the surface is particularly dirty.

5. If the surface has a thick layer of bleach and oil buildup, a plastic scraper is helpful in removing the excess material.

6. Apply the neutralizer (part B) to the surface. Ensure that the whole surface is covered. Scrub the surface lightly with a soft bristled brush or Scotch-Brite pad to assist the neutralization and help remove surface contaminants. Scrubbing across the grain will preserve soft wood fiber.

7. Let this coating sit for ten minutes or so; then rinse off. Use copious amounts of water.

8. Carefully inspect the area for complete neutralization of part A. Bleach that is left on and not neutralized will continue working and will turn the surface black. If necessary, apply additional part B and rinse again. This process is extremely important. It is also why many experts recommend purchasing two parts of B for each part A.

The information presented in this chapter is intended to help you feel comfortable working with either varnish or oil. The instructions, although somewhat generic, should work for most of the paints, oils, varnishes, and bleaches found on the market. There is, however, no substitute for experience, so dig in and give it a try.

CHAPTER 5

Interior Brightwork

The previous chapter discussed the approach to building and maintaining exterior brightwork. This chapter will expand upon those materials and methods and add information that will be helpful when doing interior brightwork projects. Maintaining interior surfaces with varnish or oil varies somewhat from doing so for exterior brightwork. For instance, cabin soles need durable finishes to withstand hard use, while interior bulkheads typically do not. Neither surface is subjected to exposure from the sun as much as exterior brightwork.

Materials

Many of the materials used for exterior brightwork projects—pots, strainers, and tapes—are the same for interior projects. Below are a few additional items you might use.

Varnish

The varnishes used on exterior brightwork are also sometimes used in boat interiors. This is particularly true with teak and mahogany finishes. Lighter woods, however, are normally finished with a clearer varnish than the darker

woods. Polyurethane-based varnishes, either one- or two-part, work especially well because they are clearer than standard varnishes.

Rubbed-effect varnishes are prevalent in yacht interiors. Thinner than their glossy counterparts, they also normally do not contain the UV-protecting additives of exterior varnishes. They are, however, often very forgiving. They apply easily and dry to a surface that will hide a number of sins.

Hinckley currently uses a combination of Hinckley or Epifanes high gloss for buildup and Pettit Ultra-V-Gold Satin #2065 satin for the last two or three coats on warm woods. Z*Spar V975 satin sheen varnish is used on light woods such as ash.

The experts at Hinckley are always testing new and different materials to use on cabin soles as well as other finish areas. The current standard for soles is two coats of System Three clear epoxy, followed by three or more coats of Rivale Max-Glass, a two-part polyurethane varnish. The combination creates a highly durable finish with an unusually strong bond to the surface of the wood.

One experimental finish under consideration replaces the System Three epoxy with Duratec Crystal Clear Coating, which is then covered

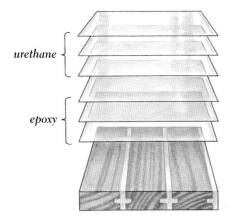

It takes many coats of epoxy and urethane varnish to develop a cabin sole finish in Hinckley yachts.

with the polyurethane topcoats. It is a polyester resin with little color and is catalyzed with MEK (methyl ethyl ketone) hardener for faster cure times than an epoxy base would have. What once took up to three weeks to finish (with a two-part polyurethane) now can be done in two to three days.

Oils

Many production boats come with oiled interior surfaces. In my opinion, unlike the use of oil for exterior brightwork, an oiled interior surface is functional—and it certainly is an easier finish to build. Although a couple of coats of oil will do, it is worth the effort to develop a polished oil finish on bulkheads. The finish will hold for years with minimum care.

Oils for interior surfaces are similar to exterior oils except that they don't have the same UV protection. Hinckley currently uses Watco oil for interior finishing.

Stick with a good linseed or tung oil. Products with a tung oil base are the most prevalent. Some oils are clearer than others; the final finish color is very much the owner's preference.

Brushes

There is ongoing debate about which is better—a foam or natural bristle brush. Hinckley varnishers seem to favor the Epifanes china bristle or the Coronoa Heritage natural bristle brushes and usually use the 2-inch size. For tough-to-reach areas, they use a Torrington #20 artist's brush.

Tack Rags

With most finishes, the Gerson tack rags I've recommended earlier will work well for interior projects. When using polyurethanes, however, use the tack rags sold by U.S. Paint for use with Awlgrip varnish, or the rags sold by Sterling for their polyurethane paint systems.

Stains and Fillers

Boatbuilders will often use a stain on new wood to provide a more uniform color. The stains are the same as those used on nonmarine woodwork and are available in many different colors.

Fillers are typically used to hide blemishes in wood. Occasionally, stain and filler are blended to provide a mixture that will both color and fill rough grain on a wood panel. Years ago, Hinckley used a filler-stain on mahogany interiors; the tendency today is to use less filler. These materials may be necessary in an interior to blend new work to old. Interlux #42 is commonly used in many older boats with mahogany bulkheads.

Varnished Bulkheads and Trim

The trim on most Hinckley interiors is varnished with a satin finish. You'll occasionally see some painted trim, but most boatowners hate to cover up that beautiful and expensive wood for which they paid so dearly. More and more owners are now requesting some gloss varnish, too, rather than doing everything in the traditional rubbed-effect finish.

Applying varnish to interior surfaces requires more initial effort, but it will yield improved surface life and, in my opinion, improved appearance. The specific materials needed for varnishing an interior will vary with the type of wood. Mahogany and teak are often covered with a traditional golden-colored varnish. Lighter colored woods, such as ash and birch, are coated with clear varnishes. Warm woods, such as cherry, are done either way. Stains and fillers are occasionally used in these applications.

Preparation

Interior brightwork preparation needs to be carried out in slightly gentler fashion than that for exterior brightwork, for two reasons: The surrounding surfaces are highly finished areas, and the surfaces themselves are often thin veneers that can be damaged easily. Pardon my repetition of many of the steps outlined in Chapter 4 (Exterior Brightwork), but they are so important.

1. Remove all fabric components (cushions, curtains, rugs) and any other easily soiled materials. Place protective covering over anything that you don't want to damage. Consider putting masking paper or cardboard on countertops and other horizontal surfaces.

2. Clean the surface to be varnished with a mild solvent such as denatured alcohol (stove alcohol) to remove as much surface oil, dirt, and sealant as possible. Allow the surface to dry thoroughly.

3. Carefully tape the areas to be varnished. I recommend taping a bulkhead-to-corner post (plywood-to-solid) joint if you are going to use a harsh (rougher than 220-grit) sandpaper on the corner post. The solid corner post or trim will handle the deep scratches; the plywood veneer probably will not. After you see the glue under a veneer starting to appear through the scratches, it is too late. A common problem in the production of boats is for the edges of plywood to be sanded too vigorously. The plywood then has to be replaced or reveneered—not a pleasant prospect for the boatowner or yard.

4. Sand the surface to smooth the grain and remove unwanted finish features, using 120- to 320-grit paper. The choice of grit will depend upon the surface type and condition. Remember, it will not take long to sand through a lovely plywood face veneer with 120-grit sandpaper. That surface should already be quite

smooth; 220- or 320-grit paper will work nicely.

Take the time to thoroughly sand the full surface; that is, do not breeze by the small indents and corners. Your effort now will save you time later—you'll have less sanding to do and will probably get by with fewer coats of varnish to get a nicely sealed finish.

5. Vacuum the surface and surrounding area. Trust me—any dust that is left around will end up in the varnish surface. Hinckley personnel often place a room fan in an overhead hatch with a furnace filter placed on top of that to apply positive pressure to the interior cabin. This helps push dust out and inhibits exterior dust and other pollutants from entering the cabin. It also stirs up any dust that *is* in the cabin, so clean extra carefully and let the fan run for awhile before final cleanup and varnishing.

6. Tack the surface lightly with a quality tack rag, such as the ones made by Gerson or Red Devil.

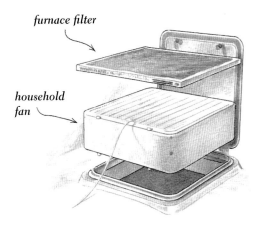

furnace filter

household fan

When you are varnishing, a household fan placed over a hatch with a furnace filter taped over it provides a supply of air to below-deck areas. The air pushing in moves dust out of the cabin and helps prevent other dust-laden air from entering.

Stain and Filler Application

1. Apply any stain or filler at this point. Most stains are applied with either a brush or clean rag, but read the manufacturer's recommendations. Use the material sparingly—a little will go a long way.

2. Remove excess stain with clean, dry, lint-free rags, gently wiping the surface with a circular motion. If you are using a product with a filler in the stain, do not rub too hard because it will lift the filler from the wood grain. Alternatively, wiping too softly will allow excess filler to accumulate and create an unattractive paste finish under the varnish. If you are concerned about this particular step, try a test patch in some relatively out-of-the-way location. Better yet, make a test panel out of a small matching wood piece.

Varnish Application

Follow all the steps for varnish stirring, straining, and brushing outlined in Chapter 4 (Exterior Brightwork).

1. Apply the first coat of varnish. Depending upon the thickness of the varnish and the wood being finished, you may wish to thin the varnish with an appropriate manufacturer-recommended thinner. Hinckley varnishers use gloss varnish for buildup on most interiors, but they thin the first coat 50 percent (just as they do for the first coats of exterior brightwork buildup). On wood such as teak, which is oily and resistant to film adhesion, thinning the varnish is an especially good practice; doing so will improve the mechanical bond. On the other hand, if you choose to use rubbed-effect varnish (which is already quite thin) on a mahogany surface, it will not require much, if any, thinning; doing so would be primarily for handling and varnish flow.

   Lighting problems complicate varnishing in a boat interior. It is an excellent idea to have a strong light source that can be moved around in the cabin so you can carefully examine the film surface for potential sags and errant bugs.

A fluorescent-tube trouble light works well for this purpose.

2. After allowing the proper drying time, lightly sand the finish—220-grit sandpaper should be the roughest needed at this stage. Go easy on the corners and beware of oversanding veneers.

3. Thoroughly vacuum and reclean the surface and surrounding areas. Replace any damaged masking tape.

4. Repeat steps 1, 2, and 3 until a good base film has been established. The thinner, rubbed-effect varnish will require more coats (perhaps five or six) than a heavier gloss varnish, which will need maybe three or four.

5. When the base film has been built up, thoroughly sand the surface to remove any grainy texture and imperfections. Be careful again of any radius and veneer edges.

6. Repeat steps 1, 2, and 3 for additional coats until the desired surface and film thickness has been achieved. Hinckley varnishers apply as many as eight to ten coats of interior varnish on a new boat. This surface will hold up for many years with little maintenance.

Refinishing

It seems to me that the key to maintaining varnished interior brightwork is not so much the varnishing technique as it is knowing when to varnish. As with all varnished surfaces, it is important to revarnish before the old surface wears or breaks down. Look for any lifting areas of dead or yellowing varnish. An increase in grain on the surface is also a good indication that the finish is giving out.

   Thoroughly clean the surface to prepare it for revarnishing. Well-meaning folks often apply furniture polish and wax to bulkheads; these products work into the grain and pores of wood and create havoc when it comes time to refinish. Any polish or wax residue will affect the bond and surface of the fresh varnish. Clean with a strong detergent and possibly a chemical wax-remover before sanding. Failure to remove all contaminants from the surface will result in poor adhesion and "fish eyes" (varnish film separation).

Allowing these louvered doors to deteriorate until they needed stripping or extensive refinishing would result in a major task. Note that the use of a small brush allows you to coat one strip at a time and apply varnish evenly.

When the bulkheads are clean, follow the same steps as outlined in the buildup procedure on page 56.

Building an Oiled Wood Finish

What follows is a basic procedure for developing a fine rubbed-oil finish on interior bulkheads and trim.

Surface Preparation

1. Remove all fabric components (cushions, curtains, rugs) and other easily soiled materials. It is much easier to remove these items now than to clean them later. Spilled oil can leave a nasty, permanent stain on a cushion.

2. Clean the surface with a mild solvent to remove as much surface oil, dirt, and sealant as possible. Allow the surface to dry thoroughly.

3. Tape off areas that will be oiled to prevent sanding scratches and oil from getting on adjacent surfaces. Oil is thin and will readily splatter and drip. Consider placing masking paper or cardboard on countertops and other horizontal surfaces for extra protection.

4. Sand the surface to smooth the grain; use grits from 120 to 400. The choice depends upon the surface type and condition. For instance, it does not take long to sand through a plywood face veneer with 120-grit sandpaper. That surface should already be relatively smooth. Sandpaper with 320 or 400 grit, applied lightly, would work better. Handrails, though, may be fairly rough and, if so, would need to be sanded with 120 grit before moving on to the finer grits. When in doubt, start with a finer (higher number) grit.

Sand with progressively finer grits until you have removed all scratches with 400-grit sandpaper. The surface should be at least as smooth, clean, and dry for initial oiling as it would be for varnishing. When sanding, use a good disposable dust mask or, better yet, a mask with disposable cartridges for sanding and application. Disposable gloves are helpful as well.

5. Clean the surface and surrounding area with a vacuum. Oil application is less sensitive to dust flying around than varnish, but working in a clean environment will let you more readily see drips and other problems.

6. Tack the surface lightly with a quality tack rag such as the Gerson or Red Devil products.

Applying Oil Finishes

1. Apply the oil with a brush or clean, lint-free rag. A foam brush works well for this project. Sparingly dip the brush into the oil—a little goes a long way. Oil is thin and easily splatters and runs everywhere, so be especially careful. Keep a clean rag and thinner handy for immediate cleanup of drips and splatters.

2. Allow the oil to dry and apply a second coat without sanding. Drying times will vary with the brand, but it normally takes less than one hour in moderate weather. Follow the manufacturer's recommendations.

3. Apply the third coat of oil, beginning in a small, manageable area—3 square feet or smaller. Wet-sand the surface with 400-grit wet-or-dry sandpaper while it is still wet. The sandpaper will clog quickly, so turn the paper over frequently.

4. Wipe off the sanding waste, which is a gummy paste, with a clean cloth. Rub across the grain to smooth the surface and fill the grain with the paste. Allow the surface to dry for approximately one hour.

5. Apply at least two additional coats, then sand and wipe as in steps 3 and 4.

    The number of additional coats you apply is determined by the quality of surface preparation (that is, how well the grain was smoothed before you started oiling); how smooth a finish you want; and the surface life you want. The surface life will be affected by the quality of the sealing job. I recommend you apply two coats of oil for each sanding cycle.

Two additional tips: Using sandpaper of up to 600 grit on final coats will provide a finer finish. And remember to properly and safely store and dispose of oily rags—they present a fire hazard.

Refinishing Oiled Woodwork

It should not be necessary to frequently refinish interior brightwork that has been treated following the above process. A thin coat, or possibly two, of oil, applied annually, should do the job well.

1. Prepare the surface by washing it with a clean, lint-free rag and a mild solvent.

2. Scuff the surface with 400-grit sandpaper or fine bronze wool.

3. Apply the oil in a thin layer, using a brush or clean rag. If the first coat is quickly absorbed by the wood, more oil is required. Apply a second coat after the first has dried. Do not apply heavy coats of oil.

4. When the finish has dried, burnish it with another clean rag to remove excess oil. If the surface has been reasonably maintained, wet-sanding is probably not required annually.

Every once in a while, perhaps every six to eight years, you'll want to remove the finish with a solvent and rebuild it. Use the procedure explained in the earlier section "Building an Oiled Wood Finish."

Cabin Soles

Cabin soles create a unique problem. Almost all Hinckley owners want a clear, durable finish that does not discolor the holly in the traditional teak and holly sole built into most of their boats. They want a finish that can be cleaned easily and that is highly resistant to spills of everything from hot cooking grease to caustic cleaning materials.

If it's possible to remove a panel to be finished and take it off the boat, do so. This reduces dust in the boat's interior. What's more, a shop often has better conditions for varnishing. This panel is being sanded hard before building several coats of varnish.

Some owners like a sealed or oiled finish on their cabin soles because it is less slippery than a gloss varnish finish. I have found, however, that a slightly worn varnished sole is not too difficult to navigate on, as long as it is kept clean.

Preparing a Cabin Sole for Varnish

Preparing a cabin sole for varnish is the same as for exterior brightwork.

1. Clean the wood. If the surface is old and greasy, clean the sole with the methods outlined for cleaning a teak deck in Chapter 1 (Day-to-Day Care). If the surface is in good condition, Pettit 12120 thinner or its equivalent is acceptable for this step.

2. Tape any bulkheads, trim, or hardware that abut the sole. If you are going to use an electric sander, the tape will help prevent the sander scratching those surfaces. It is possible that you will need to replace the tape before varnishing. Remember, though, if the tape is scratched away, you have saved the underlying surface from abrasion. Use quality masking tape such as 3M Fine Line #218.

3. Sand the surface smooth with a moderate-grit sandpaper. If the wood has aged, you may need to start with 120 grit or possibly rougher, to even the grain of the wood and bring back the color or new look of the wood. Note: If your cabin sole is built of plywood, use no rougher than 220-grit paper to prevent over-sanding the veneer. If hand sanding, use a sanding block wherever possible to improve the flatness of the surface and avoid creating grooves from finger pressure.

   Steps 1, 2, and 3 are extremely important. Do not shortcut the sanding. When you apply the first coat, the wood grain will swell, which will require more sanding and removing all but the film in the low areas of the grain. Proper initial sanding of the surface will minimize this intercoat sanding.

4. If you have used 120-grit paper to start, sand again with a finer grit to remove the scratches from the previous paper. You may be able to shift directly to 220 paper. If 220 does not seem to remove the scratches, try an intermediate paper such as 150 grit.

5. Clean the work area thoroughly. Vacuum the sole and the surrounding cabin. If possible, use a fan with a furnace filter to provide positive pressure in the cabin. It will help reduce the possibility of dust coming into the cabin. (For more information on using a fan, see page 55.)

6. Retape those areas where the masking tape has been abraded.

7. Clean the surface with a thinner or other appropriate solvent to remove the dirt and oils from the surface that have accumulated during the sanding stages. Cleaning will also reduce the surface oil in a teak sole. The oil in the wood prohibits the finish coating from sinking into the grain and developing a good mechanical bond. The thinner recommended by the varnish or epoxy manufacturer would be a good selection. As a substitute for the recommended thinner, acetone also works well on bare wood; on prevarnished surfaces, try denatured alcohol.

8. *Lightly rub* the surface with a tack rag just before applying the final coat to remove the last bits of dust and dirt that have collected. Pressing hard on a tack rag will leave a sticky surface that will interfere with smooth application. Frequently refold the tack rag to keep it doing its job.

Varnishing a Cabin Sole

If you are using a two-part polyurethane varnish or a single-part varnish, mix it following the manufacturer's instructions, being particularly careful to avoid introducing air bubbles into the varnish. Do not shake the varnish. Proceed as directed on pages 44–46, following the instructions for exterior brightwork varnishing.

Applying Epoxy to a Cabin Sole

1. If you are using an epoxy base, carefully mix it in a clean container. Next, thin the epoxy as recommended by the manufacturer until it can be handled easily and will flow to a smooth surface after being applied. An epoxy mixture will be significantly thicker than a varnish, but that's okay—the flat surface of a sole is ideal for the epoxy to flow.

2. Apply the first coat of epoxy with a brush or roller. A foam roller works well for this application, and a foam brush will help the liquid flow. Your brushing technique is not as critical with epoxy as it is with varnish.

3. After thorough curing (usually less than 24 hours), sand the first coat of epoxy with 220-grit paper. If the epoxy film has not dried properly it will tend to fill or "gum up" the sandpaper, and the surface of the work will not smooth properly. Wait additional time before proceeding. Also, if you are using an amine-cured epoxy such as the West System, it is advisable to wash the surface with warm soapy water before sanding to remove the amine "blush." Other epoxies, such as the System Three clear epoxy, do not contain amine and therefore do not "blush."

   The manufacturer's instructions should recommend a normal drying time before recoating. With epoxy, as with most materials, it will vary with temperature, humidity, and ventilation.

   Clean, wash, and tack the surface again when sanding is complete. Replace any damaged masking tape.

4. Apply the second coat of epoxy, following the same procedure as for the first coat.

5. Sand the surface more aggressively with 120-grit sandpaper. The objective is to remove as much of the grainy texture on the surface as possible so future layers will flow to a smooth finish.

6. Proceed with two to four coats of polyurethane varnish, applied as for exterior brightwork (see pages 44–46). In each of these layers, the key to success is proper sanding and thorough cleaning. If those are done well, the prospect for a shining finish is greatly improved.

Buildup coats should be applied carefully to minimize brush marks. Keeping a smooth surface means not only an improved look, but less sanding between coats.

Depending on the boat's use, a properly

It is a good idea to start by brushing varnish around hardware and then work over the larger, open areas. This eliminates flow lines from the short strokes around the hardware. Note how this foam brush is being pulled from the center over the edge to reduce edge drips.

applied epoxy or polyurethane finish to a sole should last for two to three years. I have seen cabin soles in good condition that have not been refinished in many more years.

The finishing techniques described here do not vary much from those used on exterior brightwork. In both cases, the bulk of the work is in getting ready to apply the varnish—not the varnishing itself. Patience is truly a virtue when it comes to varnishing.

Topside, Deck, and Interior Paints

Topside and interior painting are projects in which owners are frequently involved. This is in part because developments in materials have made paints easier to handle and safer to use. New polyurethane paints provide high-gloss finishes with an incredible amount of chemical and weather resistance. The topside paint products discussed here are for both hull (above the waterline) and exterior deck use. Alkyd enamel finishes are used for topside and interior applications, as well.

Coating Materials

Today's marine finishes have evolved through several generations. The original marine paints were, in effect, pigmented varnishes, limited in gloss and durability. These gave way to alkyd enamels, which offered longer protection but still fell short of the ideal surface finish. To improve water resistance and shorten drying times, alkyd enamels were modified with silicone and/or polyurethane, but over time these mixtures too were found lacking in luster, and health concerns arose. Recently, newly developed urethanes and epoxy coatings have taken a dominant place in the marketplace. Health is still a concern, per-

haps more so; however, this is the focus of current advances, and users are now better informed about proper protection by manufacturers.

Single-part polyurethanes under development are less volatile and offer the wear, water resistance, and high gloss of the two-part polyurethanes. Other new products include water-based paints, which are better both for the environment and the user and are easier to clean up. This drive in the paint manufacturing industry to reduce the VOC (volatile organic compounds) or harmful solvents in paint products is spurred on by federal legislation and an increasing environmental awareness.

And then, of course, there is still gelcoat, which is basically a specially formulated pigmented resin that is normally applied when a boat is molded. Some companies, including Hinckley, are now using unpigmented gelcoat. (Hinckley uses this coating mainly on the hull. The decks are still gelcoated in the traditional fashion.) The unpigmented gelcoat permits better laminate quality control. Painting need not be done until just before delivery, giving the owner longer to choose a color and the builder a chance to repair surface scratches created during construction.

Billy Black

The introduction of urethane paints has enabled owners to obtain incredibly glossy topside paint jobs. These paint jobs are not just pretty faces; when properly applied they have good adhesion and are more resistant to staining and fading than are gelcoats.

At one time, owners of fiberglass boats considered re-gelcoating their boats rather than painting them because that first paint job often led to annual painting. Painting was not an attractive alternative because, besides lacking gloss, paints that were on the market before the 1970s generally did not adhere well to fiberglass. Recent developments in gelcoat applications have reduced, but not eliminated, the difficulty and expense of reapplying gelcoat to a hull.

The advent of the modern painting systems, primarily polyurethane, has lessened this dilemma. The bottom line now is that most fiberglass boats and, of course, all aluminum and wood boats are painted or repainted with one of these newer painting systems. Sometimes the polyurethanes are mixed with flattening agents to decrease the high gloss of the standard finish, because it shows every defect in the surface.

Development is headed toward making single- and two-part polyurethanes easier and safer to apply. Spray application of two-part poly-urethanes is recommended for professionals only. They can be difficult to handle and contain more harmful chemicals than single-part polyurethanes. Isocyanates are deadly materials that increase respiratory hazards, especially when sprayed; they are used in two-part linear polyurethanes such as Awlgrip and Interlux's Interthane Plus. None of these chemicals should be allowed to touch the skin, and respiratory protection is also important. If you decide to try spraying these paints, use full-body protection when handling them. At a minimum, use paper suits, hoods, gloves, and proper fitting and working respirators—a mask with a separate clean air supply is even better. The good news is the do-it-yourself boater can now apply these paints with a brush or roller, using different thinners and catalysts. Nevertheless, safety precautions must be followed.

Today's marine paints are a mixture of several basic components including resins, pigments, oils, solvents, dryers or catalysts, and additives. The components are carefully selected to yield the right mix for a given subsurface and atmosphere. When selecting a paint product, it is very important to consider the surface on which the paint is to be applied—you must be sure that the new coating is compatible with the old coating. The exception to this is if you are applying the first coat of paint to a fiberglass boat. In this case, it is critical that you remove any wax coating using a dewaxer before surface preparation.

Older enamel finishes might not be compatible with the thinners in a newer paint. If in doubt, paint a small test patch under the stern where it will not be seen.

Be aware, too, that if the old film is not well attached to the subsurface, it is likely that the old and new will peel off together long before the life of the newer surface is ended. Additionally, a high-gloss finish will show up all the defects in any surface that is not fair. In that case, a lower-gloss enamel might be a better choice.

Finally, the cost of a good one- or two-part polyurethane paint such as U.S. Paint Awlgrip, Interlux Interthane Plus, or Imron, among others, may be two to three times that of an enamel. Also, it usually takes longer to prepare a surface for polyurethane paint. The polyurethane, however, should last at least five years; an enamel lasts two years.

Whichever paint you choose, the successful application relies heavily on properly preparing the surface and using the right tools. Above all, remember: *Any new coating has no better adhesion than whatever is under it.*

Other Materials

Sandpaper

High-quality sandpaper not only improves the finish by giving uniform abrasion, but often pays off in longer paper life. The better silicon carbide sheets do not load up with dust as quickly as standard production sandpaper. Here are some recommended grits:

- For the initial surface preparation, including working with putties and primers, you may need grits ranging from 80 to 220.
- For the final primer and topcoat sanding, you will want grits ranging from 220 to 600. 3M Tri-M-Ite paper works well for this purpose.
- For sanding topsides and decks, 400- to 600-grit wet-or-dry sandpaper is often used.
- For topcoat repair, including problems such as removing "sags" (drips) and polishing out minor abrasions, you will want grits ranging from 220 to 600; sometimes you might even need up to 2,000-grit paper on high-gloss surfaces.

Sanding Equipment

There are three types of sanding machines commonly used in topsides preparation: (1) a disc sander using a "soft back" pad for the heavy fairing jobs or to remove old crazed gelcoat and putty; (2) a dual action (DA) orbital sander for standard surface and intercoat sanding; and (3) a palm sander with a vibrating or orbital motion for intermediate work. These sanders typically leave scratches in fine finish work unless a finer sandpaper is used than is recommended for the DA sander. They are, however, the most commonly used sanders for do-it-yourself boaters and often, the only ones available.

Application Equipment

Boatyards commonly use spray equipment, as do some handy boatowners. Advances in brushing systems, however, have reduced the need to use spray equipment, so I won't be addressing the full details of spray equipment setup. If you wish to use spray equipment, read the manufacturer's instructions to learn a few tips about the mixtures and the proper environment for the job. For small jobs, auto supply stores sell a disposable spray applicator that works well with paint, gelcoat, primer, and varnish.

If you are using a roller, the nap cover should be short (¼ inch); if you are using polyurethane paint, buy roller covers that are identified as

For small jobs, auto supply stores sell disposable spray applicators that work well with paint, thinned gelcoat, primers, and varnish. The Preval unit shown here has a reusable glass container that is screwed into a disposable aerosol spray head. The liquid must be fairly thin for spraying, but even gelcoat, cut with acetone, can be sprayed. Experimentation is the key. Depending on the liquid's viscosity, the power unit will work for two or more fills of the bottle; when it's used up, unscrew the power unit from the bottle, dispose of it, screw on a new power unit, and continue. Do not attempt too large a project (no bigger than a hatch cover) with this type of sprayer without having several spare power units.

polyurethane-grade mohair or foam. Be careful when you select roller covers; some will disintegrate in polyurethane thinners.

If you choose to brush the paint, I recommend using brushes with natural bristles. Chinese hog or badger hair bristles are the best. Hinckley uses Omega china bristle or Red Tree badger hair bristle brushes.

Wiping Cloths and Tack Rags

Rags and wiping cloths should be made of clean, lint-free material. Keep a good supply on hand and be sure to change cloths frequently.

Tack rags should be selected carefully for use with polyurethane paints because any residue may conflict with the paint. They are, however, usually fine for using with enamel. Hinckley uses Gerson, Sterling, or U.S. Paint Awlgrip tack rags.

Tape

A high-quality masking tape is essential. Most paint manufacturers recommend 3M Scotch Brand Fine Line tape because it leaves a clean paint line and resists paint from "bleeding" under the tape edge.

Masking Paper

Masking paper is necessary if you are going to spray, and it's not a bad idea to use it if you are brushing paint over a fresh boottop or wide striping.

Solvents and Cleaners

Use only solvents and cleaners recommended by the paint manufacturer. Many painting problems are incurred by using improper solvents.

Fillers and Fairing Compounds

Every painting system I have used has a compatible product for filling and fairing. The cost of the project dictates that you use manufacturer's products and follow the directions and recommendations.

Most paint systems have at least two types of fillers; you'll need one or both depending on the job. One filler is quite fine and will smooth easily over small defects. It will also work well as final smoothing over larger patches. The other is a thicker mixture that will fill rapidly and can be easily sanded and shaped.

Both epoxy and polyester fillers of both densities will be found. The epoxy fillers will be slightly more flexible and adhere better to most surfaces; however, they will cure more slowly than most polyester fillers. One type of filler may not adhere to another; therefore, it's recommended you stay with a manufacturer's system.

Preparing the Topsides

I cannot emphasize enough the necessity of a good surface on which to apply topside paint. The high gloss of the current generation of finishes will show the smallest defect, but if done correctly, the finish quality will be remarkable. The time invested at this stage will return big dividends. If you can't achieve a smooth surface, consider using a paint with less gloss. It will hide some of the problems and look better.

The following steps for preparing topsides are generic. They should apply to almost all types of hulls, as well as decks, although the materials will vary. I will concentrate on rolling and brushing techniques because these methods are becoming easier to use—and they are certainly easier than spraying.

My primary experience is with Pettit Paint Co., U.S. Paint, and International Paint products.

No doubt I have missed some tricks or important points that are provided by other companies. Be sure to familiarize yourself with all your paint manufacturer's instructions.

1. Start with a thorough cleaning of the topsides. If the water beads while you are washing, check for residual wax. Use lots of water and a commercial nonalkaline detergent such as Shaklee Bio Cleaner or Simple Green. Some high-grade household detergents may also do the job. It will take a strong detergent to clean the surface. Rinse with lots of water.

2. When the surface is visibly clean, use a chemical cleaner such as a dewaxer (available from your paint supplier or auto supply store) with clean rags to remove any remaining wax. Obviously, this is most important for fiberglass boats. New boats still have mold release wax on their topsides and older boats will have wax from their seasonal maintenance.

3. When the surface is wet and shiny from the washing in step 1, it will probably show areas that need fairing or at least spot filling. Identify these areas by outlining them with a thin marker or wax pencil.

Adhering fairing materials to fiberglass boats is difficult. Areas requiring a large amount of filler ($\frac{3}{8}$-inch thickness or more) may require an overlay of fiberglass fabric to hold the fairing in place. The glass would then require finer fairing on top. This might be expected, for example, in an area of collision repair. If you have such a problem, refer to Chapter 9, pages 99–104 for assistance. This type of repair is usually done before priming the topsides. For most areas, where the amount of fairing required is moderate or small, the surface is typically primed before fairing.

Priming

The name of the game with primers is adhesion. If you have not had to fair the hull and are preparing a new surface, or if you are preparing to repaint over an old paint job, you will want to use primer to secure the best topcoat adhesion. In turn, the adhesion will ensure film longevity overall and abrasion resistance locally. In other

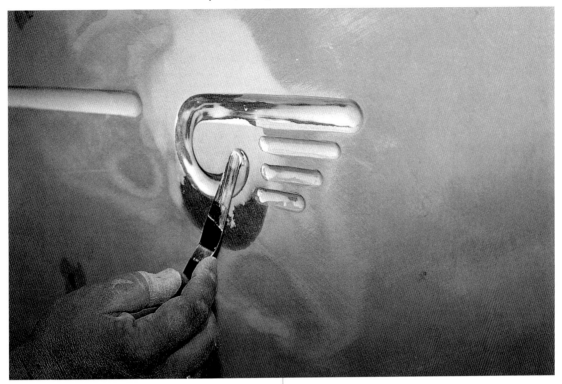

Effort spent on details such as smoothing out the cove stripes or the sheer will make a big difference in the finished paint job. For patching small defects, you can use putty made from gelcoat or any number of other materials.

words, it is almost always a good idea to prime before applying the topcoat. An exception to this rule might be if you are using an enamel product that is self-priming.

1. Carefully sand over any other fairing and earlier prime coats, striving for an even surface. Start with paper as rough as 80 grit and progress to 150 grit. Do not use a rougher paper than necessary to smooth the surface. If 150 grit works for all of the sanding, so much the better. A 150-grit surface will allow a good mechanical bond. A DA orbital sander does a good job of cutting the primer and minimizing scratch marks.

   If possible, vacuum or blow the sanding dust off the surface. If you are using compressed air, clean the air filters; contaminated air will leave water and oil splatters on the surface that will cause problems with the primer.

2. Wipe the surface in several passes. When it is visibly clean, wash it with a clean cloth, using manufacturer-approved solvent. Then, wipe off the surface with another clean, dry cloth. Work in small areas, say 10 square feet at a time. Allow all solvents time to dry at least 10 to 15 minutes before applying primer.

3. Epoxy primers are used with most new coating systems. In warm weather, when mixing or thinning the primer, you will need to stir the primer as you work to keep it evenly mixed; you may need to mix in some additional thinner to keep the primer workable. Washing out the brush occasionally as you go will also help; if you are using rollers, replace the covers periodically.

   Thinning the primer is critical. If you look carefully at other paint jobs you can frequently see where a painter's strokes started and ended. As the painter moved along, the solvent evaporated and the paint thickened. The brush dried slightly and left brush marks—which usually get progressively worse—in the paint. Some painters will try to adjust by putting more paint on their brushes, but then the paint will develop sags. Be patient—practice does make perfect.

4. Apply primer with whatever system you choose for application. If you are using the roller/brush and tip system, use at least two people for the job. One person will roll on the primer as evenly as possible with a short nap or foam roller, ending with strokes in a vertical direction; the other will lightly brush the primer with just the tip of a high quality brush, using horizontal strokes. Take care—this primer coat is a good practice session for the topcoat application.

Final Fairing

Most paint manufacturers believe that a primer base will adhere to the surface better than some of the fairing compounds. In my experience, this is certainly true with Awlgrip systems and their 545 primer. It will provide a clean, chemically appropriate bonding surface for their fairing compounds. Primers vary from one paint company to another so, when in doubt, stay with the system that matches your topcoat.

1. When the primer has dried, sand with 220-grit paper to a smooth surface. Use sanding machines—preferably orbital or blocks—to prevent finger marks and to help highlight low or high spots. Low spots will show as areas that have not been sanded thoroughly or at all; high spots will show as areas that are sanded right through. (Washing the hull at this point is helpful because the water creates a shine that shows all defects.)

2. Mark the areas that require fairing with a marker, pencil, or small piece of tape—but *not* a wax crayon. These marks will need to be removed before topcoating, so keep them small.

3. Select a fairing compound that is appropriate for the size of the spot to be faired. Mix it with the appropriate hardeners, if any, and apply

the compound with a putty knife or squeegee that is wider than the problem area. This will help "bridge" the problem.

4. After the fairing sets, sand the area with 80- to 150-grit paper, depending upon the putty and the quality of your application. Start with 150 grit and use rougher paper only as required.

5. Apply additional coats of fairing as required to smooth the area. When fairing is complete, reprime any areas that were sanded to the bare subsurface. Also, prime at least once over fairing compounds. Most paint companies recommend applying two coats over the fairing to ensure that the fairing compound does not show through the topcoat.

Preparing for the Topcoat

1. When the final primer coat is hard, usually after 24 hours, sand evenly with at least 320-grit paper. For dark hulls you might use up to 400-grit paper, because the swirl marks of coarser paper will show through the topcoat as it dries and shrinks. If you break through the primer, you should reprime that area. Some paint companies suggest having a primer layer that is almost transparent after sanding; others suggest more, but the point is not to let too much paint build up. The objective is a uniform, dry film.

2. When you are confident that you have achieved a good primer layer and have sanded so there are minimal scratch marks in the surface, prepare the work area for topcoat application. Thoroughly clean the area, including liberally vacuuming the deck and floor. Wash the topsides and, if the boat is inside, wash the floor and walls around the boat to reduce the amount of dust that might be airborne during the final coat application. Also wash any staging that has been erected around the boat. I have had many a paint job ruined by dust and needing repainting. It is hard to be too picky when it comes to cleaning the work area at this point.

   If you are outside, you will need to watch

Minor Repairs to Urethane Topcoat Finishes

Performing even minor repairs to damaged topsides or deck finishes has often been viewed as a difficult task best left to the pros. Certainly those who work with urethane paints all the time are more experienced with repairing the surfaces, but it may be worth trying a small patch or two if you are so inclined.

A scratch or nick in the paint needing touch up will most likely require some gelcoat patching as described in Chapter 8. Complete any repair work prior to starting the paint touch up. It's important to keep any repair work to as

With practice, you can touch up polyurethane paints. This repair of paint around the sheer is being done with professional equipment, but an aerosol sprayer would also work. This painter has applied a thin coat of paint and then will spray a light coat of thinner over it to blend into the surface. This reduces the amount of reworking necessary on the finished touch up.

small an area as possible to minimize the size of the paint patch. Do not buff and wax the gelcoat repair, as you will have to sand it again for primer adhesion.

After any patching, prepare for the application of primer by sanding the patch area with 180-grit sandpaper. Use the primer recommended by the paint manufacturer to achieve the best adhesion. Apply the primer with a brush (an artist's brush works well for small areas) or spray. Touch up primer in small areas with a brush.

After the primer cures (or in cases where the underlying primer was not damaged and topcoat only is being applied), prepare the area for topcoat application as follows.

Tape off the area to be painted. For a small patch, try to tape about 3 inches around the outside of the patch to protect from sanding

(continued)

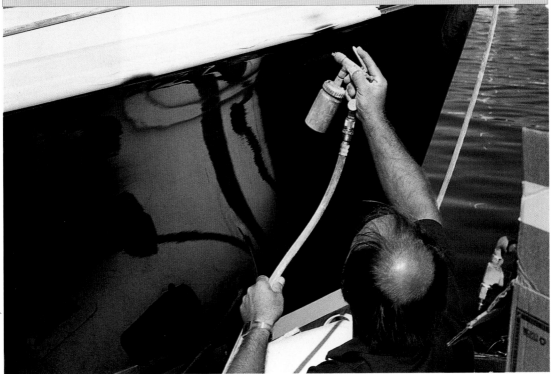

Hank Hinckley

(continued)

scratches and overspray (if using a sprayer). Use masking paper outside this layer of tape to protect the surrounding surfaces.

Sand the patch area with 400- to 600-grit wet-or-dry sandpaper. Use a sanding block to preserve the shape of the surface and prevent local hollows that are common with hand or finger sanding.

Concentrate sanding on the patch itself, but also sand with very fine paper, 1,200 to 1,500 grit, over the area just beyond the patch. This will allow adhesion of the topcoat to the area beyond the patch and help the new topcoat to blend into the surrounding area.

When applying topcoat, carefully consider the recommendations of the paint manufacturer. Spray application of two-part urethane topcoats is a concern for health and the environment and must be undertaken with proper preparation. Use the safety gear listed in this chapter and dispose of the paint waste in an appropriate manner.

If applying paint with a brush, use a catalyst and thinner recommended for brush application. Apply in thin coats and feather the edges out over the sanded area as well as possible. An artist's brush works well for small areas.

If spraying paint with an automotive touch-up gun or a disposable sprayer such as the Preval unit, spray in several thin coats, allowing a few minutes between applications for the thinners to evaporate and the film to tack a bit. Apply the paint more thickly on the patch itself and feather it out over the surrounding lightly sanded area.

Steve Smith of U.S. Paint recommends the following procedure after using a paint sprayer. Remove the paint from the spray container and replace it with thinner. Apply a light mist (or "fog") of thinner on the surface. This helps the paint blend into the surrounding finish. Obviously, this will work best when a smooth paint layer has been applied. I have seen this done and it's amazing how well it works when done right. The patch seems to disappear.

If you apply topcoat with a brush (and sometimes even if you use a sprayer), you may have to sand it a bit to smooth the surface and blend in the edges. Use 1,500-grit wet-or-dry paper sparingly.

Buff the surface for the final finish with a polishing liquid such as 3M Finesse-it. Using one of 3M's foam pads that fits on a low-speed buffer will work well for polishing the surface.

the weather carefully. The temperature may not present much of a problem, as polyurethanes can be applied in temperatures ranging from 50°F to 85°F (10°C to 29.4°C) (check your specific paint), but even a slight breeze can cause flow and dust problems.

3. After your work area is clean, solvent wash the surface with the product recommended by the manufacturer. Often, this is the same system as recommended with the primer. Use two cloths, one for solvent wash and the other for wiping. On bigger jobs, replace these cloths regularly for best results. Be sure to allow time for all solvents to evaporate before proceeding with the painting. The solvent's instructions may recommend a specific waiting period.

Applying the Topcoat

1. If you are using a two-part paint system, carefully measure the components and thoroughly mix. Be sure to use a brushing/roller catalyst for hand application, and spray catalyst for spray application. As with any paint, stir thoroughly. Many of these mixtures require a waiting period for the chemical reactions to begin before you can begin painting. Follow the manufacturer's instructions—they are critical to uniform application.

2. If necessary, thin the paint for ease of application. Use of a viscometer may be recommended, although it is more important when spraying than brushing. Viscosity is measured

by timing a given amount of fluid flowing from a hole in the bottom of a special cup. The time is often given for a Zahn Cup, which should be available from an auto supply store, or for a cup that is available at Sears. The measurements are guidelines, though; your final mixture may need to be adjusted for temperature and humidity.

Here are two more things to remember. First, as with the primer, the thinner will evaporate as the paint sits in a bucket and may require more thinning and/or stirring as you go along. Second, if you apply topcoats in an atmosphere outside the temperature and humidity ranges specified by the manufacturer, expect a dulled finish.

3. The procedure for applying the topcoat is the same as recommended for applying primer (see pages 66–68). The topcoat will often be significantly thinner than the primer and will be applied in a lighter coat, but the application methods are the same. If applying by hand, again use at least two people for the job—one to roll on the paint and the other to brush it out—and try to always keep a wet edge to the paint. It is easier to keep a wet edge when you work in a relatively small area. If you are having trouble with the paint drying before you "tip" it with the brush, adjust the thinner/solvent, work in a smaller area, or add another brusher so the process goes faster.

4. Finally, don't rush the curing of the topsides. Some polyurethane paints will require several days to cure. Picking up your boat with a Travelift too soon will cause adhesion problems and scratches. Obviously, if you are lifting the boat, the better padded the straps, the less the stress on the paint finish.

The new generation of marine paint systems is a real boon for do-it-yourself boaters. These materials are a big improvement from the paints of just a few years ago. With patience and care, you can obtain an exceptional finish. Still, because marine paints are often composed of toxic chemicals, proper application equipment, painting conditions, safety equipment, and disposal of residue and waste are critical. Once again, the safety and health aspects of the process cannot be overlooked. Do not proceed with using these materials without the proper protective equipment.

Renewing a Cove Stripe

Renewing a cove stripe is an important project that really helps a hull look its best. The process is not difficult for either a painted or a gold leaf cove. Here are some ideas if you wish to rework yours.

Repainting the Cove Stripe

A painted cove stripe, like the topsides, will last longer and look better if it is properly prepared before it is painted. It is hard to beat urethane paints for color and durability, but they are only as good as the connection they have to the hull.

Some more accomplished painters will sand and paint a cove stripe without using masking

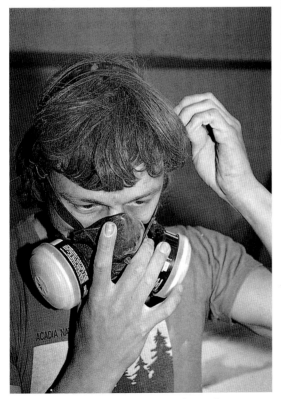

A properly fit respirator is a must when using most newer paints.

Applying Vinyl Lettering or Graphics

Repainting the topsides of your boat will bring new life to the exterior, but it also means that you will need to redo the name, port of hail, and any other lettering or graphics that have been removed. One alternative to repainting or gold leafing is to use vinyl lettering or graphics.

Seen more and more on larger yachts, vinyl lettering has become popular because it is inexpensive; may be installed by the owner; has a long life (six to eight years); may be removed easily; and has computer-generated symmetry and precision. There is one marine application that vinyl lettering is not suitable for—it usually will not stick to inflatables.

Phyllis Aschenbrenner of Acadia Sails in Southwest Harbor, Maine, has had a great deal of experience creating and applying vinyl lettering. She says that vinyl application has come to include more than just lettering and wild graphics. Today, it is even possible to incorporate photography into vinyl transfers. And for those who like gold leafing, faux gold leaf is now available.

The vinyl transfers are designed on a computer. Simply give a designer a pattern of the transom or of the curve(s) that the lettering is to follow, and he or she can make adjustments to the design on the screen before cutting the lettering.

Applying vinyl lettering is easy:

1. *Clean the surface; any grit that remains will poke through the vinyl.*

2. *Remove any wax from the hull surface, using a dewaxer from a paint manufacturer.*

3. *Place the lettering on the transom and position as well as possible. Tape the upper edge of the lettering to the transom and step back to check the alignment.*

4. *Once the alignment is correct, lift the lettering up and peel off the adhesive backing.*

5. *Press the lettering carefully against the hull, striving to avoid air bubbles. A hint from Phyllis: Use a solution of soapy water—one or two drops of soap to a spray bottle—so the lettering can slide. The adhesive is not water-soluble so you can move the lettering around until it's exactly in place. Squeegee the lettering to smooth out the air bubbles and ensure adhesion. If air bubbles persist, prick them with a pin and try to press them down.*

Multiple colors or outlines may require additional layers, which are handled in the same fashion as the first. If a boat name is extra long, or a graphic too large to easily handle without wrinkling, it may pay to cut the large piece into smaller pieces. The tape on the top of the piece will keep the positioning of the name in place.

For lettering that is to be installed inside a window or port, have the computer operator reverse the lettering; the exterior view of the finished product will be correct.

tape. If the cove is well indented, this is easier to do, but taping the cove still provides a neater job. Therefore, the steps below include suggestions for taping.

1. Clean the cove and the surrounding area. Remove any wax with a dewaxer.

2. Tape the hull along the top and bottom edges of the cove. Carefully tape around any designs included in the cove detail. The tape should be of stout enough composition to withstand some sanding.

3. Sand the cove with 180- to 220-grit sandpaper. If the topsides have been painted recently, it may be necessary to only lightly, but thoroughly, scratch the cove surface. If the hull has older paint or gelcoat, sand the cove thoroughly.

4. Remove the tape and again clean the area. Retape the cove with a quality tape that will

prevent paint bleeding. Many yards and painters use 3M Fine Line tape for this purpose.

If the hull has been recently primed and painted, skip to step 9.

5. If the paint has been removed or the hull has a gelcoat finish, prime the cove with an epoxy primer that is recommended by the manufacturer of the topcoat you are using. U.S. Paint (Awlgrip) recommends their #545 primer to enhance the bond.

6. For the cleanest edges, pull the tape when the primer is dry to the touch, but not entirely hard.

7. Retape the cove as directed in step 4, and sand lightly with 320-grit paper.

8. Replace any damaged tape. The prior sanding may have been light enough so the tape is still serviceable.

9. Paint the cove with the topcoat. Follow manufacturers' instructions and, for additional tips, review the section "Applying the Topcoat," pages 70–71.

10. Pull the tape before the topcoat is hard.

Releafing a Cove Stripe

Releafing a cove stripe involves fewer steps than repainting but requires much of the same patience and preparation.

1. Clean and dewax the cove and the immediately surrounding area.

2. Tape the cove carefully in preparation for sanding.

3. Sand the cove lightly with 220-grit or finer sandpaper.

4. Repair or replace any frayed edges of the tape.

5. Apply a uniform coat of sizing or thin varnish to adhere the gold leaf to the cove.

6. When the sizing is tacky to the touch, but no longer wet, apply the gold (from a roll or sheet) by pressing it into the sizing. Rub thoroughly to obtain an even coating.

7. Remove the tape.

8. After the gold has set and the sizing is thoroughly dry, apply a thin layer of varnish over the

gold for added protection. Different application methods will produce different gold effects. To obtain a swirled or machined look, place the gold leaf sheet against the cove and twist the paper with pressure down on the thumb. Practice this first on a separate surface to develop the technique that gives you the desired result.

Deck Painting

Most of the preceding information about topsides painting is valid for deck painting. The smooth areas of the house and cockpit are handled the same. The biggest difference is in preparing and painting nonskid areas. Painting over a molded nonskid pattern is one way to refinish the area, although I have not been happy with the results of such work—the paint does not adhere well to the rough surface.

Painting a Molded Deck Pattern

1. If you choose to paint a molded pattern, be sure to thoroughly dewax the surface.

2. Tape off the area with masking tape to protect the adjacent areas from abrasive damage.

3. Depending on the roughness of the pattern, prepare the surface using a wire brush in addition to, or in lieu of, sandpaper. The objective is to prepare the low spots as well as the tops of the pattern to receive paint.

4. Thoroughly clean the area and retape the outside of the pattern with a high-quality tape such as 3M Fine Line.

5. Solvent wash the area with the solvent suggested for the paint selected.

6. Prime the area if necessary. Some paints do not require priming and they may be a good choice for painting deck patterns because primers tend to fill the pattern. The adhesion, however, will not be as good.

7. Sand and retape if the surface has been primed.

8. Topcoat the surface. A short-nap roller may be the best application tool for this job.

9. Pull the tape when the surface has tacked and

let the surface fully cure before walking on it.

Another suggestion is to include a flattening agent in the paint to reduce the gloss and slipperiness of the surface. If more nonskid effect is desired, include some grit in the paint to enhance its "holding" characteristics.

Painting a New Nonskid

I feel the easiest nonskid to paint and repair is the rough texture surface that is created by spreading texture or "sand" in the paint before applying it. This type of surface is often used on many custom boats and on decks where there is damaged nonskid pattern.

Here are some application suggestions:

1. Thoroughly dewax the surface.
2. Tape off the area where nonskid will be applied. I prefer to leave smooth borders around hardware and deck trim. They are easier to bed or varnish, and it's easier to clean the nonskid deck around them.
3. Prepare the surfaces in the same fashion as directed on pages 66–68 for topside painting, through the application and sanding of the primer.
4. Retape the surface in preparation for topcoating. Use 3M Fine Line tape or an equivalent high-quality masking tape.
5. Now you have a couple of options. One is to roll on a layer of topcoat with a foam roller, then sprinkle with grit material in an even pattern. A shaker like the one often used for cinnamon sugar works well. Then, after that has tacked well, apply a thin topcoat to seal in the grit.

   The other method is to mix the grit into the paint before rolling it on, which works well only if you frequently stir the mixture to keep the grit evenly spread throughout the solution.
6. Pull the tape when the surface has tacked and let it fully cure before walking on it.

Interior Painting

Painting interior surfaces of boats with newer enamels is not as complicated as dealing with the new exterior paints. Application techniques typically are similar to topside finishes, but most interior paints are single-part products and handle more easily. Here are a few things to consider when choosing an interior paint:

- Interior paints can be high gloss, but a less shiny finish, such as eggshell or flat, often works better. A low-gloss surface will not show imperfections in the subsurface or paint film as much as a high-gloss surface. They will, however, be a little harder to clean. Hinckley typically uses a medium-gloss finish, usually gelcoat, in lockers and bilge areas, and a semigloss finish for interior bulkheads.

- If the selected paint does not contain a mildew inhibitor, ask your paint supplier about having some added.

- When finishing an interior with painted bulkheads and varnished trim and corner posts, varnish the trim first. It is almost impossible to remove paint splatters and smudges from trim if they get deep into the grain. Using varnish as a sealing coat can also be useful on surfaces that will be painted. Therefore, it might be a good idea to consider varnishing all surfaces before applying paint.

- When painting or varnishing interiors, try placing a fan in a hatch with a furnace filter on the top; it will provide positive pressure in the cabin and reduce the chances of dust coming in from outside of the boat.

Preparing the Surface

1. As with most paint projects, it is a good idea to begin the project by thoroughly cleaning the area. Remove all fabric components and possessions that might be damaged by dust.
2. Tape off the surface to be painted to protect surrounding areas from paint and for a sanding scratch shield.
3. Wash the surface with a heavy duty detergent or solvent to remove foreign materials that would be ground in by the sanding process. Some owners like to use polishes and waxes on the bulkheads, which spruce them up nicely. Unfortunately, these materials can create havoc

A traditional painted interior is an attractive alternative. You must plan the finishing process in advance for best results, particularly when starting with bare wood.

with new finishes being applied over them when refinishing.

4. Sand the surface. The grit of sandpaper to use depends the quality of the surface you are working on. The objective is to arrive at a 150-grit surface.

5. Patch any dents or scars in the surface with a wood filler or fairing compound. Resand patched areas to 150 grit.

Priming the Surface of New Wood

1. Apply the priming coats, using sealer or varnish. First coats over bare wood should be thinned significantly (up to 50 percent) to allow thorough wetting of the wood surface and a better mechanical bond.

2. After the first coat, sand lightly to knock down the roughest of texture. After the second and third coats, the sanding can be increased to allow the smoothing of the overall surface while leaving the grain of the wood filled.

Preparing and Applying the Topcoat

1. When the grain is filled and a complete film of the priming material is left after sanding, change to 220-grit sandpaper and sand the surface for the final coats.

2. Apply the topcoat or -coats of paint. Two coats or possibly more will be required for covering the wood color if you are applying over a transparent undercoating such as a sealer. One coat may be all that is needed if you are applying over a primer system that used the topcoat paint itself. As with other varnishes and paints, buildup will give longevity to the film. Extra coats are worth the effort. Hinckley applies two to three coats of paint after applying two to three prime coats.

Refinishing Interior Painted Surfaces

Interior finishes applied well and in sufficient thickness will last for many years. You'll know it's time to refinish when you begin seeing areas with abrasion, openings in the wood grain, fading of colors, or crazing and cracking of the surface.

The process for refinishing interior surfaces is the same as for when you are starting from scratch. Be especially careful to remove any oils or contaminants from the surface before sanding. If the surface has extensive crazing, it's best to remove it and again rebuild from scratch.

Patching interior surfaces is difficult at best. Unless the surface is new, fading and surface contamination will make the color match tricky. More often than not, refinishing a whole panel is required.

A Word about Overheads

Once in a while a boatowner will desire the smooth fiberglass overhead that is found on older Hinckleys like the Pilot 35 and the Bermuda 40. These finishes are the result of long hours of fairing and sanding.

On new boats, the inside of the cabintop is ground when the deck is still upside down, which saves a great deal of painful sanding. It can be done later, but allow plenty of time for resting while sanding.

The fairing process is the biggest step in this job. A polyester fairing compound that sands well is a big plus. Automotive body compound such as Bondo will work; however, I prefer to mix my own compound of resin and microballoons for the process. This way, I can easily control the thickness of the putty. A power sander and protective clothing, respirator, and glasses are musts.

With the exception of the additional fairing required, the preparation and painting process is basically the same as for other interior surfaces. Here, as on other potentially imperfect surfaces (trust me, you are not likely to get it perfect), I recommend using semigloss or even flat paints for coatings because they are better at hiding the finish.

Handling and Pulling Masking Tape

What a terrible feeling it is to finish a paint job with no dust or brush marks and then have the masking tape lift the edge of the new finish or even lift the finish underneath! Here are a couple of hints to make handling and removing tape easier.

1. The first step in easy tape removal is to use the proper tape. Make sure that you use quality tape that is appropriate for the task.

2. When applying tape, make sure that the edge of the tape is securely attached to the surface.

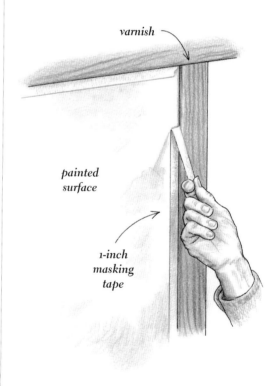

varnish

painted surface

1-inch masking tape

When removing masking tape from painted or varnished surfaces, be sure to pull the tape back on itself, not perpendicular to the surface. Pulling the tape incorrectly increases the chance of lifting the very surface you are trying to protect.

Run your finger along the edge to seal it well. This will prevent the finish being applied from bleeding under the tape.

3. Think ahead about the removal of the tape. If you can, at places where you know you'll want to start lifting a piece of tape, fold it back upon itself to make a small lifting tab; this will ease the process of starting the tape when it is time to remove it.

4. When done with the coating process, wait until the surface is tacky to remove the tape. The timing is critical. Pulling the tape too soon will let the coating flow into areas that the tape was supposed to protect. Pulling the tape too late is risky because the surface of the coating might already be too well cured and will tear as you lift the tape.

   The longer a film takes to cure, the longer it is safe to leave the tape on. The less time needed for curing, the greater the need to remove the tape promptly to reduce the possibility of pulling the film off.

5. When pulling the tape, start with an end and pull the tape back almost on itself. This will allow for a sharp cutoff of the coating film and will reduce the tension on underlying surfaces to lift with the tape. Pulling perpendicular to the surface is inviting trouble.

6. With long pieces of tape, allow the tape to fold over and adhere to itself as it pulls off—the resulting loops of soiled tape are easier to handle. This is especially important when they contain wet paint or varnish.

7. Have a bag ready to receive the soiled tape, and place the tape in the bag immediately.

Bottom Paints and Barrier Coatings

In this chapter we will look at materials and application methods to protect the bottom of your boat and provide antifouling. Whether you are looking for protection against basic marine growth or ways to obtain the slickest bottom in the fleet, it is important to understand the options available.

As anyone who has scanned a yachting magazine knows, the sophistication of today's bottom paints spans a large range. Some of the systems available are recommended for professional application only; others are basically the same paints that have been available for decades. At any rate, today's technology includes development of water-based paints, Teflon paints, and so-called "permanent" bottom coating systems of 100 percent copper, either sprayed or applied as sheets. Hinckley has had limited success with these "permanent" systems, but because they are for the most part only professionally applied, I will not discuss them here.

Carefully choose the materials you will use in bottom painting. You will have to consider a number of tradeoffs: cost, longevity of the coating, and performance.

Bottom Paints

In the past few years, there has been a lot of legislation and technical development in the bottom paint market. Tin and TBT (tributyltin) products have been pretty much legislated out of use on pleasure boats, except on aluminum boats and boats longer than 82 feet. It was not so long ago that tin and TBT seemed to be the answer to concerns over arsenic and mercury-based products. Copper seems to be the answer today, and the more the better; it is added to any number of mixtures. Copper and aluminum, however, are not compatible materials—putting copper paint on an aluminum boat will promote corrosion.

Today, there are materials with generic names like polypeptide polymer, controlled solubility copolymer, and epoxy polyamide. These new materials combined with familiar alkyd enamels and modified epoxy paints, make a wide field from which to select the right antifouling paint for your boat.

Often hidden below the shiny topsides, bottom coatings are working to protect the hull and to repel unwanted growth and creatures.

Although there seem to be many types of bottom paints with varied characteristics and costs, I break them down into two basic groups depending on how they work to prevent antifouling.

The first group consists of the more traditional type of paint that allows leaching of the toxicant as the material ages. The rate of leaching is controlled by the water temperature, salinity, alkalinity, and other environmental factors, as well as the composition and application of the paint. Bottom paints are available in various degrees of surface hardness. The softer, usually less expensive paints are recommended for slower moving boats. The harder paints are used for faster or racing boats. They may be burnished for an ultra-smooth finish.

Bottom paints possess varying degrees of antifouling properties as well. Why not always purchase the paint with the greatest antifouling properties? Cost. The metal added to the paint drives the cost up.

The second group of bottom paints consists of ablative paints, which are the newer polymer or copolymer paints. These paints "ablate," or wear off, as they are used, exposing new paint surface and toxicant to protect the bottom.

Ablative paints have an advantage over conventional bottom paints: They are less subject to the vagaries of water temperature, salinity, and the like. The bottom slime that builds up while a boat sits at a dock usually washes off once the boat gets moving. Further, ablative paints reduce the buildup of paint as they wear off and require, in most cases, little or no sanding before recoating. Manufacturers recommend applying a first coat of these paints with a contrasting color (often called a "signal color") to indicate when bottom repainting is required. Finally, ablative paints are not affected by exposure to air, which allows them to be applied at any time that is convenient. Alas, there is a price to pay for these nice features. Ablative paints are as, or slightly more, expensive than the better, conventional hard copper paints. When the costs of materials and labor for recoating are weighed, though, these paints may not be out of line for your boat.

Hinckley often uses Pettit Trinidad paints, which have a high cuprous oxide content (up to 75%) and that seem to stay potent for as long as any conventional antifouling paints. I can remember my father's Hinckley 49 returning to Maine from Florida after sitting in a canal for the better part of the winter. With nine or so months on the Trinidad paint, it was unusually clean.

Compatibility of Bottom Paints

Whichever bottom paint you choose, make sure that it is compatible with any sandless primer and solvents you might be using, as well as with any other materials that are on the bottom—including old bottom paint. Compatibility is particularly important if you are changing brands or generic types of antifouling coatings. If you are recoating an ablative paint, your problems will be minimal. If you are changing to an ablative paint from a conventional bottom paint, chances are you will need to do some additional preparation, perhaps including completely removing the old bottom paint.

If you are concerned about compatibility, ask for help from a yard or paint supplier, or test the paint in some small areas before painting the entire bottom.

Barrier Coatings

It has become almost the norm to use a barrier coating before painting the bottom of a bare hull to prevent migration of water into the fiberglass laminate—especially when the hull is manufactured with traditional polyester resin. The old saw, "An ounce of prevention is worth a pound of cure," is certainly true in the case of barrier coatings.

Blistering bottoms on fiberglass boats have led to the development of a new technology. For years, builders, as well as owners, thought fiberglass was pretty well immune from the ravages of water exposure. Not so, as everyone knows today.

Experience with osmotic blistering has induced many builders, Hinckley included, to look for better alternatives to the traditional polyester resins for laminating hulls. For some years, epoxy resins were considered the best approach, but epoxy is costly and difficult to work into the glass fabric. Continued research has demonstrated that vinylester resin is a better material for the job. It is water resistant, workable, and more cost effective than epoxy. Hinckley now uses vinylester resins consistently in hull construction. Some other builders do likewise or use vinylester resins in the outer layers to provide an improved water barrier.

The use of vinylester resin is worth considering for anyone comparing prospective boats for purchase, but is not of much help for the owner of a boat manufactured with polyester resin who wants to prevent blistering. Applying an epoxy-based barrier coating is a viable tool to protect polyester hulls from moisture problems. Modern materials, which require moderate effort to apply, are reasonably economical when considering the cost of blister repair. Additionally, the use of a primer/barrier coat is recommended for use under most current bottom paints. It improves the bond of the paint and serves as a water barrier.

Epoxy-based barrier coatings are typically offered in systems. That is, there are a series of products that work together to provide a water-resistant barrier between the hull and the bottom paint. If you are considering stripping the paint on your boat or are starting with a new bottom, you should seriously consider using one of these systems as insurance against bottom blistering.

There are both dedicated systems and additives for familiar products that may be used for barrier coatings. One popular dedicated system is the Interlux InterProtect Barrier Coat System, which offers three basic two-part products. Inter-Protect 1000 is fairly thick and is used for initial sealing and minor fairing. InterProtect 2000 products are primarily roller- or brush-applied coatings. InterProtect 3000 products are recommended for spraying and can be applied in temperatures as low as 32°F (0°C).

In the category of additives for familiar products, Gougeon Brothers now offers a copper additive for their epoxy resin to improve the water-barrier qualities of the resin and to add some backup antifouling protection to the barrier coat. This may be a good idea for those who are rebuilding their bottom finish after blister repair work. Any of these alternatives involves a multiple layer coating applied directly to the hull.

Materials and Equipment

Fairing Compounds and Putties

Fairing compounds and putties are used to repair small damaged areas and crazing in the gelcoat and underbody surface. Many polyester-based compounds are available, as are vinylester- and epoxy-based materials. The vinylester and epoxy have better sealing properties for bottom protection and therefore are more highly recommended.

When selecting these materials, compatibility is important. After using epoxy materials, you should stick with other epoxy materials. Polyester- and vinylester-based compounds do not adhere well to epoxy. Fortunately, the reverse is not true. Epoxy does adhere to both polyester and vinylester.

Thinners

Use only manufacturer-recommended thinners with bottom paints. Thinners are, for the most part, highly volatile chemicals. Use them sparingly.

Dewaxers

If you own a new boat and are applying bottom paint for the first time, consider using a dewaxer to remove mold release products. Most manufacturers of bottom paints make a dewaxing product.

Many yards use acetone for dewaxing. Interestingly, Pettit Paint specifically cautions against using acetone for this purpose; they believe that it does not do an adequate job. Their dewaxer is #15095 Fiberglass Dewaxer. Interlux offers #202 Fiberglass Solvent Wash.

Sandless Primer

With the growth of concern over blistering, removing too much bottom gelcoat by oversanding has also become a concern. The use of primers that reduce or remove the need for sanding has addressed this problem. Interlux makes #AL200 Fiberglass Primer for this purpose. Other companies offer similar products. They are designed to provide enhanced adhesion of the paint to the subsurface without the mechanical bonding that happens on a sanded surface. These products are also a lot easier on the crew than sanding.

A key thing to remember about using these primers is that they have a definite, specific window for overcoating. For example, #AL200 should be painted over in not less than two hours, nor more than three.

Masking Tape

Masking tape used while bottom painting should have the same characteristics as a good tape for varnishing or topside finishing. It should not allow bleeding of the paint under the tape edge, should not react with solvents, and should permit easy removal without lifting other finishes. Hinckley uses 3M #233 or #218 tapes for this purpose.

Sanding Papers and Equipment

Common sandpaper grits for use in preparing a bottom, either new or already painted, are 80 to 120. Typically, rougher grit will remove too much material. If you feel you need extra cutting ability, perhaps you should be stripping the bottom.

Sanding can be accelerated by using either an orbital sander or a dual-action grinder with a soft pad and adhesive sandpaper discs. Before using a sander, be sure that there is not a yard rule or local ordinance prohibiting exposed bottom sanding. Old bottom paint is not the best material to have floating around.

For the racing boater who wants a burnished bottom, wet-or-dry sandpaper of 320 or 400 grit is helpful. With hard paint and lots of elbow grease, these grits will allow you to develop an extremely smooth bottom. Spray application of the paint will also assist by giving a relatively smooth starting surface. However, rolling on paint before wet-sanding is acceptable.

Paint Brushes and Rollers

Use larger paint brushes for bottom painting than you would use on other surfaces—say, 3- or 4-inch widths. Also, use a fairly stiff bristle, because the weight of the paint will overload the softer bristle used in other marine paint and varnish brushes.

Generally, a short-nap roller cover is recommended for use with bottom paints, because some paints contain solvents that rapidly decompose standard roller covers. Read the label directions for warnings and specific recommendations.

Paint Strippers

Chemical paint strippers are a bit more user friendly than sanders when it comes to both the environment and the time involved to remove bottom paint. All of the major marine paint manufacturers make chemical strippers. Interlux makes Pintoff #299 and Pettit offers #9030 Paint and Varnish Remover (for fiberglass).

Some new products have recently come on the market and look interesting. Peel Away Marine Safety Strip, manufactured by Dumond Chemicals, and NO SWETT Stripper from Nutec Industrial Chemical provide an environment- and user-friendly method of removing bottom paint. These products do not contain many of the harmful chemicals of other strippers such as methylene chloride or caustics. They are applied by brush or roller or, in some cases, airless spray. Hinckley has used both of these products with success and currently use NO SWETT.

Miscellaneous Painting Equipment

Other painting equipment for the do-it-yourself boater normally include roller trays, paper or metal paint pots, rags, paint strainers, and tarps or heavy plastic film to catch waste.

Preparation and Application Procedures

Because the exact procedure for paint preparation varies from paint to paint, these steps are necessarily generic. All bottom paints are toxic to one degree or another, so personal safety and environmental concerns are important. Do not begin a bottom painting project without adequate protection. (See page 89 for more information on safety gear.)

Preparing a Previously Painted Bottom

The following steps cover the process of preparing a previously painted bottom to the point where it is ready for application of a barrier coating or bottom paint.

If you have a boat with old bottom paint, your first task is to evaluate the condition of the bottom: Is the paint well adhered to the bottom? Is there an excessive amount of paint buildup (typically evidenced by thick, scaling paint)?

If the paint surface is in good condition, and you are using the same type of paint as previously applied, you will only have to clean and lightly sand (120 grit is good) the bottom before recoating. If you're using an ablative paint, only cleaning may be required. If the old paint is poorly adhered or thick and scaling, you need to consider giving it either a thorough sanding (see the following step 1A) or, for the more severely deteriorated bottom, stripping (see the following step 1B).

1A. Sanding a bottom that is in poor condition is usually done with 80-grit sandpaper. Before sanding, determine if sanding is allowed where you have your boat. Many boatyards permit sanding bottom paint only indoors or in special containment areas to control the dust. Others allow only wet-sanding of antifouling paint—which is certainly one way to reduce breathing concerns.

If owner-sanding is allowed, hand sand or use equipment as specified above. If you use a sander, work carefully. Overzealous sanding will cut into the gelcoat and/or laminate and harm the fairness of the surface. It will also increase the potential for moisture absorption by the bottom.

A dual-action sander is a good tool for most bottom jobs. It is light, and its motion reduces the scratching of the gelcoat compared with other sanding methods. Many models also provide for a vacuum attachment, which helps control the dust. For heavier jobs, you may need a grinder with a "soft back" pad attached. Use a low-speed grinder and proceed slowly. It is a tiring job; no doubt fatigue in your arms, shoulders, and back will dictate slow progress and light pressure on the grinder. Make sure you wear the proper personal protection equipment for this work. Bottom paint is toxic stuff. A white paper suit and hood with gloves, as well as breathing protection (a well-fitting, two-strap dust mask or, better yet, a respirator), and, of course, safety glasses are musts.

If paint stripping is not required, go to the section on applying bottom paints, pages 87–89.

1B. If you determine that stripping the bottom is appropriate, there are alternatives to sanding to consider. As noted, marine paint manufacturers now make paint strippers for fiberglass. After application they must set for a period before being stripped off with a putty knife or scraper.

When using a paint stripper, use a drop cloth under the work area to control waste and for proper disposal. Also, tape off the bottom at the boottop, using wide tape or tape and masking paper to ensure that stripper does not get on surfaces it can harm. When the stripping is completed, be sure to wash the hull with water or a neutralizer, if so directed in the stripper product's literature.

As mentioned on page 82, there are some alternatives to traditional chemical strippers, including Peel Away Marine Safety Strip, a system that involves applying a chemical to the bottom paint.

The chemical coating is then covered with a fabric or paper cover that reduces the coating's exposure to air and enhances the performance of the system. It is left on the bottom for a period of 2 to 24 hours. The time will be determined by the amount of bottom paint to be removed. The chemical coating will continue to work if left on, and additional coatings should not be required.

When a test patch reveals that the paint is ready to lift, slide a broad putty knife along the hull, removing the paint and laminated cloth at the same time. Be sure to place the waste materials in a container or plastic bag for disposal.

Finally, wash the surface with Peel Away

All Purpose Cleaner and Surface Prep, or use mineral spirits and a coarse synthetic wool pad to remove the last paint residue.

Another stripping product, NO SWETT Semi-Paste Stripper, is usually applied by airless high-volume/low-pressure (HVLP) spray. It can also be applied by roller or aerosol for small jobs. The product develops a seal on the surface that keeps the stripper working. Unlike the Peel Away system, there is no fabric cover. The material is removed by a scraper or putty knife after setting from 15 minutes to three hours, depending on paint type and thickness.

Chemical strippers make the job of bottom-paint re-moval easier than grinding off the paint. Be sure to choose a stripper that is not so aggressive that the un-derlying material (often gelcoat) is harmed. And take care to contain and properly dispose of drippings and scrapings.

NO SWETT has a liquid product for final cleaning that is applied with a rag or nonabrasive, chemical-resistant pad. The advantage of the NO SWETT system seems to be the speed of action. The flip side of the equation, however, is that the Peel Away product is less likely to affect underlying gelcoat if left on the surface too long. Hinckley notes that both of these products appear to soften underlying epoxy coatings if allowed to set too long. The epoxy surface, though, hardens again after a day or so. I have used the NO SWETT system with great success.

2. When the bottom is free of old paint, carefully inspect it for signs of voids, blisters, crazing, or other damage. Most blisters can be repaired by carefully removing the damaged gelcoat and fiberglass and rebuilding the area with an epoxy resin–based product. Many products are available from marine paint suppliers for repairing local underwater damage.

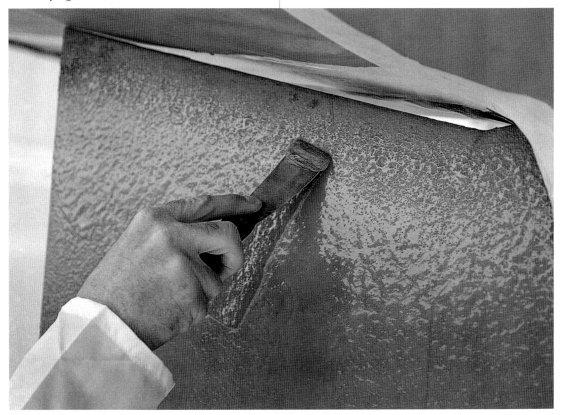

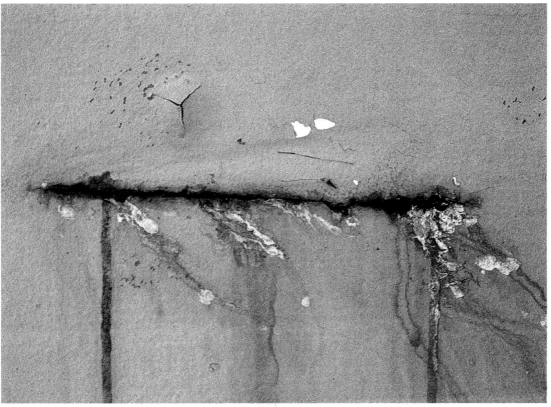

*Shown here is an open seam at the keel/ballast inter-
face. The seam should be opened and dried, then
filled with a flexible sealant. The blister above the
seam also needs repair.*

3A. When the old paint has been removed and
damaged areas repaired, carefully sand the
bottom with 80-grit paper in preparation for
applying the bottom barrier coating or paint.
This step is important and should be done, I
repeat, *carefully* to avoid oversanding the gelcoat or any repairs.

3B. An alternative to sanding on bare gelcoat is to
use a sandless primer. It is important, though,
to apply the primers exactly as indicated. Most

*(right) Larger areas such as this rudder may need
significant sanding or laminate stripping to remove
damaged fiberglass. This rudder has been treated
in spots but is not far from requiring more radical
treatment.*

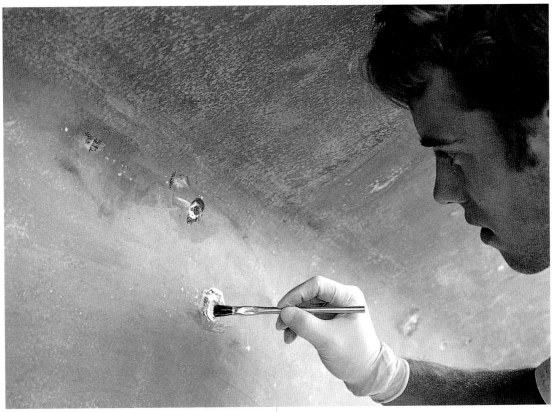

After drying and cleaning a small blister, apply an epoxy sealant to the area to seal the fiberglass. This also provides a good base for epoxy fillers and primers to be added later.

have a minimum and maximum period before you can overcoat and this period may vary with the material to be used in overcoating the primer. For instance, Interlux #AL200 must be coated in no fewer than two hours nor more than three when using Interlux Micron CSC or Bottomkote paints; when overcoating with Viny-Lux, Super Viny-Lux, or Regatta Balto-plate, the AL200 should dry overnight.

Preparing a New Bottom

If your boat is new and unpainted, your first step is to remove the mold release and other foreign materials from the surface.

1. Wash the surface with a wax removal solvent or thinner. Some paint manufacturers recom-

mend using a thinner for the job. The objective is to remove as much of the wax from the bottom as possible so sanding will not grind the wax into the surface or, if using a sandless primer, to make sure it will adhere well.

If the surface is particularly dirty before starting the chemical wash, a soap and water washdown will save on the amount of solvent you have to use.

2A. After removing the mold release agents, sand the surface with 80-grit or finer paper. Your objective is to create a thoroughly sanded, smooth, frosty surface while removing as little gelcoat as possible. Using an orbital sander is cautiously recommended, but a grinder, even with a soft pad, is not. It is too easy to oversand.

2B. As an alternative to sanding, apply a sandless primer such as Pettit #6999 or Interlux #AL200, both of which require careful adherence to strict overcoating times. To be honest, I have always been uncomfortable with these products' claims that they provide the same adhesion as a sanded surface, but others have told me they used them and obtained excellent results.

Using a sandless primer may not be appropriate if you intend to apply a barrier coating on the bottom (which I strongly recommend) before you apply your bottom paint. Check with the barrier coating's manufacturer.

3. If you sanded the bottom, wash it with thinner to further clean the surface before applying the paint or barrier coating. Allow sufficient time for the thinner to evaporate prior to proceeding.

4. Fix minor defects that may exist in the bottom. On a new boat, these may be unfaired fittings, joints in the keel/ballast seam, or scars from shipping. Make sure any materials you use are compatible with the other coatings you will be using.

When finished with this step, you are ready to proceed with bottom coatings. For more information on bottom repairs, see pages 97–98 in Chapter 8.

Applying a Barrier Coating

Barrier coatings should only be applied over clean, fair gelcoat or fiberglass. They are not intended for application over a painted surface.

To apply a barrier coating, follow these steps:

1. Proper mixing is important in the application of these coatings because they are typically high in solids that rapidly settle out of the solution. They also are two-part mixtures that require adding part A and part B in specific quantities. You must measure the quantities carefully for proper curing. Finally, proper mixing is followed by a rest period to allow the chemicals to start working together before being applied to the surface.

2. Pour the mixture into a shallow roller tray for ease of application, to slow down the chemical reaction, and to allow the maximum amount of time for application. Roll the barrier coating on in even layers. With most brands, you will need to apply more than one layer.

3. If a coating cures beyond the allowed "recoating window," you will need to lightly sand the surface and proceed.

4. Recoating will be required by most systems to build up the necessary thickness that ensures a proper insulating layer for the bottom. Read the instructions carefully to determine the recommended dry film thickness and the necessary number of coats to achieve that thickness.

The cost and hassle of applying a barrier coating may initially seem high, but when laid alongside the potential costs and hassle of repairing a blistered bottom, they are modest. Commercial blister repair costs are currently running up to $300.00 per foot.

Applying Bottom Paints

When the bottom is ready to receive bottom paint, there are a number of ways to apply it. More and more yards today are spraying bottom paint, but the equipment and facility to do this properly and safely may not be readily available to the do-it-yourself boater. Overspray on other boats would be a problem for most yards. More than likely you will elect to roll on the primers and bottom paint.

For best results, apply bottom paints when the temperature is 50°F to 80°F (10°C to 26.7°C) and the relative humidity is less than 65 percent. You will need to adjust the amount of thinner you mix with the paint based on the weather and amount of time required to paint the surface. Warm, windy weather will promote rapid evaporation of the solvents. Even in normal weather, if the application period is long, significant amounts of solvent will evaporate, leaving the remaining paint thicker and more difficult to handle.

1. Tape the bottom carefully. If you are going to spray the bottom, cover the topsides and other surfaces you don't want to expose to overspray. If there is tape already on the boat from stripping or barrier coat application, replace it. Tape should never be left on for an extended length of time because it might then lift underlying finishes. Also, the tape may be damaged by other finishes or sanding and not perform as expected.

2. Stir the paint thoroughly to remix the solids. If the can is full, pour one-half of the paint into another container. Add thinner to each, if necessary, and stir thoroughly. Either combine the paints again or pour them directly into a paint tray. Later, you will need to stir most paints again because the solids will settle if they're not frequently mixed. Additional thinning may be required if the solvent is evaporating quickly.

3. Apply paint. If you elect to roll on the paint, roll it on in a random pattern using a high-quality roller—which must be solvent resistant. If you are going to brush or "tip" (smooth out) the paint after applying it, finish rolling with an up-and-down stroke and then use a high-quality brush. This job is easier with two people—one to tip the freshly rolled paint, which sets up quickly.

4. Allow adequate time for the paint to cure before placing a support against it or moving jack stands. If you have to move jack stands or cradle supports, do so with extreme care. Don't hesitate to ask someone to help.

It's common practice to touch up the unpainted pad areas as the boat is being lifted for launching. Paint manufacturers say this is a mistake: The paint will not dry properly, nor will it perform as it should. Most paints should be allowed to dry overnight prior to launching. The reality is that most of us do touch up shortly before launching, and with most paint it's okay. Marine paint manufacturers recommend that bottom paint should not be exposed to air for more than 60 days before launching. The exception to this is ablative paints, which are relatively immune to air exposure.

Many boatowners are satisfied with the surface created by rolling bottom paint on with a short-nap roller. You can obtain a better job by brushing the still wet paint. This process, often called "tipping," works best with two people, one rolling vertically and one brushing horizontally right behind.

5. In most cases, a second coat of bottom paint is recommended. Do as directed in steps 1, 2, and 3 above.

Taking Care

A final word about safety and the environment. Some of the materials discussed in this book are highly toxic both to you and the environment. When sanding a bottom, wear protective equipment: white paper suits (they're also great for keeping the dust off of you and saving clothing), rubber gloves, paper helmets, dust masks, and safety glasses. When painting a bottom, pay particular attention to breathing equipment, eye protection and, with some materials, hand protection. Carefully read the instructions that come with the materials.

Sand boat bottoms in areas where the residue does not fall back into the water. Even old bottom paint has a good deal of toxicity left when sanded, and a concentration of such dust in shallow shoreline waters is not good for marine life.

Disposing of solvents presents another problem. Many boatyards have arrangements with subcontractors to remove and dispose of paint solvents, and that may be your best bet. An auto body shop might also be a resource for disposing solvents.

Stripping waste and sanding dust can be harmful to the environment. Check with a local yard to determine the required disposal procedures in your area.

Common Bottom Paint Problems

Understanding all the variables that affect a paint's performance is the first step in rectifying a problem. The Pettit Paint Company's Technical Bulletin #105 lists some of those variables:

- Low water in harbors means a boat might sit in mud or hit bottom *occasionally.*
- An influx of fresh water from heavy rains brings in silt, dirt, and nutrients.
- Water temperatures above or below average affect toxicant release.
- If the salinity of the water is too low, it will slow toxicant leaching.
- Chemicals (or pollutants) in acid or alkaline waters affect leaching of toxicant.
- Applying too little paint will affect its performance.
- Bad slime conditions cause the paint to seal up.
- Presence of electric current neutralizes antifouling paint.
- Not observing proper immersion times will affect the paint's performance.
- Improper surface preparation will cause the paint to peel.
- Porous fiberglass will cause blistering in the paint film.

PART 3

Hull and Deck Maintenance and Upgrades

CHAPTER 8

Maintaining Fiberglass and Gelcoat

For the most part, when we think of maintaining fiberglass we think of preserving the integrity and beauty of the gelcoat—the colored resin on the outside of the fiberglass laminate that is, therefore, the original cosmetic surface of hulls and decks. Basically, gelcoat is the same resin or material used to laminate the structural part of the boat, but with color pigment added. Gelcoat is normally applied by spraying it into a newly waxed hull or deck mold before the fiberglass laminations are applied. Therefore, it becomes an integral part of the molding. Gelcoat is important to the boat because, without pigment, the resin in the structural laminate will eventually break down from exposure to ultraviolet sunlight. This chapter discusses common maintenance procedures to preserve the gelcoat finish. If followed carefully, they will protect the surfaces and prolong the gelcoat's life.

Waxing Gelcoat

The first sign of gelcoat deterioration is when it starts to "chalk" or get hazy, a normal occurrence for unprotected surfaces. In the early stages, chalking is not cause for alarm. It will occur fairly quickly (in a matter of a few months) on even a new boat if the surface is exposed to hot sun. The common preventive step and early cure is to wax the surface. Waxing provides two benefits: It cleans the surface of contaminants such as built-up dirt or acids, and it applies a protective finish to the surface.

Gelcoat should be waxed at least once a year in the north and more frequently farther south. If the gelcoat surface has deteriorated substantially, it may be prudent to use a buffing compound before waxing.

Waxing a boat is an easy exercise. Here are a few ideas that may be helpful.

Wash and Wipe

Any protective coating—wax, varnish, or epoxy—must be applied to a clean surface. Neglecting to clean the gelcoat before waxing it will reduce the life of the new finish. The wax will be contaminated right from the beginning with grit and other deposits that are on the deck, and grit will be ground in by the rubbing or buffing motion used when waxing. In the end, you'll find small scratches in the gelcoat, which are especially apparent on topsides with dark gelcoats.

Use a good quality boat soap to wash the topsides (see pages 2–3 for recommendations), and remember to rinse thoroughly. With most waxes, it is not important that the deck or other surfaces be perfectly dry before waxing.

There are many waxes on the market, and most that are silicone or carnauba based will protect the surface well. I like a silicone wax such as 3M Ultra Performance Paste Wax. Some contain polishing compounds; others contain Teflon which, although typically harder to apply, usually leaves a longer-lasting finish. Unless the surface has apparent chalking, use a product *without* polishing compounds—there's no sense in accelerating the wear on the gelcoat.

1. If applying the wax by hand, use small circular motions. If you are going to use a buffer to polish, you should always apply the wax by hand. Limit the application to a relatively small area. On a hot, dry day, 4 square feet may be enough. On a cloudy day, you might be able to get away with 10 or 12 square feet. With most waxes, the idea is to allow enough time for them to haze over before buffing out.

    Apply the wax with either a foam pad (often supplied with paste waxes) or a clean rag. Some manufacturers recommend using a dampened pad or rag. Read and follow the manufacturers' directions for variations. Change the rags or clean the foam pad regularly to avoid scratching the surface with grit picked up in the process.

2. After the wax dries, gently wipe it with a soft clean rag, then go over it again with another. Remember to keep using clean rags. The second wiping can be more rigorous; doing so will provide a clear uniform surface with a minimum of streaking. If there is streaking (dark hulls are particularly susceptible), apply a second coat of wax.

If you are using a buffer, keep the buffing pad clean. Use a pad cleaning wheel occasionally to clean and fluff it. Finish the job with a clean soft rag.

A couple of other things to keep in mind when waxing: Allowing wax to get on exterior brightwork can lead to a varnish problem. Either tape off the brightwork, or complete all brightwork refinishing before waxing, or both. Additionally, don't wax any nonskid areas of the deck. Slippery nonskid is a hazard to safe passage at sea.

Use circular motions when applying wax to ensure even coverage. Keep the working area relatively small to prevent wax from overdrying before buffing.

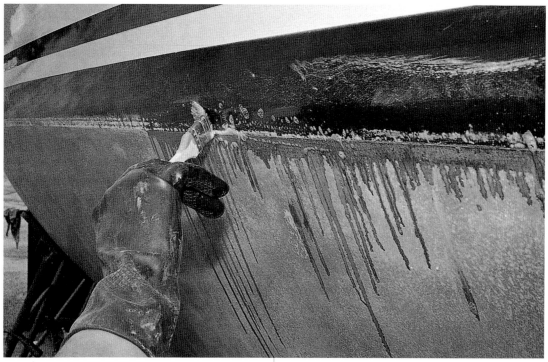

You usually can remove stains on boottops with a little buffing. However, a cleaner is necessary when calcium is built up. Try a mild solution of muriatic acid or a commercial cleaner such as Y-10. Aid the future care of the boottop area by waxing the surface. Try to keep the wax off areas that will need frequent repainting, such as bottom surfaces.

Using a Polishing Compound on Gelcoat

If the chalking has advanced to the point where the surface is dull and wax alone will not restore it, consider using a polishing compound. Use a mild compound, though, so you do not abrade too much gelcoat. The original gelcoat may be less than ¹⁄₆₄ of an inch thick, and it will wear through after repeated abrasive treatment. Resurfacing with gelcoat or paint is expensive.

Follow the instructions included with the compound. They usually suggest applying the compound in small areas of perhaps 4 square

feet, followed by wiping off and buffing with a soft, clean cloth. If you use a buffing machine, be extremely careful that the compound does not overheat the gelcoat—that will lead to surface distortion or abrasion of the coating. When using a buffer, apply the compound in small globs over the area to be buffed and, with the buffer at low speed, spread the compound. Keep the machine moving so that any heat that is built up can dissipate. Clean or exchange the pads regularly. Finish the process by carefully wiping the surface to remove all of the polishing compound. Then, wax the surface as described on page 93.

Dealing with Stains

Stains in gelcoat can be impossible to remove with polishes because the porous nature of gelcoat can allow stains to pass right through the surface. Abrasive compounds will remove the gelcoat at the same time it removes the stains. When faced with a stain, try a bleaching cleaner on the stain before buffing or waxing. Common household acidic cleaners such as toilet bowl cleaners may do the job; commercial products such as Y-10 are also available.

Gelcoat Repair

Depending on the severity of the problem, fiberglass repair might be limited to gelcoat repair or it might also involve structural work. If the damage is deeper than the color layer, it may be necessary to first follow the procedures described in Chapter 9 (Minor Fiberglass Structural Repair) before repairing the gelcoat as described here. With a little practice, most boatowners can easily repair small scrapes in gelcoat; larger sections that need to be repaired demand a bit more patience and the know-how to spray gelcoat, but are not difficult to accomplish. If you're filling scratches to prepare for painting the topsides or deck, you may not need to use a gelcoat putty. Refer to Chapter 6.

You can apply and spread gelcoat in a number of ways. This includes spraying, using an artist's paint spreader, or using a shaped tool for areas such as the cove stripe. The disposable sprayer shown here is spraying thinned gelcoat that has been cut approximately 50 percent with acetone.

The materials needed for most gelcoat repairs should all be available through your local marine chandlery. If you need to buy the gelcoat itself, contact your builder. One of the most time-consuming parts of gelcoat repair is getting the materials. Therefore, it may pay to collect the materials ahead of time—especially the gelcoat—and store them.

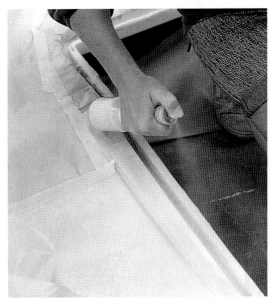

Matching Gelcoat

As I mentioned earlier, gelcoat is a pigmented resin used as the exterior protection and cosmetic layer for fiberglass laminate. Because the color of the gelcoat needs to match as closely as possible the color of the surface being repaired, you might want to contact your boat's builder to see if the original color is still available. Once in a while, a builder will provide extra gelcoat with the boat, but if the boat is more than a year old, the potential for a perfect match is low. Time and the elements combine forces to start the fading of gelcoat the day a boat leaves the plant. A well-maintained surface will, of course, be easier to match than one that's heavily oxidized, and a

light-colored gelcoat is generally easier to match than a dark one. Expect some matching problems. I have seen some experts specially tint or color gelcoat to match a faded color. It helps, but is difficult to do and requires a level of skill that few possess.

Catalyst

A catalyst is the material that, when mixed with gelcoat, causes a chemical reaction that heats and cures, or hardens, the gelcoat. The most common catalyst sold with gelcoats is methyl ethyl ketone peroxide (MEKP). It is available both clear and in a red color (the red catalysts are useful in laminating applications), and in 30 percent and 60 percent solutions. The 60 percent clear is the preferred catalyst for use with gelcoat and the one you will find in most marine stores. The 30 percent mixture is not as "hot" as the 60 percent.

Proper preparation of an area for repair is critical to good adhesion of the patch.

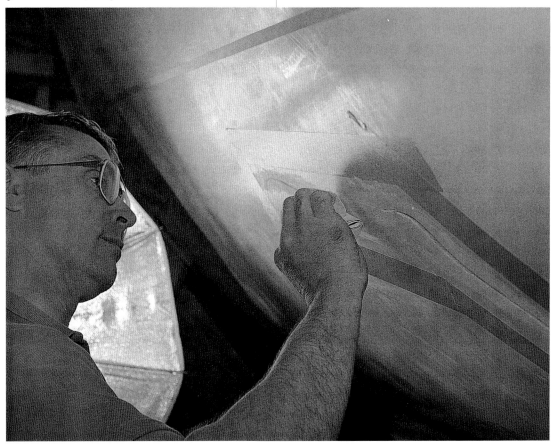

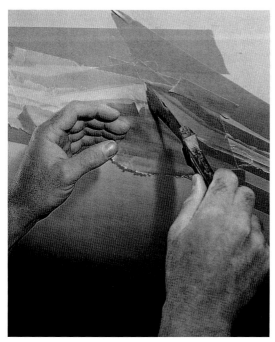

Applying waxed paper over a small scratch helps smooth out the surface and improves the cure of the gelcoat by sealing the surface.

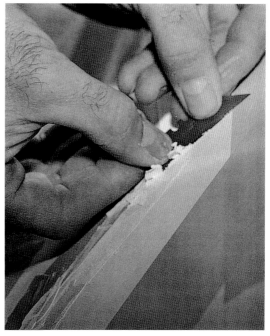

Trimming excess material off the edge of the patch as it cures reduces the amount of sanding required later. This in turn reduces the likelihood of sanding through the patch or surrounding area and having to gelcoat again.

Sandpaper

The best sandpapers for repairing gelcoat are the finer grained—220, 400, and 600 grit. If you want a smoother finish, there are even finer grits available. Purchase only wet-or-dry sandpaper for this job because the paper will get wet. Wet-or-dry sandpapers do not shed their mineral abrasive when moistened, and the paper backing is waterproof, which prevents curling and decomposition when immersed. 3M Tri-M-Ite wet-or-dry sandpaper is a good selection for this type of work.

Other Tools and Materials

Clean tuna fish cans or disposable paper pots work well for mixing and applying gelcoat. Other materials you might want to round up include: stirring stick, waxed paper, small throwaway brush, 1-inch putty knife, buffing compound, wax, acetone, masking tape, measuring vial for catalyst, and rags.

Repairing a Small Scratch

For a scratch that doesn't penetrate deeply into the laminate, the following procedure would be appropriate:

1. Clean and tape the area around the scratch. The taped area should be as small as possible to contain the patch while still allowing room to sand and work.

2. Sand the scratch to remove foreign matter and loose gelcoat. Do not sand the whole area.

3. Wash the area with acetone for maximum cleanliness.

4. Mix the gelcoat and catalyst as the directions indicate. If none are provided, mix 1 to 2 percent of catalyst to gelcoat—that's about one drop of catalyst in a thimbleful of gelcoat. If

you are using a wooden stirrer, it is important to wet it with the gelcoat before adding the catalyst. With small quantities of gelcoat, wooden stirrers will absorb a substantial amount of the thin catalyst and slow the cure, or hardening, of the gelcoat.

5. Apply the gelcoat on the scratched area with the stirrer, brush, sprayer, or putty knife. Cover the whole scratch and overlap the sanded area somewhat. The gelcoat will shrink as it cures, so apply more than it looks like you need to fill the crack.

6. Cover the patch with waxed paper and gently smooth it out with a putty knife to seal the gelcoat from the air. Gelcoat is air-inhibited, which means that its surface does not cure entirely if exposed to air. The fact that gelcoat is air-inhibited is valuable in the molding process (new construction); that quality allows the laminate to better bond with the gelcoat. Wax is added to some gelcoats and, as the gelcoat cures, the wax floats to the surface to seal the gelcoat from the air. Waxed paper serves the same purpose, and it helps shape the patch and reduce sanding. Waxed paper does no harm if the gelcoat already has wax added.

7. Allow to cure, which may take from 15 minutes to one hour. When the waxed paper is removed, some of the excess gelcoat may be removed with a sharp knife or razor blade, but beware of cutting the surface too low, especially if the gelcoat is still hardening.

8. When the gelcoat has hardened enough to sand, sand the surface with the finest-grade sandpaper that will remove the excess—220 or 320 grit will probably be required. Keep the tape in place or renew it to protect the surrounding gelcoat from scratches.

9. When the surface is flush, sand the patch with progressively finer-grit wet-or-dry papers up to 600 grit. For example, if you start with 220 grit,

Buff the patch with compound to bring back the like-new luster. Use a slow-turning buffer, not a sander.

use 320 or 400 grit next and then 600 grit. Then buff out to a high gloss finish.

10. If the surface is below flush, you may need to repeat steps 2 through 9.

On a warm day, the entire process of repairing a small scratch may take only a couple of hours, including drying time. But beware of cold or damp weather! The gelcoat may never cure. Most patchers prefer not to work in weather below 60°F (15.6°C). And note that it is a lot easier to patch well-cared-for gelcoat than faded or chalked gelcoat, so keep that gelcoat waxed!

CHAPTER 9

Minor Fiberglass Structural Repair

Repairing large structural fiberglass damage is often best handled by professionals, not so much because of the difficulty of the job, but because of the equipment and time needed for the project. There are, however, a few types of repairs that might be made by a boatowner without undue problems. This chapter will give you the information you need to feel confident in starting such projects. If you feel comfortable making these repairs, then by all means, take on that storm-damaged dream boat.

The following jobs are fairly common around boats, and all are within the realm of reasonable tasks for a handy boatowner:

- damage to the hull as a result of rubbing against a piling or dock structure;

- repairing the fiberglass taping that has become detached from a bulkhead;

- reinforcing a weak or spongy deck section.

The steps I've outlined for these projects will provide an overview of the basic procedures used in fiberglass repair, many of which can be applied to other projects, too.

Materials

Before beginning a primer on fiberglass repair, allow me to introduce you to the materials that are commonly used in jobs beyond gelcoat repair in "glass" boats. These are the basics. For those of you who are experts, pardon me for not getting into the nuances of some products. No doubt I will get in trouble with some folks for not mentioning their pet material. There are some dynamite new products on the market for boat repair, but many are not commonly available to the boatowner, and some require special equipment to apply.

Fabrics

The fabrics of fiberglass, or the real glass in the process, are commonly found in three styles: mat, cloth, and woven roving. Each is a different assembly of extremely thin glass fiber.

Mat is glass fiber that is chopped into pieces approximately 2 inches long and then pressed together and held with an adhesive material. Mat is not as strong per pound as fiberglass cloth or woven roving, but it serves as filler and binder for the other materials in many laminates. Mat is often made in weights of $\frac{3}{4}$ to 2 ounces per square

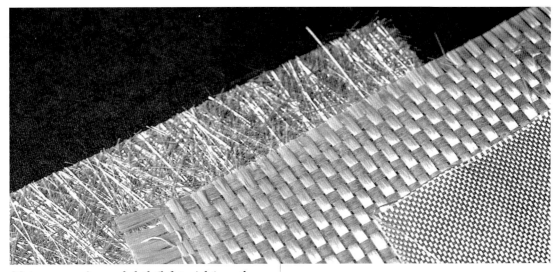

Mat, woven roving, and cloth (left to right) are the basic reinforcements used with resin for building and repairing fiberglass boats. Special materials such as unidirectional and carbon fiber fabrics are also becoming common.

foot, but the most common weight to purchase for repairs is 1½ ounce.

Cloth is a fabric made of long glass strands, woven together in a matrixlike linen fabric. It is smooth and, because it requires little resin to saturate it and hold it in shape, it is a strong fabric for repair work. Cloth fabrics commonly come in weights of 4 to 10 ounces per square yard or more. Ten-ounce cloth is the most common for repairs.

Woven roving is the heavy woven fabric that provides the bulk of the strength in most boat hulls. It looks like heavy fiberglass cloth and usually comes in weights of 18 to 24 ounces per square yard. Woven roving is normally used in alternate layers with fiberglass mat.

There are more and more special fabrics on the market today. Some are combinations of the fabrics described above, used to streamline the lamination process, and some are high-strength, special-purpose fabrics. Unidirectional woven roving and graphite fiber materials are two examples of new products. These materials are not often required for everyday repairs, but they have their place.

Resins

As strong as the fabrics are that we use in fiberglass repair, they are of little value without resin to hold them in shape. Resins are thermosetting plastics, which means that they harden when heated. The heat is generated by a chemical reaction between a promoter that is added to the resin when it is manufactured, and a catalyst that you add when you mix the resin at the time of use. Although resins provide some strength to the matrix, that is not their primary function. They are used for form retention and to hold water out.

There are three common types of resin used for marine work: epoxy, vinylester, and polyester. Epoxy is a very strong and flexible resin with excellent properties for use in the marine environment. It is, however, expensive and its cost has limited its use in the construction of fiberglass boats.

Vinylester has gained popularity lately as a good laminating resin that absorbs less water than polyester resins. It is less expensive than epoxy and, with its improved water resistance, is becoming common in hull construction. Builders are hoping it will be a solution to the problem of bottom blisters. It is often used for the first few (outside) layers of a hull and occasionally for the entire hull.

Polyester is still dominant among the resins used today. It is easy to work with, comparatively inexpensive, and widely available. I will concentrate here on repairing fiberglass with polyester resins. It is acceptable in some cases to use different resins in different applications for your boat. This should be done with some care, however. Not all resins get along well with other resins. For example, if you have an area that has been laminated with epoxy resin, do not try to laminate over it with polyester. It will not adhere well. Interestingly, epoxy will adhere to cured polyester lamination.

Core Materials

Core materials—the most common being plywood, balsa, and foam—are being found more and more in boat construction. They are built into the lamination to strengthen, lighten, and/or insulate. The core spaces the inside and outside skins farther apart and, in so doing, substantially stiffens the laminate.

Plywood is used most often in small, flat areas of decks on production boats. It is an inexpensive core material that performs reasonably well. Although it is the heaviest of the three, it's often the least expensive. It also has the least resistance to rot.

Balsa wood, specifically end-grain balsa, has found favor with many builders. It is used in decks and hulls. The strength of laminate is very high when balsa is used as a core material, due to balsa's light weight and compressive resistance.

The foam cores used today are also light. They typically are the most expensive of the cores and have more flexibility than balsa and plywood.

Core materials must be considered carefully in repair work, because damage to the core must be dealt with—along with the fiberglass skins—and sometimes core damage can be difficult to diagnose.

Tools and Supplies

The following materials are needed or helpful in fiberglass repair jobs:

gelcoat (colored resin) in the appropriate color
catalyst (60 percent MEKP is preferred)
small container(s) for mixing and application
stirring stick
waxed paper
small throwaway brush
3-inch disposable roller
sandpaper, both fine and coarse grit
buffing compound
wax
acetone
masking tape
measuring vial for catalyst
rags

A word about safety: The fumes given off from the resins and their companion solvents are flammable and toxic. These products should be handled carefully and used in a manner to prevent accidents. It is highly recommended that you ventilate any area in which you are fiberglassing. Additionally, use a good respirator and wear safety glasses.

Hull Damage

Remembering that we need to fix damage caused by a piling or dock, let's get down to business. The first thing to do is to assess the damage.

1. Carefully examine the area from the inside as well as the outside to determine the full extent of the damage. It is important to realize that, because fiberglass is a laminated composite, the damaged materials may extend well beyond the area that is easily identified. For the purposes of describing this repair, assume that the hull has been punctured in a small area and there is not a lot of damage beyond the hole. Mark the damaged area. I suggest that you use masking tape, if possible, because ink markers may leave lines that are difficult to remove and are hard to see once you start sanding.

2. Cut out the obviously damaged laminate. You will probably want to start with an electric saw and then use a grinder, if available. If they are not available, lots of elbow grease and heavy-grit sandpaper will be required.

    Finish the hole with a taper of 12:1. In other words, if the damaged fiberglass is ½ inch thick, the sanded area all around the hole should be 6 inches wide. If there is a core, the taper should be based on the thickness of the fiberglass skin on either side of the core. If you are going to replace the core, you will need to

This sketch shows the layout of a repair involving a hole of 3-inch diameter in the hull. The top-right view shows how, in a cored hull, both the inner and outer fiberglass skins should be tapered (to accept the new laminate) prior to installing the replacement core piece. The bottom-left view shows how a backing plate could be used in a solid-laminate hull to provide a surface to laminate against. The bottom-right view shows how the fabric should be cut in increasingly larger patches, both in cored and solid-laminate repairs

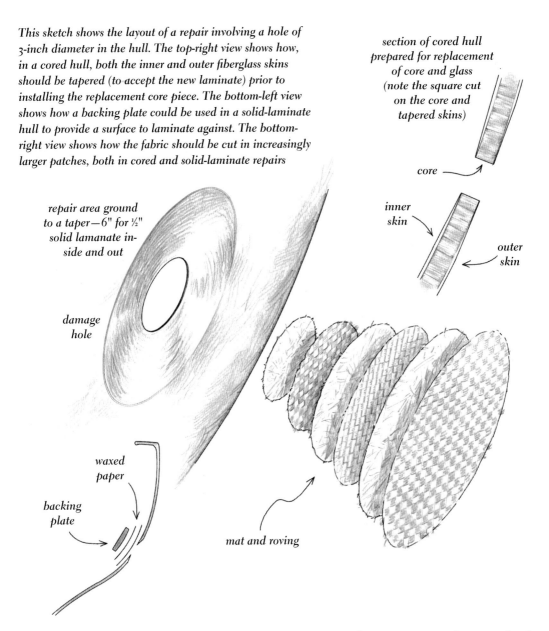

section of cored hull prepared for replacement of core and glass (note the square cut on the core and tapered skins)

core

inner skin

outer skin

repair area ground to a taper—6" for ½" solid lamanate inside and out

damage hole

waxed paper

backing plate

mat and roving

prepare the remaining core in the original laminate to receive the replacement core piece you are going to install. That process normally requires carefully cutting the old core in a pattern that will allow the close fitting of a new piece.

3. Clean the work area and wash it with acetone to remove foreign oils and materials. Retape the patch if necessary.

4. Precut the appropriate replacement laminates to sizes that allow the patch to taper in the same configuration as the feathered fiberglass on the boat. For example, if the hole to be patched is 3 inches in diameter, and the sanded taper around the hole is 3 inches larger, the first fabric layers should be cut just slightly larger than the hole; the next layers might be cut 1 inch larger, and so on.

The laminate composition and thickness should be determined by observing and measuring the existing laminate thickness and order at the cut or ground edge. It will most likely be alternating layers of mat and woven roving. It would seem that the laminate should match exactly; however, as the patch will have a "secondary bond" to the original hull, it will not be as strong as the original. Therefore, a bit more laminate should be used on the inside of the hull to spread out the load. In figuring laminate thickness, remember that two layers of 1½-ounce mat and one layer of 24-ounce woven roving cure to about ⅛ inch.

5. Apply a backing on either the inside or outside of the hole to laminate against. A piece of Formica or cardboard with wax paper taped to it will do the job. You will remove the backing as soon as the initial laminates have cured on the opposite side of the hole.

6. Mix the resin following the directions provided, or use approximately 10 to 20 cc's for each quart of resin used. Mix small quantities, and favor the heavy side with catalyst amounts in cooler weather and less in warmer weather. Cool weather for fiberglass is 60°F (15.6°C) or below. Be careful in warm weather. I remember overcatalyzing resin while glassing in an autopilot bracket many years ago. It was summer in Florida and mighty hot under that cockpit. The resin caught fire and caused a few anxious moments.

7. Wet the damaged area with the resin and apply the first and smallest laminate to the hole. I suggest that you start with mat if you are repairing a mat/woven laminate; doing so will permit better adhesion of the patch and allow easier removal of the air from the new laminate. Apply resin to the patch until the fiberglass fabric is saturated and as much of the air has been pushed out with the brush as possible. It might be impossible to remove all the air from the patch because the patch area may have rough edges. Apply additional layers of fiberglass in similar order to the original laminate, moving progressively to the larger pieces.

Do not apply more than six layers of fiberglass at one time—three or four are better. Fewer layers keep the heat buildup down and therefore reduce the possibility of distorting the patch.

8. When the patch has hardened and cooled, remove the backing and sand the rough edges smooth. The inside (or outside if the inside was done first) laminate should now be applied, following the procedure as directed in step 7.

9. The patch is finished by alternating laminate on the outside and inside until the patch is built up to the appropriate thickness. It is important to alternate sides when laminating and not to build up too much in one area at one time. Besides the heat distortion mentioned above, polyester resin shrinks substantially as it cures, and the shrinkage will tend to distort the patch.

10. When the buildup of the laminate is complete, sand the surfaces until they are smooth and the outer surface is ready to gelcoat.

11. Gelcoat, because it is quite thick, is best applied with a spray gun outfitted with a spray tip that has a larger orifice than is typically installed on an off-the-shelf spray gun. Most boatowners do not have that equipment. Fortunately, there are some other options: Thin the gelcoat so it will spray with a Preval disposable sprayer (available in chandleries and auto parts stores); or apply the gelcoat with a brush, roller, or both. When you apply gelcoat with a brush or roller, the surface will be less smooth than if it had been applied with a spray gun. You will need to work harder and more patiently to get a smooth finish, but you can certainly achieve the desired results. Start the finish process by washing the area with acetone to achieve maximum cleanliness.

12. Mix the gelcoat and catalyst following the directions provided. If none are provided, mix 1 to 2 percent of catalyst to gelcoat. Stir the mixture well and then thin as required if it is to be sprayed.

Apply the gelcoat evenly over the patch. You may find that it is effective to initially apply the gelcoat with a roller, then draw a brush across the wet surface to help the material "lay down." It is important to cover the whole patch and overlap the sanded area somewhat. The gelcoat should be applied thicker than needed because it will shrink as it cures.

13. Most gelcoat is air-inhibited, which means that it does not entirely cure if exposed to the air. Wax is added to some patching gelcoats and, as the gelcoat cures, the wax comes to the surface to seal it off from air. If the gelcoat you have applied does not have wax added, you might try lightly covering the patch with waxed paper or spraying the patch with a water-soluble film (called "PVA," for polyvinyl alcohol) sold by some fiberglass supply stores. PVA is a thin liquid and will spray through a disposable spray kit.

    If you are not comfortable with any of the above ideas, despair not. Everything except the surface of the patch should cure without these treatments. A bit of extra work is created by the tacky surface gumming up the sandpaper, but with patience you can achieve a nice surface finish.

14. When the gelcoat has hardened enough to sand, sand it with the finest grade sandpaper that will remove the excess gelcoat. For the first time, 220- or 320-grit sandpaper will probably be required. Keep the tape you applied as directed in step #1 above in place, or renew it to protect the surrounding gelcoat from being scratched.

15. When the surface is flush, finish the patch with 600-grit wet-or-dry paper and buff to a gloss finish.

16. If the surface is not flush, or the fiberglass underneath is still visible, you might need to repeat steps 12 through 15.

Bulkhead Taping

Our next project is repairing the separation of the glass tape that holds a bulkhead to a fiberglass hull or deck. If the fiberglass tape has separated from the wood on a bulkhead, and if the tape is rugged and still well adhered to the hull, resin may be injected into the seam between the tape and the bulkhead. Then the bulkhead may be bolted or screwed through the tape and eliminate the need for a new tape job. For times when this is not feasible, here is one recommended procedure to repair that problem.

1. Remove the old tape by cutting and sanding away the glass. Sand all surfaces where the new taping will need to adhere. Try to analyze and fix the source of the problem. If it was not a faulty tape job in the first place, the problem will likely reoccur. Remove from the bulkheads any paint or Formica that will interfere with the taping. Glassing over these materials is a common reason why the bonding fails.

2. Cut new fiberglass materials for the new bonding. Make the strips small enough to work with easily. Murphy's Law dictates that the glass tape will always fail in the least accessible spot. On a nonstructural bulkhead the tape should be approximately 3 inches wide for the first strip of mat. The next strip might be 4 inches, and an additional one might be 5 or more inches. The preferred laminate for a medium-sized cruiser is the following: $1\frac{1}{2}$-ounce mat; 18-ounce woven roving; $1\frac{1}{2}$-ounce mat; 18-ounce woven roving; and $1\frac{1}{2}$-ounce mat again. Some builders use more, some less.

3. Use masking tape and paper to protect the work area—it will get messy. Wash the surfaces with acetone, if possible, to remove any foreign matter that might affect the bond. *Note:* In confined spaces, be sure to ventilate everything as well as possible. Health and fire dangers are present. Wear a respirator when working with these materials.

4. Mix the resin and catalyst according to the manufacturer's directions. Wet the surfaces to be taped. With this type of repair it is possible to wet the fiberglass material in place, but most often it is easier to pre-wet the material on a sheet of cardboard and put it in place several layers at a time. Remember to place the layers in the right order, with the narrowest pieces on the inside.

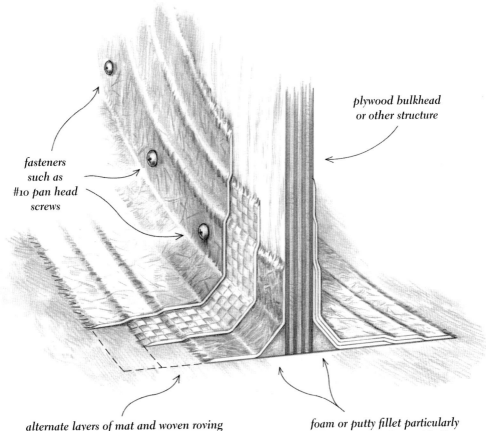

fasteners
such as
#10 pan head
screws

plywood bulkhead
or other structure

*alternate layers of mat and woven roving
or combination fabric*

*foam or putty fillet particularly
important with cored hull*

Several laminates are used in most bulkhead-taping applications. Structural bulkheads will require more laminate than non-structural pieces. Shown here is a laminate that would be used on a structural bulkhead in a 40- to 50-foot yacht.

5. When all the material has been installed and while the fiberglass is curing, trim any excess fiberglass fabric with a razor knife when the resin has gelled, or partially hardened, and has not yet become rock solid. You will get a better-looking tape job and eliminate most, if not all, of the finish job of grinding off excess fiberglass.

(right) Shown here is the placement of bulkhead taping, using a fabric that combines mat and a directional roving to simplify the process.

6. If you need to clean up rough glass, use a grinder with discs of 80 to 120 grit. Use the finest grit you can so as not to take away too much of the tape just applied. Work primarily on the edges, staying away from the inner angles that must have good strength. In fact, if possible, clean up your work by hand sanding, and then paint, if necessary, with an appropriate paint.

Deck Reinforcement

Finally, we'll repair a soft deck. Soft decks are usually caused by one of two problems—either a thin laminate or, if the deck is cored, delamination of the top or outside laminate from the core. Delamination is difficult to repair; however, if the laminate is thin, adding a stiffener will help.

If there is adequate space under the deck, con-

This picture shows a half-tube being laminated on a panel for stiffness. The same process can be used to stiffen decks, hulls, and interior components, such as liners.

sider fiberglassing a stiffening beam to its underside. The beam can be as simple as a cardboard tube that is sliced in half and glassed over with several layers of mat and woven roving. The beam should run under the deck in such a way as to decrease the width of unsupported deck surface. It is amazing how fast most springy decks will stiffen with just a bit of extra support, and they gain little added weight. The fiberglass methods are the same as described earlier in this chapter, but here are some additional hints:

1. Remove any interior woodwork or coverings to allow clear access to the area. Clean the area in which you will be installing the stiffener. Remove old paint and gelcoat and wipe with acetone.

2. Cut a cardboard tube, or other material such as balsa, to create the shape of the beam to be fiberglassed. The idea is to reduce the panel size of the weak area. The tube should be fit to the underside of the deck and taped (masking tape will do) in place temporarily. If the deck

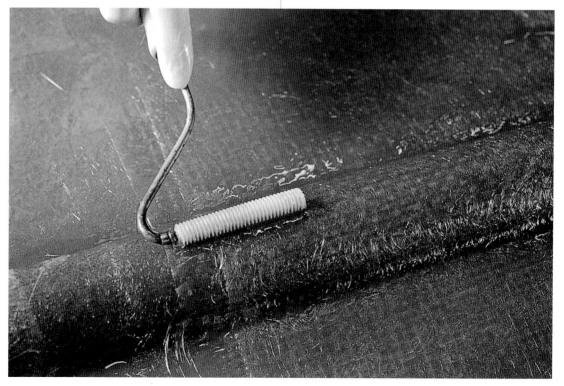

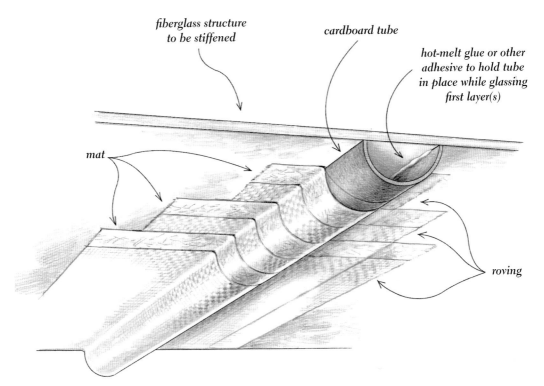

fiberglass structure
to be stiffened

cardboard tube

hot-melt glue or other
adhesive to hold tube
in place while glassing
first layer(s)

mat

roving

This is a typical laminate arrangement used on a stiffener. The material can be laminated over a half-tube or other shape, such as a rectangular section.

has any distortion, it should be reshaped (corrected) with temporary braces if possible.

3. Cut staggered layers of fiberglass to cover the stiffener. The first layers should cover the stiffener and spread out to approximately 2 inches on either side of the stiffener. The next layers should extend 4 inches, and so on. Keep the pieces small and manageable. If you have a brace 4 feet long, do not hesitate to use four or five 1-foot-long patches if you find it easier. I

do. Placing a 4-foot laminate on an overhead surface is no fun.

4. Mix the resin and wet out (saturate with resin) the fiberglass fabric on a piece of cardboard. Laminating the tube in place will take time because the laminates may have to be installed in layers to prevent them from falling off.

5. Finish with sanding the rough edges and painting or gelcoating the surface if desired.

As I mentioned at the beginning of this chapter, these repairs are certainly not the only types of fiberglass repairs that the boatowner will run into. They are, however, offered as a way to illustrate several methods of repair.

Repairing a Nonskid Deck

There was a time when a little bit of sand thrown in the last coat or two of deck paint was all that was necessary to create a nonskid surface. The system worked, even though it was a bit rough on the knees and pants. Then we invented plastic boats. The paint and sand didn't stick well enough anymore, so builders had to come up with a bunch of new ideas to keep us from falling overboard or, even worse, from spilling coffee on our new cockpit cushions.

The deck pattern is an important part of your boat's finish, and boatbuilders are always experimenting with new deck patterns. They have come up with everything from a fine, delicate pattern—which looks good in the showroom—that wouldn't keep a napkin from sliding off a flat table, to a deep, rough pattern that will remove three layers of skin from your knee when you kneel on it. Without fail, all deck patterns wear away, crack, or are in the wrong place for you; eventually, they must be repaired. There are many ways to approach repairing a boat's nonskid pattern. Some are easy, some aren't. What follows is a discussion of a few possible solutions.

Repainting a Random-Patterned Nonskid

If your deck has a random nonskid pattern with a texture similar to the old-fashioned sand method mentioned above, there are some new materials on the market that you should check out. Among them are Awlgrip Griptex fine and coarse nonskid particles, Pettit Skidless Compound, and Interlux Polymeric NOSKID Compound. These fillers are designed to be compatible with their manufacturer's paints (and with similar products from other companies). They offer several advantages over sand: They are lighter, can be sprayed with valve oriface equipment, and are sandable when it's time to refinish again.

Applying these new nonskid materials is not difficult, but if you are old-fashioned and smart, you'll read the directions. Most often, they go something like this:

1. Tape off the area where the nonskid is to be applied.

2. With a solvent, clean the surface of all oils and waxes.

3. Carefully sand the surface with 150-grit paper to remove the old paint or chalked gelcoat to allow proper adhesion to the deck. Oversanding will create more work and endanger the deck's fairness.

4. Wash the surface again with a solvent to remove any contaminants.

5. Mix the paint and nonskid in correct proportions (read the instructions again) and stir them well to ensure a thorough and even mixture. If you don't stir enough, your finished deck may look like a mill pond with an ant hill in the middle. You might also consider adding a flattening agent to reduce deck glare.

6. Evenly apply the mixture with a roller (different naps make different patterns and degrees of roughness; I recommend a short-nap roller), using a random pattern.

7. If necessary, apply a second coat. If the first coat is not fully cured, you may be able to do this without sanding again. Refer to the paint manufacturer's information for recoating times and preparation suggestions.

8. Occasionally, a covering coat without abrasive is applied to further seal the surface. This will provide a protective layer over the abrasive-filled layer. Use good judgment to avoid creating too smooth a surface.

The Mold Method of Pattern Repair

If you own a fiberglass boat and the deck pattern is uniform, such as a diamond pattern, you may be able to repair damage by creating a mirror image (called a mold) of an undamaged deck pattern area. The mold will enable you to build a replacement pattern or re-form the pattern in a patched area. This method works well if you have a fairly large section of molded-in deck pattern in good condition and want to replace a smaller section, or patch a hole in the existing pattern.

1. Locate a section of deck pattern that is in good condition and that is larger than the area you need to patch or replace. (It is possible, but

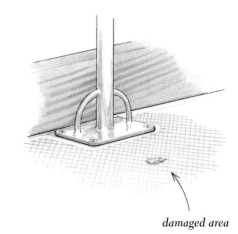

damaged area

Small chips in a molded-in deck pattern, caused by air in the initial laminate or by dropping something on the deck, are almost inevitable. Occasionally you need to rework an area after removing a fitting.

more difficult, to replace a large area starting with a smaller one.) This section will become the master mold for a new deck pattern.

2. Prepare the master pattern area by carefully cleaning it with mild detergent and a soft-bristled brush; then tape off the area to delineate the working area.

3. With a soft-bristled brush, apply multiple layers (four or more) of mold release wax, following the manufacturer's instructions. Often, substantial time must be allowed between coats to allow the wax surface to completely cure. Applying the wax is the most important part of the process. If you mess up the waxing, it's likely that the mold you build will stick to the master pattern underneath. If you doubt whether or not you have applied enough wax, add more. The only downside of overwaxing is filling the pattern (which would take a *lot* of wax).

Polyvinyl alcohol (PVA) is very helpful in this application. PVA is a water-soluble liquid that forms a film between the wax and the gelcoat that you will be applying to create the mold. PVA should be available from a fiberglass supplier; it is worth the search for this project. It is applied with a small spray gun (the small spray kits with disposable propellant cans available at auto supply stores work well), or can be brushed or applied with a rag. Only a very thin layer is required.

4. When everything is ready, mix the gelcoat with the hardener and apply the mixture evenly over the surface. Spraying is the best method, but brushing is often the only option. The trick is to make the application as air-free as possible. Air that is trapped by the thick gelcoat will create small cavities in the mold surface.

5. When the gelcoat has cured at room temperature, usually after two to four hours, it should still be sticky on the surface so it can chemically bond with the laminate placed against it. You will need to apply several layers of fiberglass mat to the surface to enable the mold to be removed from the deck area and hold its basic shape. The mold should be at least one-eighth of an inch thick and should not exceed one-quarter of an inch. You'll want some flexibility in the mold because you might have to flex it slightly to fit a deck camber that is different from the area it was taken from.

6. Remove the mold from the deck. It should come off easily but may require some starting help from some wooden wedges inserted around the edges. Trim off the rough edges and allow the surface of the mold to cure in the sun for at least a couple of days.

At this point, there are a couple of ways to proceed with the repair. If the damaged area is large, you may wish to remove a substantial portion or the entire pattern and replace it. If the area of damage is small and in the middle of a large pattern area, you may wish to patch the existing pattern. I prefer to replace an entire section of pattern if at all possible because it's usually difficult to match the colors and edges when patching.

Replacing an Entire Section

1. Remove the damaged pattern area very carefully. Tape off the deck around the pattern and sand off the pattern entirely. Be sure to maintain a smooth, level surface for the new pattern to fit to.

Mold Method Simplified

Here's a way to simplify the mold method of pattern repair for very small holes or chips. This procedure is basically the same as the one outlined above for larger repair areas but substitutes a small silicone-and-plywood mold for the fiberglass one used there.

Follow the instructions on page 109 for preparing the pattern area the mold is to be taken from. Instead of brushing on gelcoat and applying fiberglass to produce a mold, spread a bit of silicone on the surface and press a piece of plywood onto the silicone while it's still wet. This will create a sort of "rubber stamp" of the pattern. Proceed as described above for the larger mold.

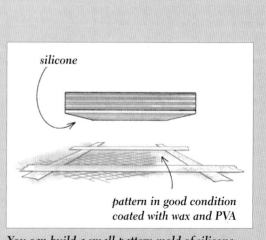

silicone

pattern in good condition coated with wax and PVA

You can build a small pattern mold of silicone and plywood for patching small areas such as drill holes and chips.

2. The mold surface is prepared in the same manner as the deck was to build the mold (see page 109). Remember that you are working in reverse (on a mirror image) when taping. Because the mold is usually new and its surface has probably not entirely cured, put extra emphasis on waxing and using PVA. The new pattern piece that you will try to remove from this mold will be thin and, if it sticks, it will be a bear to remove without doing damage.

3. Mix the gelcoat with the catalyst and spray or brush it on the mold surface. Coat an area larger than the patch area—you will later trim the new pattern to fit. Be extra careful to work the gelcoat into the pattern to reduce the possibility of trapping air in the deeper areas of the pattern. Do your best to smooth out the gelcoat—it will ease the application of the fiberglass fabric.

4. Apply one or two layers of fiberglass mat. Some folks recommend using one layer of mat and one of fiberglass cloth. I like using mat exclusively because I sand the underside of the new deck pattern before gluing it down to ensure a smooth deck, and mat sands reasonably well.

5. When the mat is fully cured—after at least four hours—carefully pull the pattern from the mold. It is easy to crack the thin pattern piece, so take your time and be patient.

6. Trim the pattern to fit the area of the removed deck pattern. A jigsaw with a metal or plastic cutting blade works well, but a wood blade will often shatter the edge of the pattern.

7. Sand the back of the pattern to smooth out the bumps that might be caused by overlapping fabric, extra resin, or rough laminate.

8. Dry fit the new pattern and tape the deck around the outside of the pattern. This will prevent the resin, which will be used as glue, from ending up where it is not supposed to be. When the pattern is in place, fit plywood and weights to hold it down while the resin (applied later) cures. Be thorough in this step. It is important to have adequate support and weight to reduce the potential of waves in the pattern when it is glued.

9. Mix the resin, catalyst, and a thickener for the resin (ground fiberglass dust works well if it is clean). Apply this mixture to the pattern piece and to the deck, spreading the mixture around evenly and completely. Any voids may leave pockets where moisture will collect in the completed repair. The moisture will freeze and you will once again have a damaged deck.

10. Reinstall the deck pattern piece, place the plywood and weights (fit in step 8 above) on top of the pattern, and recheck the alignment. With the resin in place it is easy for the pattern to slip out of alignment.

11. After curing, clean the edges of the pattern with sandpaper and patch them. Use gelcoat that matches either the pattern color or the background deck color to build a hollow radius edge to the pattern. Tape off the pattern edge and the deck on the outer edge of the radius. Using a finger as an application tool works about as well as anything; a tongue depressor or ice cream stick works, too. Match the size and shape of the radius on the rest of the boat if possible. Take your time applying a good smooth radius; doing so will mean less sanding later.

This system produces a fine repair. I have used it on new and like-new boats, and it's almost impossible to tell that the deck has been patched. With older boats, it is tough to get an exact gelcoat match. Often, a bit of white has to be added to the base color to get the faded look of aged gelcoat. If the color match is unacceptable, consider painting the pattern over the entire deck. See Chapter 6 for more information.

Patching a Small Area

Now, let's look at making a patch in an existing pattern. I should begin by saying that I have never seen this type of patch done so well that it disappears, but a few have been hard to find.

1. Place the deck pattern mold in place on the deck over the area to be repaired. The pattern

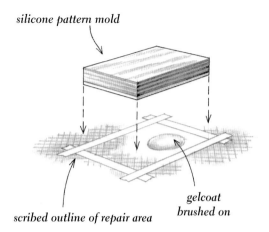

silicone pattern mold

gelcoat
brushed on

scribed outline of repair area

Dry-fit the deck pattern mold to the deck over the patched area. It should "index" into the pattern. Use masking tape to mark its location; this helps relocate the mold when it is placed into the wet gelcoat.

should fit exactly, and ideally the mold will fit tightly on the existing deck pattern. When you have ensured that the match can be made, remove the pattern and prepare it for use by waxing as described in step 3 on page 109.

2. Remove the damaged area of pattern. If your deck pattern has lines etched in, use the lines to delineate your patch area. Keep the patch as small as possible. Use masking tape to mark off the area. I've found that it's a good idea to place cardboard around the damaged area to pad the rest of the deck pattern from dropped tools. A die grinder bit with a pointed end works well to remove the outside areas of the patch. The inner areas can be easily removed using one of those small (1½ inch to 2 inch) sanding disc tools that fits a drill, available in hardware stores. Enough of the surface has to be removed to permit a healthy layer of patching gelcoat to be applied and not be squashed out when the pattern mold is placed on top.

3. Now tape off the prepared patch area. Wax the pattern area immediately adjacent to prevent

the patching gelcoat from sticking where you do not want it. Use PVA if you have it.

4. Place the mold over the area again to check out its best position. When you are satisfied that the mold fits exactly, tape around the outside of the mold to ensure that you can easily replace it in the same position. Remove the mold from the deck and, if possible (by measuring from the tape on the deck), mark the mold surface with the outline of the patch. Then remove the masking tape from and carefully clean the patch area. The masking tape will leave a sticky residue. Be sure to avoid contaminating the waxed area around the patch with any cleaner used.

5. Mix the gelcoat and catalyst and get ready for the most difficult steps. Brush the gelcoat on the patch area and, if you have been able to mark the mold, brush gelcoat on the mold surface. You may feel that just painting the deck with gelcoat will suffice, but it is difficult not to trap air in the pattern on the mold when it is put down in place. This creates air bubbles in the surface.

6. Place the mold down on the deck, being careful not to press overly hard in one area—doing so will create a hollow in the patch. In fact, if you are working on a relatively flat area, place a piece of plywood over the mold with moderate and even weight on it.

7. Use the mixed gelcoat left in the application container as a guide to determine the hardness of the gelcoat in the patch. When it has cured adequately (in relatively warm weather it should take about an hour) pull the mold off the deck. A cold surface will slow the curing process considerably. If in doubt, let it cure longer.

8. The patch will require a lot of detailing (fine sanding) around the outside to match it as well as possible to the old pattern. A small triangular file works well to shape the outer edges of the patch on most geometric patterns. If the patch has not filled in completely, you may wish to try again. Practice makes better in this endeavor, so don't expect too much your first time out.

When All Else Fails . . .

In a clearly defined area, such as a cockpit, an alternative to repairing the deck pattern is to install teak decking or another premade pattern. Teak is expensive, but the finished product is beautiful and functional. The details of laying a teak deck would constitute another chapter, but the process is not all that difficult. It is now possible to make a pattern of the area to be decked over and send it to a company (such as Teak Decking Systems of Sarasota, Florida) that will assemble the decking, complete with trim, on a thin plywood underlayment, all ready to be glued down.

Premanufactured deck patterns are also available. Treadmaster is an often-used pattern but may be a bit too "commercial-looking" for some folks. Ask at your boatyard or chandlery about alternatives.

These jobs may seem a bit complicated for the beginning boat repairer. They do require some time and, in some cases, a lot of patience. Give some thought to undertaking any of these projects and plan your work carefully.

CHAPTER 11

Boat Improvement Projects and Upgrades

This chapter offers upgrade ideas and projects that a boatowner may wish to undertake. The projects are not too complex; you shouldn't have any problem tackling them if you have basic carpentry skills. Even if the ideas presented here aren't appropriate for your boat, the methods they employ are valuable for other projects and upgrades.

The projects include:

Building a Hatch

Building a Dorade Vent

Preventing and Repairing Deck Leaks

Portlight Repairs

Installing High-Load Deck Hardware

Repairing or Replacing Veneers

Building and Installing a Battery Box

Building a Hatch

Constructing and installing a beautiful wood-framed hatch is a good project for a boatowner/woodworker. Reasons to build a new hatch include: improving a boat's ventilation system; providing a new escape route from down below; enlarging an existing hatch; or simply improving the look of an existing hatch. Although there are many hatch designs that work well, I'm going to give instructions for building a fairly straightforward, flat-topped hatch that might have either a wood or plastic top.

Building a hatch requires a modicum of woodworking expertise. Tools required include a table saw, bandsaw, router, and a few basic hand tools.

(opposite page) The addition of components such as this double Dorade box enhances both function and beauty.

This hatch-and-Dorade-vent combination is similar to those found on many Hinckley yachts. It provides both light and ventilation to the interior. Note the hinges on the forward side of the hatch. Hatch pins can be removed from the aft hinges and inserted in the forward ones in order to change the angle of opening. This position will draw more air below, but with the hatch hinged on the forward side it will better protect the opening from rain or spray.

It is definitely a workshop job and would make a good winter project.

Materials

You will need some teak for the hatch and deck frames—use 1½-inch or 2-inch stock, or laminate 1-inch. If you do not have a surface planer, ask your supplier to plane the stock. The exact amount and thickness you need will be determined by your design.

The top of the hatch could be ¼ teak, planed down to ⅞ inch or perhaps ¾ inch, depending upon the size of the hatch. Plexiglas or Lexan also make good tops. They are available in a variety of colors and have the benefit of letting in some light. Again, the thickness will depend on the size of the hatch, but ⅜ inch to ½ inch are good for most offshore yachts.

There are several good glues, including Resor-

cinol and Weldwood Plastic Resin, on the market, but epoxy seems to be the glue of choice today.

Design

First, determine the location of the hatch and the size of the hole through the deck. Next, draw a full-size plan view and cross section of the hatch and frame to help you envision the size of the pieces and the necessary materials. I also recommend making a pattern of the deck crown that is in the way of the hatch to help you precut the frame. Check the crown pattern at both the front and back of the hatch—two patterns may be necessary for a better fit.

Finally, locate and sketch on the drawing the hinges, hatch dogs, and any hatch support hardware to check space conflicts and alignment of all the parts.

Prefabrication

Start construction of the hatch by cutting the stock for the frames. If the hatch is to replace an existing hatch that has a raised deck frame with the right proportions, the hatch frame itself is all that is required. If not, you will need to make two frames—one to fasten to the deck, another for the sides of the hatch cover.

The frames should be cut to fit the highest section, plus a little additional for fitting. That is, if the deck has a crown where the hatch is to be

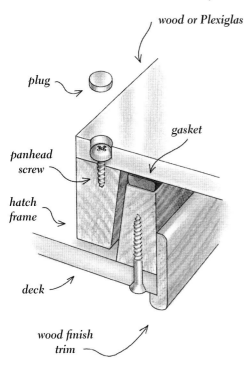

wood or Plexiglas

plug

gasket

panhead
screw

hatch
frame

deck

wood finish
trim

*This simple cross section shows how a hatch and
hatch frame (hatch coaming) installed on a deck
might look. Beveled edges and fiberglass frames
spruce up the design a bit, and transparent or
translucent Plexiglas or Lexan tops provide both privacy and light. If the gasket is attached to the hatch,
it will not be as susceptible to damage when pulling
items through the hatch.*

the pieces as required. The fore and aft side pieces
could be cut on a table saw with the blade tilted;
the rounded end pieces are best cut on a bandsaw.
Sand the edges and reassemble, using glue. When
each frame is glued, ensure that the top of the
frame is flat. A good, level workbench is helpful.

If the top is to be solid wood, it's almost without question that you'll need several pieces of
wood, edge glued, to obtain the necessary width.
Cut the pieces for the top with an eye to matching the grain and avoiding splits. Join the pieces
using a glue joint made with a router and cutter
that makes a matching glue joint on each piece,
a wood spline, or perhaps wood biscuits.

While the top is being glued, you can hold it together by using long pipe clamps or by fastening
two straightedges to the workbench, slightly farther apart than the top is wide. Place the hatch top
between the two straightedges and press wedge
pairs between one straightedge and the glued top.
This will put a lot of lateral pressure on the top.

Fit the top to the frame carefully and fasten
with allowance for the top to float a bit (a wood
top is likely to swell some across the grain, and
oversizing the holes through the top will allow for
some movement). Having said that, I have known

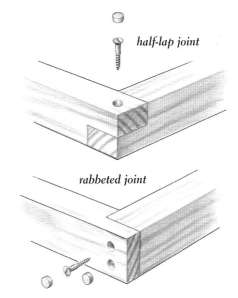

half-lap joint

rabbeted joint

*These two joints are commonly found on hatch
frames as well as other types of marine joinery.*

installed and the top of the hatch is to be flat, the
outside edges will be higher than the center. This
will be true of both the hatch cover and deck
frame. If the hatch is to be installed on a flat boss
where there was an existing hatch, the sides may
be the same all the way around.

When the stock is cut for the frames, mark and
cut the corners to fit. Join the corners with either a
half-lap joint or a rabbeted joint (for wider stock).
Follow your full-scale drawing by laying the pieces
down on the plan view to ensure that everything is
the right length. Assemble the frames with fasteners only—do not use any glue yet.

Use the deck crown pattern to mark the frames.
Disassemble the frames and cut the crown into

some carpenters who glue the tops down with no problems.

If the top is Plexiglas or Lexan, cut it with a saw and drill with slightly oversized holes to prevent the screws from cracking the plastic where they pass through it. Pan head or round head screws are preferred in plastic, because they do not crack the plastic as easily. If you are using flat head screws, countersink them slightly below the surface, install them until snug, and then back off just a bit.

Installation

Installing the hatch requires some refitting on the bottom edges of the deck and the cover frames, unless crown patterns were carefully made and used.

Start by removing any interior overhead trim and liners that are in the way of the new hatch. Dry fit the hatch and mark the deck cutout (outside of the frame), as well as the external footprint of the deck frame. If the hatch is to be located where there is now deck pattern, at the very least remove the deck pattern that is in the way of the hatch frame. You might want to extend beyond the frame to match the smooth borders used around other deck equipment.

Cut through the deck. Drill a starting hole within the cutout lines and cut with a jigsaw, using a grit-edge blade. If there is core in the deck where the hatch is being installed, remove it and replace it with solid glass at least where the hatch hole is cut and where fasteners for the frame and hinges will pass.

Drill the deck, without the frame in place, from the top down. The line you drew earlier of the outside of the hatch should help you to accurately position holes. After locating the holes in the deck, drill the hatch frame by going below and drilling up through the deck holes into the hatch frame. Be careful not to drill too far and come up through the frame—unless you are going to bolt the frame in place, which may not be a bad idea for a foredeck hatch. I like to see fasteners on 6-inch centers at least. Bed and fasten the frame in place. *Note:* If you are going to varnish the hatch, before installation seal the bottom with at least a couple coats of varnish or sealer.

Dry fit the hatch frame, and then place the hatch top onto the frame. Insert a spacer for the gasket and thin spacers along the inside gap to help center the top on the deck frame.

Position the hinges and other hardware, drill, and fit. Disassemble the parts, seal and varnish if required, then reinstall the hatch using good bedding compound or sealant.

Finally, reinstall any overhead components and trim the inside of the hatch with wood that matches other interior trim. I often use teak on the hatch interior trim, even when the existing interior wood is mahogany, ash, or some other kind, because teak is tougher for standing up to exposure and abrasion.

Building a Dorade Vent

The instructions for building a Dorade vent (see photo, page 115) are very similar to those given for building a hatch. Designed by Rod Stephens in the 1930s for the yacht *Dorade*, the vent has a clever water trap that prevents water from flowing down below, while at the same time allowing air to circulate.

The exact design of a Dorade vent box should match the boat. The sides and ends may be straight or sloped and made of ¾-inch teak. The top may be wood, plastic, or other strong material. The drawing shows the critical parts of the box. If you use a Plexiglas or Lexan top, be careful attaching the vent—the top can crack from fasteners, and the installation has to be strong enough to handle green water and the occasional crewmember falling against it. Translucent tops do, however, add a bit of light below without sacrificing privacy.

The tube that extends through the deck can be plastic, metal, or fiberglass. Add a screen to the tube to keep out bugs. Keep the tube far enough below the top to allow adequate air circulation, but not so low that water can easily slop over. Some tubes are cut at an angle with the higher side closer to the vent on top.

Depending on the placement of the Dorade vent on deck, you may want or need to add a guardrail because vents are susceptible to being caught on and bent by lines. This is particularly true of the larger metal vents that catch the most air.

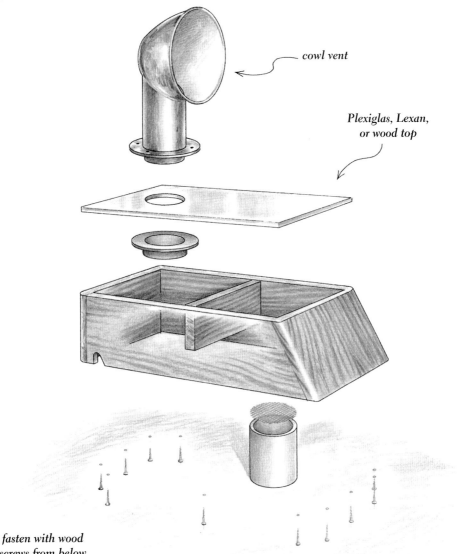

cowl vent

Plexiglas, Lexan,
or wood top

fasten with wood
screws from below

The components of a Dorade box. The box should be drained on either the outboard side or aft, depending on the slope of the deck. A screen installed on the tube that passes air below is a requirement if you sail where there are lots of bugs. Tops made of plastic or wood work well. Fasten the box in place with wood screws inserted up through the deck into the box sides.

Preventing and Repairing Deck Leaks

Knowing how boaters enjoy deck leaks, and also knowing how those leaks mysteriously appear over the winter, here are a few ideas about preventing and repairing deck leaks.

Installing a Companionway Flap

During inclement or cold weather, the hassle of putting in and taking out dropboards every time someone uses the companionway soon wears on a sailor's patience. A practical solution suggested by John Melchner, owner of the yawl Jocar, is to install a canvas flap in the companionway.

John writes, "We have made a simple Dacron flap that attaches to the forward side of the lip at the after end of the companionway hatch. It is attached with Velcro so it is easily removable . . . but we only rarely do that, to wash it."

Movement in and out of the companionway requires only lifting the flap onto the hatch cover, sliding the cover back, closing it again, and pulling the flap down. The Velcro seals the sides and lead shot in a bottom pocket pulls the flap down and prevents it from sagging in the center. Pretty neat solution.

John is looking forward to modifying the design by making a flap with a clear plastic center so he can see in or out when the flap is down, and another flap with screening that lets air in and keeps bugs out.

When installing or reinstalling a deck fitting that is likely to leak, look carefully at any backing plates that are used to help secure the fitting. All too often I find that an inadequate backing plate

This stainless steel backing plate is not likely ever to have a corrosion problem. Although aluminum probably is the most common backing plate material, wood, fiberglass, and stainless steel are used as well.

has been used for a fitting that takes a fair amount of stress and the fitting can move, breaking the seal that was originally in place. A good backing plate is larger than the base plate of the fitting on the exterior surface. It should seat well on the underside of the deck so that it does not move and loosen, which would allow the exterior seal to break.

If the fitting is a new installation, consider

This deck fitting is being installed with a liberal dose of sealant around the fasteners. Note the bevel to the edges of the holes on the right. These bevels allow extra sealant to remain around the fastener and improve the water barrier.

tapping the fiberglass for the fasteners. This will reduce the space around the fastener for water to leak through. Do not, however, allow this tapping, which may look secure on a new installation, to replace proper below deck backing, washers, and nuts. Additionally, before installing any fitting, new or old, slightly counterbore the fastener holes at the outside surface of the deck so the sealant can build a superior washer around the fastener–deck-fitting interface.

For the best installation, use small spacers (such as paper matches or a small piece of Formica) to hold a fitting slightly off the deck while the sealant cures; this will prevent the fasteners from squeezing out all or most of the sealant when they are tightened. When the sealant has cured, remove the spacers and fill any voids left by the spacers. Finally, tighten the fasteners again to prevent movement of the fitting. This process takes longer than just spreading on sealant and tightening the fitting, and some might argue that using a thin gasket, with or without sealant, does the job just fine. Either method works if well executed.

Repairing Portlights

In many modern boats it is easier to replace the whole portlight than to replace only the glass or plastic. Some ports, though, are specifically designed so the frames are used again—you replace only the glass or plastic. Plastic ports are easier to install but scratch more readily. I will discuss glass here, but plastic is installed in basically the same way.

If you are replacing the entire port, be sure to carefully clean and smooth the frame and seat for the glass before you reinstall it. When installing, bed the glass in sealant (see table) and use small spacers between the glass and seat to

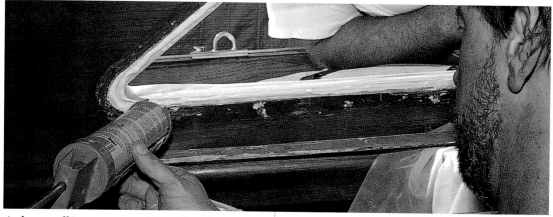

A clean caulking groove or rabbet and a liberal coating of sealant are critical for good portlight bedding. Air trapped in the glass-to-frame interface can provide pathways for leaks.

prevent the glass from squeezing all the sealant out. You will remove the spacers later and fill any voids.

When installing the retaining ring for the glass, loosely position all of the screws, then slowly tighten them in an orderly pattern, alternating from side to side of the ring to maintain even pressure on the glass. Do not overtighten. Most cabin sides are curved, so you will be bending the new glass into place. As in many of the small maintenance projects around a boat, patience in this operation is important. I remember a boatowner who went through three large custom-shaped portlights before getting one to stay in without cracking—a result of not taking the time to carefully clean the portlight glass seat before reinstallation. The culprit was a small bump that consistently cracked the glass.

When installing Plexiglas or Lexan ports, see

Recommended Sealant Usage

	Silicone	Polyurethane	Polysulfide
Deck hardware (removable)	x		
Deck hardware (permanent)		x	
Teak deck seams			x
Windows	x		
Through-hull fittings		x	
Deck-to-hull joints		x	
Through-bulkhead gaskets	x		
Hull-to-keel seams		x	
Protective covering (cotter pins)	x		
Exterior wood trim (removable)	x		
Exterior wood trim (permanent)		x	
Interior wood trim	x		

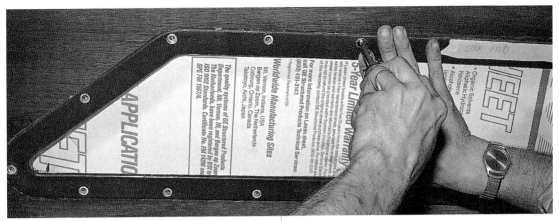

Installation of an inside frame on a glass portlight must be approached with patience. The curved sides of many cabin trunks are a problem for the flat glass. First, install the fasteners with only enough tension to hold the frame and glass in place. Then, slowly tighten the fasteners a little at a time.

that the new plastic is well covered. Cleaners and some sealants will mar the surface. Uncover after the port is cleaned up.

Installing High-Load Deck Hardware

Properly installing hardware is of paramount importance to all boaters. On sailboats, for example, winches and cleats need extremely strong mounting. On sportfishing boats, outriggers and fighting chairs are good examples of equipment that require special attention. The stresses these types

A Helping Hand

If you've ever had to go forward on your boat during a good blow—and who hasn't—you know that every handhold is welcome. It doesn't matter, though, if there's a gale blowing or if the water is smooth as glass—dodgers are natural magnets for hands looking for support. And as a boatowner, you know how quickly grubby hands can soil Sunbrella.

Parker Rockefeller, owner of a Hinckley SW-42, suggests installing a stainless steel grabrail at the forward edge of your dodger. He points out: "The grabrail enables crew to move forward with solid footing and stops people from constantly grabbing the dodger . . . I can't tell you what a wonderful addition this is!" Parker covered the grabrail in leather to prevent slipping. You can attach a grabrail to a dodger support either parallel to the deck or at an angle. Hinck-

ley often installs rails on the aft dodger bow for a cockpit handhold.

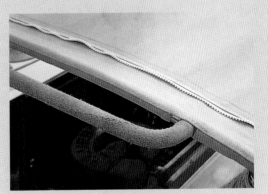

These dodger handles are in just the right place for crew support. However, they put additional stress on the dodger and require that you consider the overall strength of the dodger frame.

Windlasses, bow cleats, and mooring bitts all see heavy loading. On some boats this area of the deck is built without core and with extra-heavy laminate to help distribute the load. Internal bulkheads and external structures such as the bowsprit also help to spread stress over a larger area than just the base of the hardware.

of equipment and hardware experience are terrific; improper installation could lead to failure of the fitting or the structure around the fitting.

Consider, for example, the installation of an outrigger base on the cabinside of a sportfishing boat. The cast base might be 4 inches by 5 inches and bored to accept four ⁵⁄₁₆-inch flat head fasteners.

After you have decided where you wish to locate the fitting, make sure that you can access the back of the surface where the fitting is to be

(opposite page) Winches are a prime example of high-load hardware requiring you to consider both the amount and direction of loading. Backing plates are important, but the structure of the deck must be able to handle the load as well. If a winch is to be placed on a lightly built cabin top, reinforcement of the deck laminate may also be necessary.

installed. If an interior liner prevents you from reaching the interior surface, you will need to remove it. When deciding where the base is to be installed, make sure that the portion of the deck that will be bearing the load is strong enough to support it. If you have any doubts, ask the boat manufacturer. If the area where the base is to be installed is fastened to the main structure (such as a ventilation fairing), you must make sure that the fasteners of the substructure are strong enough to support the loads that will be placed on them.

The installation will vary with the design of the structure on which the fitting is to be mounted. For instance, the cabinside might be made of solid fiberglass laminate or cored with balsa, plywood, or structural foam.

If the cabinside is solid fiberglass with sufficient thickness to handle the load, the procedure is easy. Briefly, all you have to do is drill the cabinside for the fasteners, fit a backing plate, and through-bolt the fitting using a proper bedding compound and/or gasket. The bolts should be fitted with flat washers, lock washers, and nuts.

A common backing plate used in hardware installations is made of ¼-inch-thick aluminum. It should be cut larger than the fitting with which

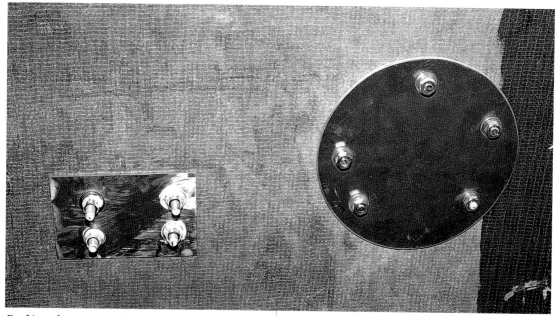

Backing plates on winches and cleats should be larger than the hardware they are backing, in order to prevent stress concentration at the hardware edge.

it is used to distribute the load. If the backing plate is the same size as the fitting base, the load on the fitting will tend to cut the laminate in the same place on both the inside and outside of the laminate, which will speed the deterioration of the laminate and lead to its cracking.

If the cabinside laminate is of insufficient thickness to support the outrigger load, you must add more laminate. The extra fiberglass should spread the load evenly over enough area to prevent distortion and failure. Any laminate that is added should be cut in layers of increasing size to distribute the load. The smallest laminate patch should be slightly larger than the backing plate.

Give careful consideration to the size, thickness, and composition of laminate reinforcement. For example, adding ⅜ inch of laminate to a cabinside that is ¼ inch thick may work just fine. If the extra laminate is not tapered correctly, however, and stops next to a pilothouse window, you can almost count on the window developing a leak. In this case, I recommend installing the base fitting somewhere else or, if reinforcement is to be

added, making sure that it covers a larger area to prevent distorting the cabinside near the window.

Now, let's look at installing the same fitting on a cored cabinside. Cored laminate is a great weight saver, but if moisture penetrates between the skins it may lead to deterioration of the core and a rapid weight gain of the laminate. There are several approaches to preventing that from happening.

If the skins are relatively thin on either side of the core, it may be best to remove the inner skin and core in the area of the fitting, taper the resulting hole, and laminate a new inner skin against the outer skin. The cabinside will then be a solid laminate in the area of the base fitting. If the additional laminate overlaps the inner skin on all sides of the fitting area, the stress will be evenly distributed to both skins. In most instances, this is the best solution to the core problem.

Another approach where the skins are quite thick might be to build in fiberglass compression tubes, tying the skins together where the fasteners will penetrate. This will prevent moisture from seeping into the core and fasteners from distorting the skins and crushing the core when they are tightened.

Place the fitting on the outer skin and mark the fastener positions. Bore through the skins and core with a smaller drill bit than the one you'll use for the fasteners. From the inside, carefully bore through the inner skin and the core with a hole saw of larger diameter (for a ¼-inch bolt, make the new boring ¾ inches). The pilot hole from the first drilling should provide centering for the hole saw. Be extremely careful not to cut any of the outer skin with the hole saw. Remove the inner skin and core in small increments to ensure that the outer skin is left intact. Next, place masking tape on the outside of the outer skin to cover the fastener holes. (This prevents the resin filler from leaking.)

Fill the holes from the back with resin that has been mixed with small, finely cut fiberglass (choppings). Make the choppings by cutting fiberglass material into ⅛-inch to ¼-inch lengths. When mixed with resin, these fibers add strength and help keep the resin from draining out of the hole. Fill the holes until they are level with the inner surface of the structure. You might need to apply the material in multiple layers. Doing so will let the material stay in place while it is curing, and the heat that is built up in the smaller mass will be less likely to distort the outer skin.

When the holes are filled and the fiberglass is cured, sand the interior of the skin until it's flush. Laminate the interior area with multiple layers of fiberglass, each slightly larger than the preceding one. As mentioned before, the smallest laminate should be slightly larger than your intended backing plate.

Finally, remove the tape from the exterior and rebore the original mounting holes. Install the fitting as described on page 125. Although this method is not as strong as the one previously discussed for a cored deck, it may be easier to accomplish in many out-of-the-way areas.

Remember to counter bore the exterior surface adjacent to the fitting. You will build up sealant around the fastener and improve the gasketing effect of the sealant.

The key to wrapping up the installation process is deciding how to finish the interior. If the fasteners end up showing inside a locker where they are not eyesores, great. If the backing plate and fasteners end up right in the middle of your beautiful teak cabin liner, not so great. One option, perhaps the preferred one, is hiding the intruders—a wood covering block is a good way to go. Be forewarned, though: Someday, the fitting you installed will need to be removed or tightened. And, of course, it might leak. You must be able to access the fitting. Installing a covering block with screws and plugging the holes with matching wood plugs is neat, but will be a problem when you need to get to the fitting. It may make sense to let the fasteners for the cover plate show.

If you must let the backing plate and fasteners show, consider using cap nuts or blind nuts to finish off the through-bolts. Blind nuts are hollow fasteners with threaded interiors that accept the through-bolt; their surface is similar to a screwhead and typically has a Phillips-style cut. They are low profile and make for a neat job. If you use blind nuts, drill larger holes in the backing plate than those required by through-bolts; you must make clearance for a blind nut's hollow shaft.

Hardware installation problems can be solved in many different ways. One of the best sources of ideas is to survey the better-built boats at boat shows. Regardless of how you decide to proceed, be sure to think through the design and execution of your installation before you start. Good luck!

Repairing or Replacing Veneers

Ever look at your boat and think that, although she still fits your needs functionally, it would be nice to have a new, fresh interior that's free of dark stains? Or perhaps you would like to have an oak finish rather than teak in your cabin. Or maybe there's some damaged veneer around the companionway or galley that is unsightly. This section will look at the methods for applying wood and plastic veneers. I'll concentrate first on wood veneer. It is more demanding than plastic, but the methods of application are similar.

The application of either wood veneer or plastic laminate is usually a straightforward process, although it takes a bit of planning to do a first-class job.

What is Required?

Wood veneers and veneering tools are available from a number of sources, including catalogs from the Woodworker's Store and Constantine's. Some large hardwood lumber wholesalers, building supply stores, and furniture repair shops also carry, or can obtain, wood veneer.

The veneers commonly used for reveneering are ⅛ to ¼₀ inch thick. That's not much to work with, but it means the veneer can be easily shaped around corners. Some veneer is available with a backing of plastic or paper film; we have used both and find that the paper-backed veneer has been easier to find and its cost is reasonable. It also handles well. The backing strengthens the veneer and helps prevent glue from bleeding through.

When planning a veneer job, particularly when it's your first time, order extra veneer. You will need it so you can adjust the veneer to match colors and grain and to have small patches to practice on.

Contact cement, epoxy glues, and hide glues are some of the choices available to apply veneers. Contact cement works with simple pressure and is perhaps best for the amateur.

Additional materials needed are the following:
short-napped roller
masking tape (light-to-medium sticky) or special veneer tape (available from the Woodworker's Store and others)
razor knife with sharp blades
straightedge (preferably metal)
thinner/cleaner for the contact cement
laminate or veneer roller
sandpaper
sealer for the subsurface if the veneer is being applied to new wood.

Reveneering a Small Bulkhead or Cabinet Face

If this is your first veneering project, I recommend that you begin by veneering a piece of ply-wood instead of an interior component. Use a one-foot square piece to get the feel of working with the veneer and the tools. The following steps describe the method for veneering an interior component; the process you use on a test piece should be the same.

A good choice for a first veneering project (after the test panel) would be a cabinet face that has water damage and is small enough so it will not require a seam in the veneer. (Adding a seam in veneer is an additional complication that is nice to avoid on the first run.)

The steps required to complete the project are layout, patternmaking and cutting, surface preparation, gluing, positioning and rolling out air, trimming and cleanup. Here are some thoughts on each.

Layout of the Job

Layout of the job requires five steps: 1) measuring the area to be veneered; 2) removing any trim that, when replaced, will hide the edges of the veneer; 3) figuring the placement of seams, if any; 4) determining how to place spacers so that the veneer and the bulkhead do not come in contact before they're supposed to; and 5) setting up and clearing a work space.

A few notes on each step:

- When measuring the area, be conscious of the grain patterns—you don't want to order a 3×6 sheet of veneer with the grain running in the wrong direction. Also, don't forget to allow for trim material on the edges of the veneer.

- Removing trim simplifies the fitting process. On cabinet faces, there is usually some molding and there is often a nosing piece near the sole. If possible, remove door frames and any other detachable furniture. The idea is to cover as many edges as possible and reduce the number of tight areas where you'll have to fit something by hand.

- If the panel requires any seams, try to place them where they can be as short as possible or where cutouts for doors or equipment reduce the exposed seam.

- Using spacers is important to prevent the

veneer and the subsurface, once they are covered with contact cement, from coming into contact and sticking together before they are correctly aligned. Repositioning is almost impossible. The spacers' placement and removal must be carefully planned because they must be removed slowly as the veneer is worked into place. (I'll talk more about using spacers a little later.)

- If the piece being veneered can be removed from the boat, the work area should be large enough for you to lay out the piece to be veneered and the veneer itself for gluing. It certainly is possible to place each piece on a work bench one at a time, but not as convenient. The work area must be warm enough for the glue to dry and clean enough to keep dust off of the surfaces being glued.

- If the piece cannot be removed from the boat, you can get by with a work area large enough to accommodate only the veneer. The surface in the boat, however, must be clean and warm enough for gluing.

Patterning and Cutting Veneers

Most removable panels can be easily placed on the veneer for marking. To make a pattern of a nonremovable panel to use in cutting the veneer, use heavy building paper cut to fit or strips of thin wood (¼-inch plywood works well) glued together with a hot-melt glue gun. Either will provide an accurate pattern. An alternative method, but slightly less accurate, is to use a tick strip.

Regardless of which method you use to transfer the shape to be cut onto the veneer, spend some time considering the placement of the pattern. You'll want to make good use of the veneer's grain, taking into account any defects, and you'll want to match surrounding wood grain.

After marking the veneer, cut it with a razor knife (in some cases, scissors will do). Leave a little extra on edges that will overhang when applied and in openings like doorways. These can best be trimmed after installation. Allow for

extra veneer to go under adjacent trim if it was removed. Straight edges that will show should be cut with a razor knife and straightedge.

Surface Preparation

Assuming that the veneer is going over old woodwork, you will have to remove any old or worn finishes. The quality of bonding for the veneer is

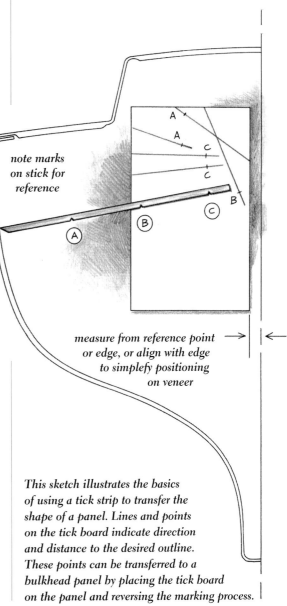

note marks on stick for reference

measure from reference point or edge, or align with edge to simplify positioning on veneer

This sketch illustrates the basics of using a tick strip to transfer the shape of a panel. Lines and points on the tick board indicate direction and distance to the desired outline. These points can be transferred to a bulkhead panel by placing the tick board on the panel and reversing the marking process.

no better than the surface it is bonded to. This is true for both the smoothness and the adhesive life. If the veneer bonds to varnish that is falling off, the veneer will come off with the varnish.

If old finishes are not in good condition and well adhered to the underlying structure, sand and strip them. If the sanding requires going to bare wood, it's a good idea to prime the surface of the wood—varnish is not a bad primer for this purpose.

If there are irregularities in the surface that will show through the finished veneer, sand and fill them with a quality wood filler. For larger fairing jobs, an autobody fairing compound will do the job and it will dry quickly and sand easily.

Carefully wipe the veneer and the surface being veneered with a clean rag before applying contact cement.

Applying Glue

A word of advice about using contact cement: Some types of contact cement are highly toxic. Carefully read the manufacturer's safety precautions and follow them closely. If you do not have a respirator, get one and use it.

Apply contact cement on both surfaces with a short-napped roller. Roll in even strokes for an even, smooth cover. It may be helpful to thin the cement slightly to improve its flow characteristics. Lumps in the cement will show through the veneer. Check the cement can for the recommended thinner.

Apply the cement to the veneer and to the surface being veneered. Allow to dry to the touch. If the coverage is extremely light, it may be prudent to apply another coat. This is where your experience in working with the test piece will be of use.

Positioning and Rolling

Now that both surfaces are covered with contact cement, it is very important that they do not touch each other before they are correctly positioned. This is where the spacers come in. Where you are placing the veneer determines what types of spacers will work. I often use long wood sticks placed every 4 to 6 inches as barriers. They hold the two pieces apart while the most exacting

alignment is done. If, for instance, I am veneering a cabinet front and there is a corner post where the veneer is to stop, I attach the veneer at the corner post first and remove the spacers one by one, working away from the corner post. As the spacers are removed, the veneer is smoothed against the underlying surface. Utmost care must be taken that air is not entrapped by the process. It is difficult, if not impossible, to completely remove air bubbles later.

One downside of using wood sticks is that they might leave small chips behind. In some cases, it's better to use plastic sheets that can be slowly pulled out from between the laminate and the face. You must decide for yourself which is the better method, based on clearance and experience. If you decide to use spacers, consider fitting the veneer before you apply the glue so you can see how the spacers will work.

When the veneer is in place, roll the surface with a small-diameter veneer or laminate roller to firmly attach the veneer to the underlying surface. If air bubbles are going to appear, it will be at this point. With luck, there will only be a few. Start rolling from the same spot where you began applying the veneer and work across the surface in a methodical pattern.

Trim and Cleanup

As mentioned earlier, once the veneer is in place adhesion is almost instantaneous. Therefore, it is all right to trim the excess veneer almost immediately. Use a veneer trimmer if you have one, but a razor knife and straightedge may work almost as well.

Lightly sand the veneer, but remember that it is thin and you could easily sand through it—don't use anything rougher than 220-grit paper; 320 would probably be better. Next, if the surface is to be varnished, apply a sealing coat of varnish; or if not, use oil. Apply oil sparingly to prevent overwetting the veneer and causing wrinkles. After you have built a few coats of the finish, replace the trim and complete the application of varnish or other finish.

You now should have a surface that looks like it just came out of the factory—or maybe better!

Incorporating Seams in Veneers

Occasionally, you may run into a panel that needs to be reveneered and that is too wide for a single sheet; therefore, you will need to join the veneer sheets. Joining may be done either on a workbench or in place.

To join veneer on a workbench, place the veneers face side up on the bench with the grain aligned as you would like and with a slight overlap (¼ inch or more). Lift the edges of the veneer and place a piece of either masking tape or veneer tape under the seam. If possible, place some tape on the edges of the veneer to hold them in place. (Thin push-pins work, too.)

Place a straightedge on the seam and cut through both pieces of veneer. Lift one side of the veneer at a time and remove the cut scrap. Check the realignment of the veneer edges. If the alignment is tight, gently place a piece of tape along the face of the seam to hold the two pieces together and in position. Proceed with the application of glue and installation as directed on page 130, but do so with great care to prevent the two pieces of veneer from moving.

Splicing veneer pieces in place is not much different from splicing them so on a workbench—the veneer panels are patterned and fit with overlap. To prevent the seams from attaching until the cut has been made, you can either create a barrier—waxed paper will work—or omit gluing on either side of the splice for about 1 to 2 inches. When the joint has been cut, remove the barrier or lift the edges and apply the glue. Next, attach the veneers at the seam, working the edges together with a veneer roller.

Dealing with Corner Posts

There are a number of ways to apply veneers at a round corner. One option is to have the veneer go right around the corner and end at some panel side or other trim. This is easily accomplished where the corner post or corner trim is flush with the surrounding panels.

On many boats, however, corner posts and trim stick out beyond the adjacent plywood surface. In those situations, applying veneer is easy because the raised trim provides a natural stopping place for the laminate.

If the veneer is to stop at the corner post and the bulkhead surface is flush with the adjacent trim, the problem of blending in the sides of the veneer becomes slightly more difficult. Consider oversanding a section of bulkhead adjacent to the corner post to allow the edge of the laminate to taper into the post. If the taper is smoothly finished and extends over a large enough area— 6 inches or more—the adjustment will be difficult to detect.

Replacing Plastic Laminates

Most of what is mentioned here about veneer application is appropriate for installing a plastic laminate such as Formica. The steps for making patterns and preparing the surface are the same, as are the procedures for gluing. Splicing and trimming plastic laminate, however, is not the same. Laminate is usually cut with a saw or laminate trimmer to obtain a straight edge.

Removing Old Laminates

Although it is possible to laminate right over an old laminate, it's better, I believe, to remove the old surface. It really is not difficult to remove damaged plastic laminates. Here are some pointers on the process.

Both on bulkheads and on countertops, the laminate is usually applied with contact cement, which will soften with the judicious use of heat. A paint stripper heat gun will work fine but, like many other tools, it can be misused, so take it easy with the heat. A fire can ruin your whole day.

First, remove any trim from the surface and edges. Protect the adjoining surfaces from scratches and heat by applying tape or, even better, strips of plastic laminate. Start by heating a corner of the old laminate and slowly lifting it with a putty knife. Be patient! A fair amount of glue will likely be left on the surfaces underneath the laminate. You can scrape it off later or remove it with an adhesive remover. As the laminate begins to lift, heat the surrounding area and slowly work across the surface. With large areas, it may be helpful to place wood spacers under the old laminate as it comes up; they will prevent the laminate from reattaching itself if it falls back against the old surface.

Cleanup and Surface Preparation

When the old laminate is removed, clean the underlying surface with an adhesive remover or a thinner recommended for use with the glue. Then, sand the surface to obtain a clean, smooth start for the new laminate.

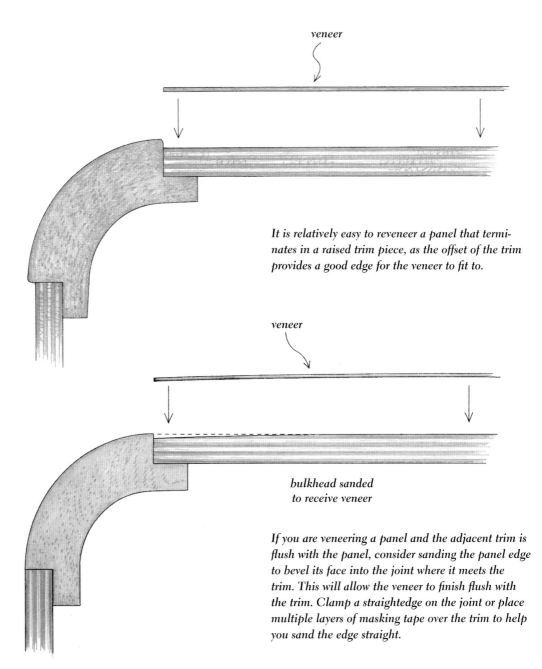

veneer

It is relatively easy to reveneer a panel that terminates in a raised trim piece, as the offset of the trim provides a good edge for the veneer to fit to.

veneer

bulkhead sanded to receive veneer

If you are veneering a panel and the adjacent trim is flush with the panel, consider sanding the panel edge to bevel its face into the joint where it meets the trim. This will allow the veneer to finish flush with the trim. Clamp a straightedge on the joint or place multiple layers of masking tape over the trim to help you sand the edge straight.

Installing New or Replacement Laminates

Proceed with the patterning, cutting, and application of either replacement or new laminates as described on pages 128–131 for veneer. The principles of using trim on the edges to simplify the installation fit remain the same. The thickness of laminates, when they are being added to the surface, may require adjusting the trim a bit when it is reinstalled.

Applying veneers and laminates requires a modest amount of skill but can pay big dividends in improving the interior finish quality or look of a boat. Start small and give it a try.

Building a Battery Box

Whenever you need to add a battery to your existing bank, you also need to give careful thought to where it will reside. Lead-acid batteries, in particular, should have a solid, corrosion-resistant box that will hold the batteries in position, contain spilled fluid, and channel explosive gasses from the boat's interior.

A relatively simple solution is to purchase a plastic battery box, strap it into an appropriate location, and install a vent. However, if you are expanding an existing system, using a battery for which a plastic box is not available, or want a more secure restraining system, consider building a fiberglass-lined wooden box.

A battery box should be solidly constructed and lined with fiberglass to support the weight of the batteries it holds and withstand potential chemical exposure. The top should provide a way to secure the batteries in case of knock-down or rollover. Battery boxes near a potential ignition source should be vented to outside air.

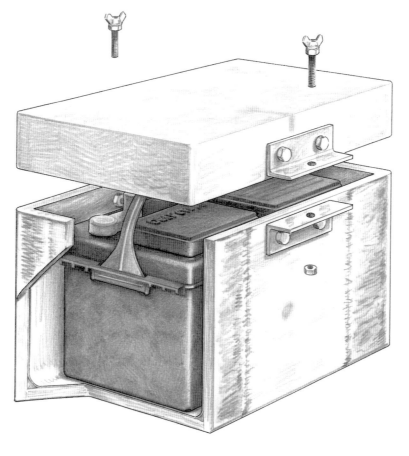

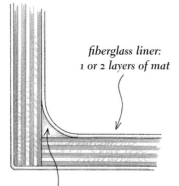

*fiberglass liner:
1 or 2 layers of mat*

*Fill with polyester putty if using polyester resin
for liner. Form ½" radius fillet to assist with
laminating glass and to strengthen joint.*

*This sketch shows a cross section of a battery box
with a fiberglass fillet and liner. The basic fiberglass procedures outlined in Chapter 9 should be
used here.*

For years, Hinckley has used a simple box
arrangement constructed of ½-inch marine-grade
plywood with a fiberglass liner. To build one, measure the battery size and add ½ inch clearance on
all sides of the battery on the inside of the box.
Allow for a minimum of ½ inch clearance in
height. (In a multiple-battery installation, figure
the clearance around and between batteries.) It is
important to allow heat to dissipate when the batteries are charging. For example, if a battery is 16
inches long, 7 inches wide, and 9½ inches high,
the box should have inside dimensions of at least
17 inches by 8 inches and be 10 inches high.

Construct a basic box, using small screws or
nails to hold it together. If you are careful, you
can build the whole box as a unit and then cut
off the top on a table saw. Be careful, though, not
to place any fasteners where the cut is to be made
to remove the top. Once the box is constructed,
resin coat the inside of the box and line it with
one or two layers of fiberglass mat or cloth.

Two important points to remember: Using
polyester resin is acceptable, but epoxy has more
chemical resistance and is more flexible; and filling the interior corners of the box with a resin
putty adds strength and makes lining the box eas-

ier. See Chapter 9 for step-by-step instructions on
fiberglassing.

Latches for the top of the box may be as simple
as a couple pieces of metal angle bolted through
the sides (as illustrated in the accompanying drawing), or a purchased latch. In any event, the latch
system must hold the top tightly and should be
able to hold the batteries if there is a rollover.

Batteries that are placed in a compartment with
explosion hazards, such as an engine room, should
have a reasonably tight cover system to prevent the
venting of fumes into the boat's interior. Because
gas is lighter than air, a vent placed near the top of
the box and plumbed to an exterior loop or vent
should be adequate. Hinckley has successfully inserted a piece of small-diameter pipe into a stanchion as a vent. The stanchion, of course, must be
drilled to allow fumes to escape.

Mounting a Battery Box

A battery box should be mounted as securely as it
is built. Any mounting arrangement must sustain
the loads of heavy batteries—and the momentum
developed by batteries as a boat pounds into a big
sea is tremendous. Don't skimp on this part.
When installing the batteries in a bilge or sail
locker, you may need to build mounting brackets.
Or, you may be able to build a mounting bracket
on a bulkhead or bolt the battery box directly to
a bulkhead.

Here are some tips for mounting a battery box:

- Cut and fit wood bases to provide a level plat-
form to which the battery box can be lagged
or bolted.

- It is a good idea to resin coat the finished
wooden parts before glassing them in;
doing so will improve their resistance to
moisture and enhance the bonding of
the fiberglass.

- Using the fiberglass technique explained in
Chapter 9, apply at least four layers of glass
around the supports.

- Bolt the battery box to the mounts. If you

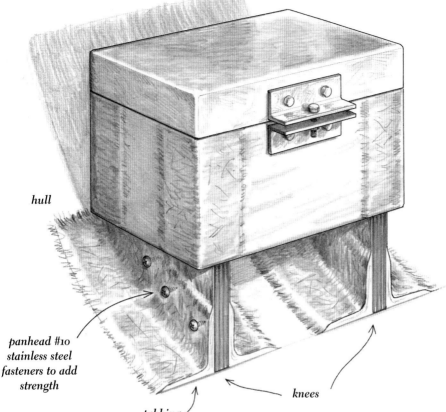

hull

panhead #10
stainless steel
fasteners to add
strength

tabbing

knees

A battery box support bracket mounted with glass tabbing. Remember, with any fiberglass project the surfaces must be especially clean. Sand well and wipe the area with acetone before glassing. This is especially important with a battery box in an older hull, where there probably is paint and oil on the hull surface. The laminate spread is more than a lot of builders use, but considering the battery weight, it is not excessive.

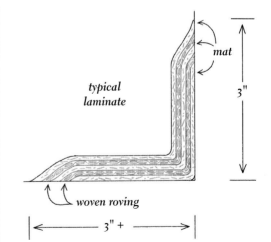

mat

typical
laminate

3"

woven roving

|← 3" + →|

cannot bolt the battery box in place, be sure that the screws or other fasteners are capable of taking the stress that they will receive. You may wish to bed them with a small amount of resin to enhance their holding power.

- Finally, connect a vent (if desired) that will remove any fumes.

Do not skimp on the glass tabbing used to attach equipment like battery box brackets. Four or more layers of glass (alternate mat and woven roving or combination fabric) are usually required to prepare the surfaces for best glass attachment.

P A R T   4

Mechanical
System
Maintenance

CHAPTER 12

Main Engine Care

Boatowners should not be overwhelmed by the basic maintenance needs of their engines—maintaining the engine and drive system in the average pleasure boat is not difficult. However, failure to do so will lead to enormous headaches and, no doubt, a real crimp in your boating budget. In this chapter I will concentrate on the maintenance of diesel engines because they are the prevailing power supply in most cruising boats.

Any maintenance program should start with education. Many engine manufacturers and distributors offer courses that teach troubleshooting techniques and basic engine repair. Pick up the phone and call the manufacturer, or ask your boatyard for information. These sessions provide information about oil changing, fuel systems, engine cooling basics, and many other related subjects. If you do not have the time or the opportunity to take such training sessions, open your engine manual and start reading. When the engine quits on you—and it will—being familiar with the equipment will help you overcome the dread of dealing with the creature in the engine compartment. You'll find that a small amount of education and logic will get you through a lot of seemingly impossible situations.

Next in priority is the need for preventive maintenance. You should stay abreast of the day-to-day care required in the operation of your engine. The following information, although general in nature, will provide an overview of the kinds of maintenance that you should perform.

Prestart Check

Check fluid levels in the engine. Cooling water in a freshwater-cooled engine and crankcase oil should be checked at regular intervals—daily if the boat is being used a lot. Transmission oil should be inspected once a week when the engine is used regularly.

Engine Coolant

When checking the engine coolant, use both sight and feel. The coolant should feel slightly oily from the antifreeze that is added to the system—and remember, antifreeze should be in the system regardless of the season. Why? First, because antifreeze increases the boiling point of water, thereby reducing the risk of boiling out all of the coolant if the engine overheats. Second, the antifreeze acts as a rust inhibitor for the interior sections of the engine that are reached by the enclosed cooling system.

If you have to add water, adding pure water in small quantities is fine. If you are losing a lot of water, however, look for the source of the loss and mix some 60/40 antifreeze/water mixture to add to the system. If the water level is low and you can't find an obvious leak, overheating might be the problem, in which case the water is being pushed out of the pressure cap. In some systems the overflow is routed down a tube to the bilge where it is difficult to see it drain.

Another potential cause of losing cooling water is a defective gasket somewhere in the engine that is allowing the water to enter another part of the engine. This can be serious. Coolant lost this way may pass into the lubricating oil or into the cylinders. Both situations spell trouble.

If it is necessary to add antifreeze or an antifreeze mixture to the coolant system, be sure to add a type that is compatible with what is already in the engine. Ethylene glycol is traditionally used; propylene glycol is environmentally friendly antifreeze. They should not be mixed. If in doubt, empty the system and fill from scratch.

Finally, don't forget to test the freezing point of the coolant, although you don't need to do this if you are filling a system for the first time. There usually is a chart on the antifreeze bottle that indicates the freezing points for different mixtures. The older mixture in the engine might have been adjusted (watered down) by the addition of water, and the ratio may no longer be as originally intended. With ethylene glycol, the mixture is tested by using a floating ball syringe that indicates the specific gravity of the mixture and, therefore, the freezing point. This specific gravity test does not work with propylene glycol; in this case you must use a refractometer to test the mixture.

Lubricating Oils

Lubricating oils in marine diesel engines operate at high temperatures and under great stress. Diesels use the heat created by high compression for ignition of their fuel/air mixture. If an oil is not doing its job, damage to the engine is likely and often catastrophic. Larger engines with turbochargers need even more lubrication and therefore require additional attention.

When checking lube oil, it is important to note that you are checking not only the level of fluid in the engine, but also the condition of the oil—both its color and texture. This inspection will help detect foreign materials that have worked their way into the system. The oil must be at the proper level—not too low or too high. An overly filled lubrication oil system can cause a diesel engine to run on its own lubricating oil rather than the fuel oil, and a runaway engine may result.

You will get a different oil level reading from a running engine than from one that's shut down. It's usually recommended that smaller engines be turned off when you check the oil; on larger engines it is especially important to know whether the oil should be checked with the engine running or not.

If your measurement indicates that additional oil is required, be sure that the oil added is appropriate for the engine. Check your owner's manual for the manufacturer's oil recommendations. When purchasing oil, always buy some extra to keep aboard; then, when oil is added you can be sure it is the same as what's already in the engine. If you have a boatyard change the oil for you, have them supply you with a couple extra quarts if the oil they use is not the same as what you currently have aboard.

Oil's color should range from clean brown to black. In a diesel engine, oil will turn black shortly after it's changed. Gray or white streaking in the oil is bad news. It probably means there is water in the oil, and it requires immediate attention.

If the oil looks okay, rub some between your fingers. A gritty feel indicates that an unusual amount of material is being worn off the engine and washed into the oil. Engine oil analysis, when used to track engine wear over time and thereby develop a history of an engine, can be helpful in the early diagnosis of a problem. Consider having it done regularly (semi-annually or annually). If a local yard cannot help you, try a truck or farm machinery service center.

It's a good idea to check the shaft stuffing box regularly. Check that the unit is secure and, if it is the style with packing, that a small amount of water (slow drip) can pass to lubricate it.

Start-Up

When starting the engine, watch for the oil pressure gauge to rise immediately. If you have an oil pressure alarm, it most likely will ring as the system is turned on (even before the engine is cranked over) and the pressure builds to a level that is above the alarm setting. If you have an alarm and it is not ringing when you start and stop the engine, be suspicious. Did someone dislike the noise and disconnect the wires?

Listen to the engine as it idles. Keep an ear tuned to pick up unusual sounds. Squealing often indicates a worn or loose belt. A knocking noise may indicate a dirty or fuel-starved injector in a diesel.

Look at the exhaust discharge to ensure the flow of cooling water through the system. A weak flow may indicate poor raw-water circulation, which will lead to overheating and excess use of fresh water in the engine. If the exhaust discharge is weak or nonexistent, shut the engine down and look for problems.

Observe the color of the exhaust smoke. Black smoke indicates that the engine is not burning fuel adequately. A clogged air filter is a common cause of this problem; injector problems should also be checked. Blue smoke indicates that the engine may be burning the lube oil—typically a result of worn rings or valve stems. White smoke occurs when there is moisture in the fuel or cylinders. When running properly, a diesel engine should not emit any smoke. Therefore, if the smoking continues after initial start-up for any prolonged period, the cause should be found and cured.

Check the gauges again to make sure the oil pressure is in an appropriate range, that the water temperature is rising to a normal level, and that the alternator is doing its job of recharging the starting battery.

Basic Engine Troubleshooting

In order to run, a diesel engine needs several systems to be operating efficiently: the cooling system (to remove excess heat); the fuel system (to provide combustion); and the lubrication system (to reduce friction). Problems that develop with engines are often, although not exclusively, in one of these basic areas.

Cooling System Problems

Probably one of the most common problems in the cooling system is overheating. Start at the beginning to analyze the problem. Visually examine the engine and cooling plumbing for leaks and other readily spotted problems. This is where your familiarity with the engine room and its components is important. If the problem is not immediately evident (for example, a broken hose), start by concentrating on the raw-water, or seawater, system.

Raw-Water System

Check the seacock or valve that controls the flow of water through the hull to the engine. Is it open? Next, examine the hose that leads to the strainer. Is it restricted? If yes, it will no doubt be necessary to close the seacock, remove the hose, and clear the path. If the problem is in the seacock, valve, or an outside strainer and if the hose length allows, you may be able to clear a restriction there by probing with a stiff wire. Reconnect the hose to the seacock, then hold the open end of the hose above the waterline. Open the seacock and probe it with a wire. If the open hose end (the end that was connected to the strainer) is below the waterline, this method will not work, because water will pour out of the hose at a frightful rate. That flow, however, may also clear a restriction if it is not too tight. If this procedure does not remove a restriction in the seacock or exterior strainer, it will have to be cleared by going over the side or by hauling the boat.

Next, examine the strainer. Is it clear? Close the seacock or valve, open the strainer, and clean it. Remove the strainer basket/filter and ensure that it is clear and correctly installed in the filter housing. It is possible to improperly install a basket in some filters, thereby restricting the flow of water. Examine the inlet and outlet of the strainer for foreign material. If the strainer is below the waterline, open the seacock slightly and allow a small amount of water to flow through to ensure a clear path to the strainer.

If everything is okay with the strainer, next check the hoses between the strainer and the raw-water pump. Use the same method as described before for checking the hose between the seacock and the strainer.

The raw-water pump is next in line and, on most engines, is easily checked. Close the seacock and remove the pump cover. Be especially careful with the gasket under the pump cover. It is an excellent idea to carry a spare gasket aboard. If the blades on the impeller are rubber, they should be supple and complete. It's not unusual to lose parts of the impeller in the raw-water pump. If parts of the blade are missing, or the im-

This strainer and seacock are easy to access and therefore are likely to be checked regularly. Can you easily perform a visual check on all your strainers?

peller appears badly worn, replace it.

It is important to note that the missing impeller parts may cause mischief downstream in the cooling system if they are not removed. A few small rubber pieces can cause havoc with the efficiency of a heat exchanger. If parts are missing from the impeller, take time to locate them by opening or back-flushing parts of the raw-water system. You may not find them all, but you will be confident that there are no further restrictions in the system. Carefully reassemble the water pump, making sure that all gaskets, spacers, and screws are back in their original positions.

Examine the heat exchanger(s) for restrictions blocking water flow. Most units are accessed by removing an end cap. Look both for restrictions and corrosion of the small interior tubes. Erosion of the metal allows raw water to mix with the engine coolant in the primary exchanger or oil in an oil cooler (usually in a smaller exchanger).

Next, examine the exhaust system. Most installations nowadays take the cooling water and discharge it through the exhaust. Systems that inject water directly into the exhaust gas section of the system might allow water to back up into the engine if the exhaust system fails or a valve is closed. Look carefully at the exhaust elbow where the raw water is injected into the exhaust. Metal erosion here is a common problem; also, the weight of the fitting can create cracks in the attachment fittings.

Another type of exhaust system cools the exhaust by running the raw water in a jacket around the exhaust gas tubing. This kind of system doesn't blend the exhaust gas and the cooling water until they are about to exit the hull. When it's working correctly, this arrangement is less likely to allow raw water into the exhaust system; however, like all exhaust systems, it is susceptible to erosion from hot water, particularly when fuel with a high sulfur content is present.

A restriction on the discharge plumbing can cause a backup of raw water through the system and cause cooling system problems. Either of these systems may have a vent or bleed-off for excess cooling water to leave the system without passing through the whole system, which may be a reason for low water discharge at the exhaust.

Another exhaust system problem that you should watch for is water entering the engine through the combustion exhaust. Both excessive engine cranking and water leaking in through the exhaust through-hull may be the source of the problem. Water will not compress and burn like fuel. If left, the water will rust the cylinders and pistons. Common symptoms of this problem are difficulty starting the engine and having the engine seize while running. Exhaust systems do not frequently cause problems, but they aren't troublefree, either.

Freshwater System

If you have not found any problems with the raw-water system and your engine has a freshwater cooling system (most do), your next step is to analyze that system.

Perhaps it goes without saying, but I will say it anyway. *Do not open the freshwater expansion tank when the engine is hot. Wait until it has cooled down significantly.* Many people have been badly scalded by the hot water and steam that sprays out of an expansion tank from an overheated engine. If the tank is located in a confined engine room, the situation can be even worse than in a car. The boater cannot always back away from the sprayed hot water. If your engine has overheated, be patient. Drop the hook if necessary (and possible) and check the raw-water system for problems, but do not rush to open the freshwater system too soon. When the engine has cooled enough to remove the expansion tank cap, do so slowly and with the aid of a towel or heavy rag as additional protection in case the coolant is still too hot. Crack open the case just a bit to allow the pressure to escape. Wait a few seconds, then remove the cap entirely if it appears safe to do so. When the cap is off, check the coolant level.

Freshwater cooling systems vary so much from engine to engine it is difficult to be very specific about how to troubleshoot them. There are, however, a few basic components you should examine: the circulator pump (breakdown unusual); the thermostat (locked shut?); and the heat ex-

changer. Also, check for good old rust or other restrictions in the cooling paths.

You should also check the lube oil for any signs of water. If coolant is getting from the cooling system into the lube oil, the oil will show gray or white streaks. Another source of problems may come from having air in the system. When a freshwater cooling system has boiled over and is refilled, air may be trapped in corners and high spots of the plumbing. Most systems have petcocks, or bleeding valves, to allow the removal of air. After filling the system with coolant, and when the engine has cooled down, run the engine at low speed with the expansion-tank pressure cap off. Open the bleeding petcocks one at a time and allow them to run until the air bubbles stop flowing out. Don't forget to look for a petcock at the hot water tank if you have one. It is no doubt heated by coolant from the freshwater cooling system. You will need to fill the expansion tank again after the bleeding. Watch the temperature gauge and, if after a few minutes things seem to be working, replace the pressure cap.

It is a good idea to have some appropriate antifreeze or antifreeze/water mixture to put in the engine if a lot of fluid is required. If it is not available, use water only but do not forget to bleed off a bit of the water and add antifreeze to the system; then test the mixture.

If the engine is still fairly hot when you are filling the expansion tank, fill it with hot coolant. If none is available, allow the engine to cool significantly. Cold water in a hot casting can be a dandy formula for causing cracks in the casting.

Fuel System Problems

Most fuel system problems can be diagnosed and cured if you carry extra filters and if the boat is not out of fuel. Clogged filters and water in the fuel are two common problems with fuel systems. Therefore, it is important for all boatowners to learn how to replace filters and, if their engines are not self bleeding (also called self purging), they should know how to bleed air from the fuel system. Diesel engines simply will not run if there is air in the fuel.

If an engine will not start or shuts down while

running, the first thing to check is the fuel tank. Got any diesel fuel in there? If yes, make sure that no fuel line valves have been turned off. In boats with multiple fuel tanks, it pays to check that the excess fuel being returned to the tanks via the fuel return line is, in fact, being delivered to the same tank that it is being drawn from. If someone has recently worked on the boat, examine the fuel lines for any bends or crimps.

If you determine that a fuel supply is available, examine the filter. There will most likely be a filter (or filters) mounted on a bulkhead near the engine as a first line of defense and a filter on the engine. If your boat does not have a high-quality filter installed in the fuel line before the engine's filter, the single best investment for your engine and peace of mind would be to install such a unit. The primary filter (the first filter in the line) often has a clear bowl so you can examine the condition of the filter and fuel in it. Many are equipped with probes that can be connected to alarms that indicate either a vacuum (clogged filter) or water problem in the filter. If the filter shows any water or sediment, it will be necessary to clean the filter and replace the filter element.

Servicing Fuel Filters

Cleaning the filter and replacing the element is not difficult. First, shut off the fuel supply line leading from the tank to the filter. This will prevent fuel from flowing out of the fuel line while the filter is apart. Most filters have a drain on the bottom that allow you to drain off at least a small amount of fuel, thereby reducing the mess when you disassemble the rest of the filter.

Next, remove the filter cover. Hinckley normally uses Racor filters that have a large handle on the top that allows easy removal of the cover. You can then remove and dispose of the filter element. Ensure that all gaskets are removed and in sound condition if you will be using them again. Remove the clear bowl and clean out any silt or moisture. Reassemble the bowl and install a new filter element.

Fill the filter with clean fuel as completely as possible before installing the top. With Racor filters it is particularly important that the filter is

completely filled. Any air that is trapped near the top of the filter will sit benignly when the boat sits level; however, when a sailboat is heeling and tossing about, the air may escape down a fuel line, halting the engine at the most inopportune time. Therefore, carefully top off the filter and tighten the filter top.

If you think that moisture or other contaminants have passed through the primary filter, replace the engine (secondary) filter's element. If you have an electric fuel lift pump, there may be a screen/element to clean or replace on that, too.

Finally, open the fuel-supply valve again and pump fuel into the system via the fuel lift pump. This pump is often manual and is located either on or downstream of the engine (secondary) fuel filter.

A 12-volt fuel booster pump is a good idea for installations where filling the filters is difficult. Installed between the tank and the primary fuel

This engine-mounted fuel filter is your engine's last line of defense from fuel problems. It is difficult to determine the status of the filter without disassembly, and, therefore, the filter is not often checked. Install a good primary filter in the line before this unit if one is not already in use.

filter, the pump can fill the filter and place a positive pressure on the system, thereby easing the process of bleeding the engine.

Bleeding the Engine

If the main engine on your boat does not have a self-bleeding fuel system, it is imperative that you understand how to remove air from, or "bleed," the system. The process involves opening small fittings—called bleed points—in the system so that the air in the lines can escape. Most engines have two or three primary locations for bleed points: at the secondary (engine-mounted) fuel filter; at the fuel injection pump; and possibly at the injectors themselves. The engine manual is the primary source of information for locating the bleed points. If the manual is not available, though, common sense and an understanding of how the fuel flows through the system should allow you to successfully bleed out the air.

Follow the fuel lines from the primary fuel filter to the fuel lift pump, then to the secondary filter, and then to the fuel injection pump. Locate the bleed points on the filter and at the injection pump. Hinckley typically paints the bleed points a contrasting color from the rest of the engine, which is most helpful in locating them. I recommend this trick for all engines—simply dab a bit of brightly colored fingernail polish on each bleed point.

First, open the bleed point on the secondary filter. Loosen the screw or bolt only slightly and use the fuel lift pump to apply positive pressure and cause fuel to flow out of the point. Watch the fuel flow for any air escaping along with the fuel. When the air bubbles are no longer coming out with the fuel, close the bleed point. Move on to the fuel injection pump and open the bleed fitting(s) there. Loosen the lower (if there are two) fitting again and allow all of the air to escape while pumping the fuel lift pump. Tighten the fitting when all the air is purged and move on to the next fitting if there is one.

If the bleeding process has been done carefully, it is possible that the engine will need no further bleeding. Advance the throttle to the fully open position and turn the engine over. If it does

not start within a few seconds, loosen one of the nuts attaching the fuel lines to the injectors (use one of the higher injectors) and crank the engine again. If any air is coming out of this fitting, you may need to repeat the bleeding process.

Here are a few helpful hints about bleeding an engine. First, the fuel lift pump is often operated by hand and also by the engine. If the engine has stopped at just the "right" point, it may have the pump mechanism in a position so it will not work by hand. If this is the case, turn the engine over quickly to release the lift pump.

Next, the diesel fuel spilled during the bleeding process is harmful to rubber and plastic components, such as mounts and wiring in the engine room. It is important to wipe up any fuel that's spilled while bleeding the engine.

Finally, the injectors are not visible on some larger engines such as the Caterpillars. On these engines, bleeding the injectors is done where the fuel supply piping attaches to the side of the cylinder head.

Any number of fuel system problems might require bleeding the engine. Coastal or offshore boaters should be comfortable with the process; any time taken to understand your engine's system is time well spent. Also, if you find water or sediment of any type in the fuel system you need to locate the source of the problem and fix it as soon as possible.

One final word about fuel systems. From time to time, the Hinckley Service Department runs across boats with old fuel in their tanks. Several boats that have been in storage for more than one year have had to have the fuel entirely pumped out and replaced before the engine would run. Keep this in mind if you have just bought or are considering buying a boat that has been in storage for an extended period.

Lube Oil System Problems

As mentioned before, the marine diesel engine operates under enormous pressure and temperature. These conditions require that an engine's lubrication system be in top-notch condition. Although oil problems are not as common as fuel problems, they are certainly of no less concern.

Ignoring a lubricating oil problem can mean engine damage, which often leads to engine replacement—or a repair bill that approaches the cost of engine replacement.

During normal operation, oil filters become clogged with sludge, moisture accumulates from the condensation created by the cold engine block, and leaks occur from internal gaskets and through the exhaust—all of which create problems with lube oil. Always check that the oil pressure comes up to the proper level when you start the engine. Changes in operating pressure may indicate clogged fittings or worn out oil. When in doubt, change the oil in your engine.

As a general rule, change the oil at least as frequently as the manual suggests; it certainly doesn't hurt to change it more often. Remember how important this simple fluid is to the life of your engine. Most boatowners should be able to change their engine oil and filters. If you encounter any problems in your oil system though, such as clogged pick-up tubes in the sump or contaminated oil, I recommend that you hire a professional mechanic; some lube oil problems require substantial disassembly of the engine.

When preparing to change the oil, run the engine to heat the oil, which makes it easier to pump or drain out. This will take longer than a few minutes—watch the engine temperature gauge to see when the engine is up to temperature. Next, shut the engine off and drain or pump the oil out of the engine's oil sump. Many boaters have installed a small electric pump connected to a fitting in the base of the oil sump to facilitate the removal of old oil. It is a great idea and an easy installation.

When you are changing the lube oil it is a good idea to replace the lube oil filter element as well. When the oil is as completely drained as possible, remove the oil filter element. If your boat has a spin-on filter element, a filter wrench of the proper size is an important tool to carry on board. Dispose of the old oil and the filter element in a proper manner. Your local garage or boatyard can help.

Clean the oil filter housing with a clean rag and check that any gaskets are properly in place if

Checking and replacing oil is pretty basic stuff for a culture that practically lives in automobiles. However, boaters should be aware of the need for frequent oil changes in boats. Moisture and long inactive periods oblige owners to change the oil a lot more often than you might initially think. Some engine manufacturers suggest changing the oil every 50 hours, some recommend it at longer intervals.

they are to be reused. Remove them if the new filter element comes with a gasket. Hand tighten the new filter element until it's in place, then tighten it about an additional three-quarter turn.

Hinckley recommends that filters designed to be installed upside down have a check valve in them to prevent the oil from draining out when the engine is shut down. Having oil in the filter all the time speeds the delivery of oil when the engine is restarted. Your dealer may be able to identify brands that have the check valve.

When installing the new filter element, make sure that the gasket(s) stay in place. Fill the oil sump again with oil that meets the engine manufacturer's specifications. Check the oil level with the dipstick while you are filling; when the level is correct, start the engine and check for leaks.

If you are changing the oil because you have found water or some other contaminant in it, you should *not* heat the oil by running the engine—doing so may cause more damage. Also, you may need to change the oil more than once to clear the system of the contaminants.

Engine Decommissioning

If you choose to have the boatyard commission and decommission your engine, ask for a list of the work that is to be done. Compare it with the recommendations in your engine manual and discuss any variations with the yard.

If you do the work yourself, start with the engine manual where you will no doubt find a section on laying up the engine. In addition, here are a few ideas and thoughts on the process.

Winterizing a marine diesel engine involves several tasks. Let's start with the oil change. It's logical to think that the oil should be changed at recommissioning, so it will be fresh for the new boating season, rather than at decommissioning. Not so. During the boating season, when the engine is in use, the lube oil picks up moisture and solids. In most instances, that's not a problem because the engine recoats its interior surfaces with oil as it runs. Over the winter, however, moisture and oil will separate and the moisture will start to form areas of rust on the engine's interior.

Changing the oil in the fall minimizes the amount of moisture and other contaminants left in the oil over the winter. When changing the engine lube oil, first heat the oil to decrease the viscosity by running the engine until it is up to normal operating temperature. Next, pump out the oil sump and replace the oil filter or filters. Make sure the replacement oil and filters meet the engine manufacturer's specifications. When the oil change is complete, run the engine a short time to be sure there are no leaks.

Some people also change the oil at recommissioning. Perhaps it's overkill, but I feel that you can not be too careful.

Next, you'll want to take care of the fuel tanks. There is a lot of debate about whether it is better to top them off or empty them when winterizing

a boat. My preference runs toward topping them off—especially when faced with a 200-gallon fuel tank that is three-quarters full. Of course, draining smaller fuel tanks is a much easier task. As a practical matter, I find that a side benefit of topping off the tanks is that the run to the fuel dock warms up the lube oil for the final oil change. The fill or not-to-fill debate focuses on the moisture that forms on the inside of a tank left partly or totally empty during the winter. If a tank is empty, the "not-to-fillers" argue, it's easier to clean the tank interior (if it has an access plate) and start with a fresh load of fuel at recommissioning. True enough—but how easy is it to get all the moisture out of a tank's interior? With a full tank, the surface that is subject to condensation is minimized.

Debate also takes place about which are the best fuel additives. I believe that most people now consider additives to be helpful for reducing bacteria growth and absorbing or reducing moisture in the fuel.

Next, replace the fuel oil filters(s). Although they frequently are left until recommissioning to be replaced, I recommend disassembling and cleaning them at decommissioning.

It is likely that your boat has two fuel filters. One will be located on or near the engine and may have been supplied with the engine by the manufacturer. There may also be another filter in the system before, or upstream, of this filter. It is important to clean both, following the instructions on page 143. Most mechanics will reassemble the filters at decommissioning. Hinckley recommends doing so when the elements are changed at decommissioning and then running the engine. Reassembly protects the fuel lines and filter parts from dirt, dust, and corrosion.

Although it is not always done for regular annual decommissioning, it's a good idea to put some oil in the cylinders. Over a long-term layup, the oil will help prevent corrosion on the cylinder interior. On a diesel, oil is inserted through the injector ports. If you do this, be careful to clean around the openings before removing the injectors. It is important that grit or other foreign matter does not get into the cylinder(s). It may be important to determine that you have, or can readily get, new gaskets for the injectors before you start. The gaskets may not survive the disassembly. When the cylinders are open, squirt a couple ounces of oil into each and turn the engine over a few times to coat the cylinder walls. Replace the injectors.

Finally, pickle the raw-water system. It is important to remove the water from the system to prevent freezing during a winter layup. First, close the seacock for the raw-water intake. Then, drain all the water you can out of the system via the drains and petcocks. Next, mix up some antifreeze solution in a bucket. Remove the raw-water intake hose from the seacock and put it into the bucket; start the engine and allow the

mixture to run through the engine. It may take more than one bucket of antifreeze solution depending on the engine capacity and exhaust system. Look for the antifreeze coloring to start appearing at the external exhaust. When you are satisfied that the engine has been adequately filled with this mixture, reconnect the hoses.

When you are finished doing all of these tasks, it is a good idea to remove a rubber impeller from the raw-water pump. The impeller will likely suffer from sitting in one position for a long period. A good extra step in the layup process is to spray the engine with a good anticorrosive lubricant. Wipe it with a rag to coat things nicely and loosely cover the engine. If possible, leave the engine room door or access open to provide ventilation.

Chapter 13

Water Systems

There was a time, not too long ago, when pressure water systems were rare on all but the biggest, fanciest pleasure craft. The drawbacks were not only the cost and availability of the equipment, but also the small volume of water tankage aboard most boats. A pressure system would have drained the tanks too rapidly, and having to pump water by hand was a good way to conserve. Today, not many pleasure boats longer than 25 feet are without a pressure freshwater system. Let's take a look at a typical water system: its components, some maintenance techniques, and a couple of ideas for upgrading your system.

The simplest pressure water systems have the following components: a pump, a water supply or tank, a piping system to deliver the water to the pump, and a faucet. Additional components commonly include a hot water tank, an accumulator tank, an inline filter, a water manifold, and various valves.

Pumps

There are several types of electric water pumps commonly found aboard most boats: diaphragm, impeller, and turbine. *Diaphragm pumps* use a flexible membrane fastened over a cavity in the pump body; it is flexed in and out of the cavity by means of a motor-driven arm. These pumps work by pulling water into the cavity as the membrane is drawn out of the cavity and then by pushing water downstream when the membrane is pushed back into the cavity. Check valves in the inlet and outlet sections prevent water from flowing back to the tank. Diaphragm pumps are often noisy, but they are quite reliable and easily understood and repaired.

Impeller pumps use rubber, plastic, or metal for the impeller, which is not unlike a small gear with large teeth. They typically have an off-center drive that draws water into the pump body on one side of the impeller's rotation and pushes the water out of the pump body on the other side. Impeller pumps are less noisy than diaphragm pumps, but they are more susceptible to damage from running dry.

Turbine pumps use an impeller as described above, except that the impeller is not in contact

(opposite page) This sporty Hinckley Picnic Boat has most of the components of water systems found on the largest offshore yachts.

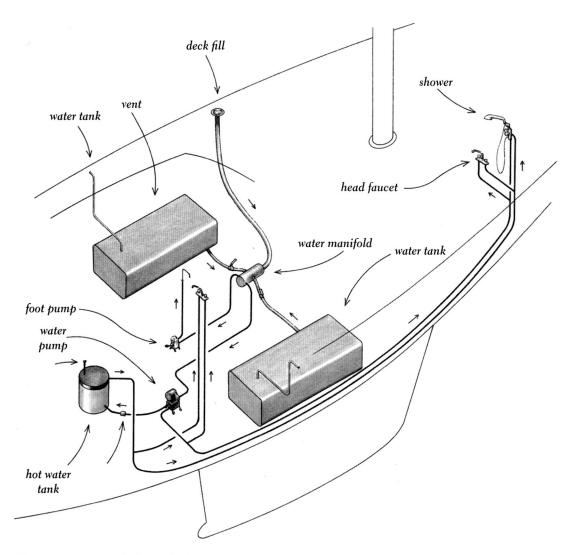

water tank

vent

deck fill

shower

head faucet

water manifold

water tank

foot pump

water pump

hot water tank

The components of a fairly standard water system on a cruising boat

with the pump body; the pumps draw water by vacuum and throw the water out by the shape and rotation of the blades. Turbine pumps are often the quietest of these pumps. Their impellers are also less subject to damage from running dry because they are not in contact with the pump body. The downside is that these pumps often have to be primed with lots of water to start pumping. This disadvantage may be minimized by locating the pump low in the water system.

All of these pumps are controlled by one of two switching devices. The simpler is a switch that is connected to the faucet; in fact, the faucet "knob" is often the pump switch. When the faucet is opened, the pump starts. This device is used on only the smallest of pumps. The more common arrangement is a pressure switch at the pump. When a faucet is opened, the pressure in the system is reduced. The pressure switch senses this and turns the pump on. When the pressure builds to a predetermined point, the pressure switch senses this too, and shuts the pump off.

In a water system with small-diameter, rigid

tubing, the volume difference between low and high pressure in the system is small, causing the pump to cycle on and off at a rapid rate. To reduce the cycling and smooth the flow of water, some systems include an accumulator tank, a plastic or metal tank with a cushion of air held in by a flexible membrane. The tank, which is placed on the high-pressure side of the pump, allows water to enter the bottom, forcing the membrane up and pressing against the air on the other side. As the water volume builds, it compresses and raises the air pressure. When the water pressure hits the high-pressure cutout setting, the pump shuts down. When a faucet is opened, the pressure in the accumulator tank pushes water back into the water system, allowing the pump to stay off until the pressure of the water in the system reaches the low-pressure setting. The system is simple and usually requires only an occasional boost to the air pressure in the accumulator to keep it working. An air fitting on the top of the tank does the trick.

Tanks

Water tanks are commonly built of aluminum, stainless steel, fiberglass, or plastic. Rubber bladder tanks are sometimes found aboard small craft. Fiberglass tanks, which are frequently used aboard fiberglass boats, are built either as integral components of the hull or as separate tanks. The water in both fiberglass and plastic tanks is subject to taste problems if the tanks are not properly constructed. All tanks, however, can lead to bad-tasting water if they are not maintained properly. This is why you should determine if your tanks have clean-out ports; if not, consider installing them. Water that sits in a tank will become stale, surfaces of the tank will develop a film, and precipitate will collect in the lower sections of the tank if they are not cleaned on a regular basis.

If your tanks do not have gauges, consider installing sight tubes or a remote reading device such as Hart Systems Tank Tender, which uses pneumatic tubes to determine water level. These simple devices will help you plan water usage.

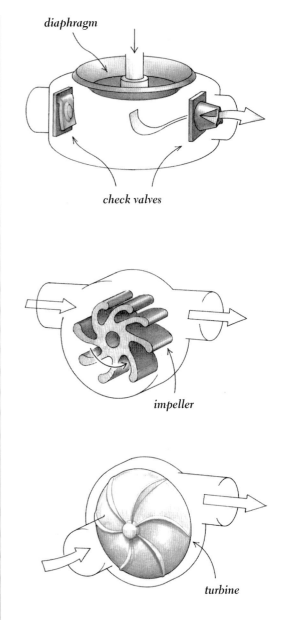

diaphragm

check valves

impeller

turbine

Pumps found in cruising yachts include the diaphragm pump, the impeller pump, and the turbine pump.

Tank Cleaning

I recommend an annual cleaning, at a minimum, to maintain water tanks. The frequency of cleaning will, of course, depend on your climate and the composition of the supply water. Those of us in the northeast typically have less growth in our tanks than those in the south where it is much warmer. I think it is hard to beat the hand cleaning of a tank interior, but for those who do not have easy access to the interiors there are products on the market that help improve the taste of water. Aquabon drinking water freshener and Sudbury Aqua Fresh are both recommended for use with fiberglass and plastic tanks. On the generic side, you can use a mild chlorine bleach/water solution to clean tanks; I'm told baking soda works also. Rinse the tank several times after cleaning.

Fills and Vents

On most boats, water is supplied to the tanks through a deck fill. The supply line should be hose or pipe of adequate diameter to allow for rapid filling of the tank or tanks. There should also be a vent line to allow air to escape from the tank; that line should be positioned to prevent water from escaping from the tank in rough seas or, on a sailboat, under heeling conditions. Water tank vents can be a source of problems on many boats. A few boats have the vent looped and drained into the bilge, and the loop is lower than the fill. The result? The vent leaks into the

bilge before overflowing on deck where it can be seen by whomever is filling the tank. If the vent is large enough, it can pass a substantial amount of water in a short time. The moral is, pay attention when filling the tanks with a hidden vent system, or modify it to drain into a sink or perhaps overboard.

Consider carrying a water filter for use when filling tanks with questionable-quality water. My father carried a double water filter mounted on a board that could hang from the lifelines. The shore hose connected to the input side, and a short hose was connected to the output. This was dropped into the deck fill. This system ensured that water entering the tanks was as clean as possible.

Water Control Valving

Water exits the tanks from water lines that should have valves to shut off the tank if there is damage to the system piping or pumps. These valves will also allow the selective use of water in a system that has more than one tank. An arrangement that works well is to fill the tanks and isolate the smaller tank or tanks—often a bow tank. When the main tank runs out of water, open the valve to the isolated, smaller tank. This system warns

---

A Simple Water Collection System

Norman H. Brown, owner of Pagan, a Hinckley B-40, picked up a neat way to fill his water tanks while cruising from Stu Brown, another B-40 owner. Norman has installed Y-valves in the deck drains just below the deck scuppers. These valves, which are normally directed overboard, are set up to be switched to supply water to the boat's tanks when there is a sufficient rain.

Norman says, "If we are anchored and our tanks are low, we wait until enough rain has fallen to rinse the decks and then throw the valves the other way so that water flows into our tanks. It never ceases to surprise me how quickly the tanks fill. I remember one cold and

rainy day when we had been cruising east of Mount Desert for a week or so. We were anchored in Cutler [Maine] wondering if the tanks would support the hot showers that seemed to be the closest approximation of heaven that could be attained under the circumstances. We opened the valves and had more water than the tanks could hold in about 10 minutes."

He adds the reminder: "Don't forget to switch the valves back before getting underway."

This seems a simple and workable solution. If you are concerned about the cleanliness of your decks, perhaps keeping a fabric water chute to feed the water tanks would work.

you that you need to refill. Using multiple tanks also adjusts a boat's trim—which may be considered either an advantage or a disadvantage. If your small auxiliary tank is located in the bow, ideally you would want to use it first to remove weight from the end of the boat. Using it as a backup tank means that it would be the last to be used, adding to trim problems.

A water manifold is a handy device if you have multiple tanks. It is often nothing more than a series of "tees" and/or "crosses" with valves attached, allowing the selective use and filling of tanks from a central location. Manifolds, if located low enough in the boat, provide a great way to drain tanks. They also may reduce the number of deck fills you require, which is a good way to eliminate the source of possible leaks.

Hot Water Tanks

For those of us who have a hard time giving up the creature comforts of home, a hot water tank is high on the list of shipboard appliances. It is right after the basic water system on my want list.

Hot water tanks are installed on the pressure side of the water pump. Most are heated by a heat exchanger that receives its heat from the water circulated through the engine for cooling. Some tanks have the heat exchanger right inside the tank; others have the heating water circulate through the tank's shell. Many hot water tanks have the option of installing a 110- or 220-volt heating element in the tank for shoreside use. Hot water tanks typically have check valves installed upstream from the tank to prevent backflow of the hot water. Additionally, a pressure relief valve is fitted to prevent excess pressure buildup if the tank is overheated.

Piping

Several types of hoses and tubing are used for piping water systems; many boats use a combination of types. Copper tubing was used for years but, although it is still used, other materials have substantially replaced it. Hoses that were available some years ago imparted a taste and generally were considered inferior for water systems.

Plastic tubing has become more accepted of late. PVC tubing, both reinforced and unreinforced, is used, as are nylon, rubber, and a material called polybutelene. When it is time to locate a clog or clean or replace the hoses, reinforced PVC tubing has the advantage of being transparent. It is not terribly expensive and is easy to work with. Polybutelene is a semi-rigid tubing assembled by hand with fittings. It has the advantage of being able to take a considerable amount of abuse, including freezing, without breaking. When you are having a hard time getting all the water out of your system at decommissioning, that's a feature you will appreciate.

Whichever kind of piping you select for your water system, make sure it is appropriate for the job. For example, thin-wall, unreinforced PVC tubing will collapse if it's used on the suction side of a pump. Instead, use a sturdier reinforced hose or tubing. And, when buying hoses for your hot water system, don't forget that they must be able to withstand high temperatures.

Fittings

Pay close attention to hose connections and the installation of fittings when assembling or repairing water system components. Hanging at anchor in a quiet cove with no noise except some rustling leaves, an occasional bird call, and an intermittent running pump doesn't make for a happy crew. A small leak in a fitting can waste a lot of precious water. It can also be hard to find. Use high-quality hose clamps. When you use double hose clamps, reverse and stagger their positions so they evenly load the fitting inside the hose and don't pinch it. If you have a high-pressure fitting that is too small to accept double hose clamps, consider replacing it. Use approved sealants as required, or use Teflon tape in screw connections if necessary.

Valves that are used in the marine atmosphere should be of top-notch construction—stainless, bronze, and even plastic are appropriate. I have an affinity for ball valves with handles that easily indicate the orientation of the valve.

Maintaining and Troubleshooting Water Systems

A properly installed water system should be a cinch to maintain. I have already discussed washing the tanks out at least once a year. In addition to that chore, consider occasionally removing and flushing, or otherwise cleaning, the hoses. The same film that builds up in the tanks can build up in the hoses. They can be hard to remove and clean, but it is worth the effort. For larger-diameter hoses, remove the hose, drop a string with a bolt or nut tied to it down the hose, and use the string to pull a rag back and forth through the hose a few times. Smaller-diameter hoses require water pressure or chemical cleaners to clean them. While you are working on the hoses, remove and clean any inline water filters, replace any rusty hose clamps, and look for cracked or deformed fittings.

At a bare minimum you should check pump impellers and diaphragms once each year. Decommissioning is a good time to do this; you'll then have time to order any parts that are needed for replacement in the spring. Even if you do not need to replace them now, consider ordering spares to keep aboard.

Impellers commonly fail because they run dry or have become old and brittle. In your inspection, look for missing pieces of the impeller or for wear on the impeller sides or tips. Either sign of wear should prompt you to replace the impeller. As you reassemble the pump, be sure that any gaskets are clean and in good condition.

One problem area to check in an impeller or turbine pump is the pump seal, which prevents the water in the pump body from getting out along the drive shaft and keeps other materials from getting in. Replacing a damaged or worn pump seal is not difficult, but it requires patience. Detailed replacement instructions should come with the pump or replacement seal, but a word to the wise: Do not strike the pump shaft, seal, or body directly with a hammer to remove or reset a

seal. Take time to find the right tool for the job. Use a block of wood to soften the blow to the shaft and, I repeat, take your time. A small nick in any of these parts will ruin them.

Many newer pressure pumps have sealed pressure switches; a defective switch must be replaced. It's advisable to carry a spare aboard, but if you do not have one you can wire the pump directly to the source, bypassing the pressure switch. This would allow you to use a manual switch or circuit breaker to control the pump. Be careful, though—if you leave the switch on you will damage the pump.

Larger pressure pumps usually have an adjustable pressure switch that may be the same as the switch used in your home if you draw water from a well. These typically have two adjusting screws for high- and low-pressure settings as well as a set of points. Keep the contacts on the points clean with a piece of fine, 600-grit sandpaper. The pressure settings are determined by adjusting the switch screws. One screw will adjust both the high and low settings; the other will adjust the pressure spread. To set up the switch, adjust the screw that controls both the high and low pressure until the pump comes on at an appropriate pressure (low-pressure setting). Then, adjust the other screw until the pressure pump shuts off at the right pressure (high-pressure setting). Be careful not to set the pressure too high. You may unnecessarily damage the system and you will use too much water. Most systems are designed to operate in the 20 to 40 psi range.

Adjusting pressure in an accumulator tank is important as well. Tanks with a built-in bladder and air fitting occasionally need recharging. You can do this by connecting an air pump to the air fitting (normally supplied) in the tank and pumping air back into the tank. If the water system is not pressurized, the amount of air pressure you will charge to is less than if the system is pressurized. A good pressure for an unpressurized system is 20 psi; for a pressurized system, 35 psi. Remember, if you set the pressure too high when the water system is pressurized, the water will not be able to push the bladder back into the accumulator and the cushioning effect will be lost.

Some accumulator tanks use an air cushion

only. These tanks are recharged by draining the tank and opening a fitting on the top to allow air to enter. When the fitting is closed, the air alone acts as a cushion. These tanks are usually not as effective as the bladder types.

One final thought on servicing pumps and filters. If you have a pump or filter that is elevated above the tanks, consider installing a valve on the upstream (tank) side of the equipment. This will allow you to prime the pump or filter with less effort after servicing.

Decommissioning the Water System

When laying up the water system on your boat, the goal is to get all the water out of the system and clean the tanks.

Many boats have been designed and constructed with a great deal of thought to draining the tanks. A drain in the low point of a tank saves a lot of pump time. Other boats have a water manifold in a low spot in the boat. There may also be a place to open up the system and let the water flow into the bilge before being pumped overboard.

Here are some hints for decommissioning your water system:

- Check the water pump and accumulator tank for water collection; drain them if necessary.

- Drain all of the outlets in the head, galley, and on deck.

- Drain the hot water tank and carefully inspect piping to and from the tank. Turn off and tape over 110-volt heating element switches to prevent them being switched on and burning out in an empty tank.

- Be suspicious of any draining lines that include a check valve; remove check valves if in question. Many yards use pressurized air to blow out the water from the lines. This works quite well, but I would caution you to be sure

to remove pumps and accumulators from the system first—their diaphragms may well be damaged from the air pressure. Keep the air pressure low. Check valves, too, may impede the process. Follow the system carefully in planning for a winter layup.

As a final precaution, it may be advisable to put something in the system's low spots to ensure that no freezing takes place. Some folks recommend good old vodka for the purpose; many people use a nontoxic antifreeze. Its your choice. I find that there is a taste to all of the antifreezes I have tried, so I prefer to spend extra time drying out the system.

Recommissioning the Water System

Recommissioning the water system should be a piece of cake if the system was properly decommissioned.

1. Drain antifreeze from the system as well as possible.

2. Rinse tanks with lots of water if possible. Drain directly overboard if the water is clear.

3. Reconnect piping, examining the fittings for signs of cracks and firm connections.

4. Test check valves by blowing in them if possible. They may stick during the layup period.

5. Reassemble the pump impellers or diaphragms if necessary.

6. Fill the system with water and test. Look for leaks and check the operation of all valves.

7. Check out the hot water tank operation, both with the engine and, if available, with the 120-VAC element.

It may take quite a bit of flushing and some tank cleaning (see pages 151–152) before all of the unpleasant tastes are gone.

CHAPTER 14

Installing a Through-Hull or Seacock

Eventually, most boatowners will want to install equipment that requires either the supply or discharge of water via a through-hull or seacock. Although drilling a hole in the hull of your boat is not the most relaxing way to spend an afternoon, the process is not technically difficult. It should be undertaken, however, with caution and plenty of forethought.

This chapter discusses several types of through-hulls and seacocks, as well as considerations in locating and installing them.

Seacocks and Through-Hulls

The term "through-hull" is typically used to define any fitting that passes through the hull of a boat. Sometimes a seacock will be called a through-hull when, in fact, it is a special valve that may or may not be used with a through-hull fitting.

For openings in the hull that are below the waterline, you should install a seacock. Seacocks can stop the flow of water into a boat when a hose or fitting in the line is damaged and leaking. As a single fitting, it is more secure and compact than, for example, a ball valve attached to a through-hull.

Another type of valve, a gate valve, which is a common shoreside plumbing fitting, occasionally finds itself aboard a boat. Gate valves are not recommended for marine use either by way of materials or design. Commonly made of iron or brass, they cannot be installed with the security of a seacock and do not allow a clear flow as a seacock or ball valve does. Additionally, their rotating handles do not allow for easy inspection of the status of the valves, open or closed. Therefore, they have no place on a boat.

A seacock can be attached to the hull by one

of several methods. First, a through-hull (a threaded fitting with a flange) is mounted from the outside of the hull and holds the seacock against the hull with its shaft, which threads into the seacock body. Alternately, two or more bolts

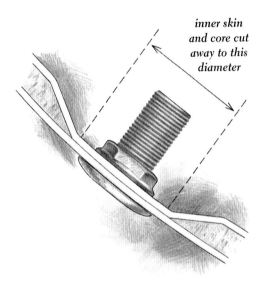

inner skin and core cut away to this diameter

Shown here is the standard surface-mount through-hull. It is used with seacocks for below-waterline installations and often are used alone when placed above the waterline.

The seacock is designed with a valve fastened to the hull so the seacock can be closed for servicing equipment or hoses, as well as to provide a shutoff if a hose is cut.

can be used to hold a through-hull in place. Bolts are typically installed with their heads flush with the outside of the hull and projecting through the base of the flange on the seacock. Many builders and owners choose to use both bolts and a through-hull for extra safety.

Both seacocks and through-hulls are available in bronze and high-strength plastic. The traditional bronze fittings have proven their worth over the years. Plastic fittings are usually made of a glass-reinforced plastic such as nylon. (Fore-spar Marelon fittings are made that way.) They offer the benefits of being lightweight and resistant to corrosion.

Two seacock styles are common. One is essentially a ball valve. Perko is one manufacturer of this style. The other has a tapered barrel in the center that can be rotated to either align the hole in the barrel with the hole in the outside casting, thus opening the seacock, or to close the hole. Wilcox-Crittenden has traditionally manufactured this style. The ball valve seacock is becoming more popular today.

When a fitting is to be installed in the boottop or above, as the discharge for a refrigeration or air conditioning system often is, it is not necessary (although it's still safer) to install a seacock or ball valve. The installation requires only that the through-hull be installed in an appropriate location and fashion.

Before installing a new piece of equipment that requires either a seacock or through-hull, you need to make decisions relating to location of the equipment, as well as the location and types of connections.

First, evaluate the need for a new through-hull. The first choice for water supply connections should be to hook into some existing plumbing. Is there a sea chest that permits multiple use of a single seacock? If so, is there an appropriately sized fitting available in the sea chest? If no sea chest is available, is there another piece of equipment with a water supply that would not be adversely affected by tapping the line for water to the new equipment?

Some pieces of equipment should not be compromised. Do not tap into the raw-water supply line for a primary engine. You do not want any

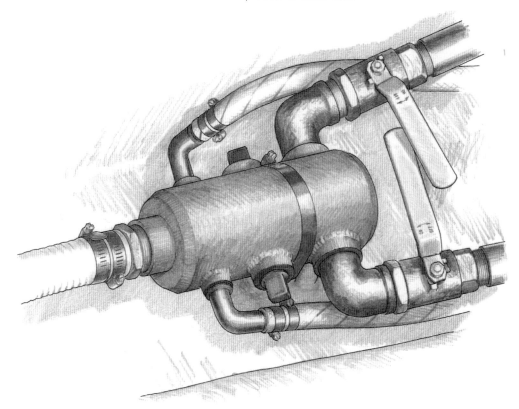

*A sea chest distributes seawater for a number of
needs, reducing the number of through-hulls required
in a boat. You can have one built or assemble one
from a collection of plumbing fittings such as tees
and pipe nipples.*

problems with its cooling. Nor do you want to interfere with generators and other equipment with
raw-water requirements and small supply lines.
When in doubt, contact the manufacturers of the
potentially affected equipment and discuss the installation. I have found manufacturers to be quite
conservative, but be forewarned that going against
their recommendations could void a warranty.

Combining water discharge lines may be
easier than combining water supply lines.
Putting a sump and a bilge pump discharge
together will not likely cause a problem—but
make sure loops and vents are designed appropriately. Construct the system to prevent water
from one pump backing through another.

Locating the Fittings

Assuming there are no currently available water
sources or discharges, look for the best place to
locate the through-hull or seacock.

Obviously, raw-water supplies must be located
beneath the waterline. On sailboats, the supplies
must be low enough in the hull to be submerged
even when the boats are heeling significantly.
Engines, refrigeration, and head intakes are examples of the type of equipment that need an
unceasing supply of raw water. Therefore, their
intakes must be down near the keel or centerline.
Although other equipment is less critical, many
pumps will lose their prime if their through-hull
connections lift above the water level when sailing. So, it is generally a good idea to keep intake
fittings low in the hull.

The negative side of placing a seacock low is
that access to it in an emergency can be difficult.
Discharges of water, such as for sink drains

and head discharges (for offshore use only), are often below the waterline; refrigeration, air conditioning, deck, and cockpit drains are often above or just below the waterline. Fittings that are above the waterline make the flow easier to inspect and reduce the danger of leaking if something should fail. Fittings that are below the waterline hide the holes and reduce the noise of the discharge water. Placing a discharge fitting just above the waterline in the boottop is a good compromise between safety and aesthetics.

Other considerations to review when locating fittings are the proximity to the equipment served and access to the fitting. Shorter hose lengths are generally a good idea, but placing a seacock where it cannot be examined or operated is a poor decision.

With head seacocks, it is customary to locate the discharge aft of the intake, so that as the boat moves or current moves by the boat, the effluent will not be recycled into the intake seacock. Similar consideration should be given to the positioning of the head discharge relative to the engine intake. Occasionally you will find a boat with the intakes on one side and most of the discharges on the other.

Carefully measure and remeasure the location for fittings to be installed in lockers. If they are to be located precisely in the boottop, measure from another fitting, sheer, centerline, and any other available reference points. Give consideration to space for the fitting itself as well as for the plumbing running to the fitting.

Installation

For owners of boats with single-skin hulls, the installation is a very simple process. It becomes slightly more difficult when the through-hull is to be installed through a cored section of a hull.

Installing a Through-Hull in a Single-Skin Hull

1. Once you have determined an appropriate location, bore a small pilot hole through the hull to use as a double check for positioning the fitting. The pilot hole will also serve to attach a fairing block later on.

2. Next, sand the interior surface of the hull in an area slightly larger (approximately 1 or 2 inches) than the base of the fitting and/or any locknuts that are to be installed. A 6-inch-diameter circle will often suffice.

3. Once the hull is sanded, you will need to construct a flat smooth surface to accept the locknut. Cut a wood disk, with a smooth surface, from plywood. The disk should be slightly bigger than the locknut. Resin-coat the disk and wax it several times to permit its removal later. Drill the disk in the center to accept a bolt that will attach it to the hull, through the pilot hole drilled earlier in the hull.

4. Dry fit the wood disk to the prepared hull surface by placing a bolt through it and then through the pilot hole. Use a bolt that has sufficient length to allow for a nut (preferably a wingnut) to be placed on the bolt where it exits the hull. Using a washer on both the inside of the disk and the outside of the hull is a good idea. If the hole is to exit in a painted boottop or topside, place either masking tape or foam tape around the exterior of the pilot hole to prevent scratching the paint. Finally, tape and paper around the inside of the disk to allow for easy cleanup.

5. Next, using fiberglass mat, build a smooth, flat surface for mounting the fitting. Cut the mat in doughnut shapes with the center hole slightly larger than the pilot hole in the disk. The exterior of the doughnut should be the same as the exterior of the wood disk. Cut and fit enough material to bridge any hollows or curves in the hull.

   Remove the facing block from the interior of the hull, wet the mat with resin (see Chapter 9 for more detailed information on handling fiberglass mixing and lamination), and place it on the surface of the hull interior. Replace the wood facing block, tightening the nut on the outside of the pilot bolt so that it compresses the mat and forms a smooth interior surface.

When the mat has cured, remove the facing block from the interior of the hull and sand any rough edges from fiberglass that may have squeezed beyond the extremities of the block. This should provide a flat, smooth interior hull surface upon which to install the through-hull.

6. With a hole saw of appropriate size—equal to the outside diameter of the stem of the through-hull—drill from both hull interior and exterior. Drilling both directions at least enough to cut the surface will prevent ragged edges from being formed as the hole saw exits the hull skin. Taping the hull exterior will also help reduce any scratching and chipping of gelcoat or paint. The great bulk of the drilling for the hole can be done from whichever side is more convenient.

7. Once the hull is bored, install the through-hull fitting with an appropriate compound such as BoatLIFE Life Calk sealant or 3M #5200 (if you don't mind it being hard to remove). I like to use polyurethane compounds. Some boatyards install a gasket underneath the locknut on the hull interior. I feel this is more important on an underwater seacock than on a through-hull; many times, the gasket is omitted in both applications.

8. If possible, once the through-hull is installed and the locknut tightened, leave the installation for a while (depending on the drying time for the sealant) to ensure that the sealant is cured before proceeding with the rest of the plumbing.

Installing a Seacock in a Single-Skin Hull

The preparation for this type of installation is similar to that described for a through-hull. Typically, a larger facing block is necessary because of the larger size of a seacock. It may be necessary to increase the amount of mat used to fill the space between the concave curve of the hull and the flat facing pad as you move lower in the boat into more greatly curved areas.

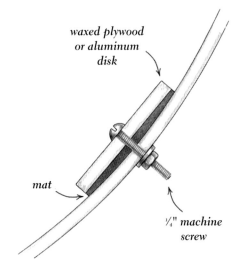

waxed plywood or aluminum disk

mat

¼" machine screw

Use this temporary jig to provide a smooth, flat interior surface on which to install a gasket and retaining nut or seacock body. A single machine screw through the center of the disk pulls it into the wet mat. When the mat sets up, the waxed disk is removed, and the hole left by the machine screw then guides the hole saw when you cut the opening for the through-hull or seacock.

Although it is fairly common to see wood blocks used for interior fairing/facing in seacock and through-hull installations, I have never been comfortable doing so because the block is constantly moist and the wood will eventually rot, leaving a loose installation. I recommend using a fiberglass fairing block—it is less susceptible to water damage and will form a homogeneous structure with the hull.

1. Prior to drilling, place the seacock on the inside of the hull and mark where the bolts will come through. It is recommended that seacocks be bolted in position whether or not a through-hull is used. Some builders rely on a through-hull to hold the seacock against the hull, but I feel strongly that this offers too much opportunity for unseen deterioration of a practically hidden joint. There is too much potential for the seacock to loosen around the through-hull and come free. Bolting a seacock does not take much longer or add significant expense.

Different seacocks have different bolt patterns. Seacocks with two, three, and four holes are fairly common. Double-check that the large center hole, as well as the fastening holes, fall in expected locations on the hull exterior.

2. Drill the holes through the hull. Drill from both sides to reduce damage to either the outside or inside of the hull.

3. From the outside of the hull, countersink the fastener holes for flat head bolts to be flush or slightly recessed.

4. Tape the fitting and the hull that is in the way of the fitting to ease cleanup.

5. Install the seacock with a liberal application of sealant. A note on sealant: Applying it can be messy. One drop of the stuff is roughly enough to cover a football field. If you want, you can apply a gasket between the seacock flange and the hull facing. I prefer this method of installation and use a reinforced red rubber gasket that prevents expansion or distortion when compressed.

    Use quality bolts—I like monel bolts, but they can be difficult to find. Silicon bronze bolts work also.

6. After scraping off the excess sealant, pull the tape and dispose of it.

7. With all metal seacock installations on boats that are bonded, it is important to connect a bonding strap or tie-wire, of at least number-four cable, to the seacock after installation.

Installing a Seacock in Cored Hulls

Coring in the hull makes seacock installation slightly more complicated. The objective when installing a seacock in a cored hull is to prevent moisture from migrating into the core. This is accomplished by removing the core in the area where the seacock will be installed. If a seacock is installed without removing the core and sealing the exposed edges, water can enter the coring material and migrate between the core and the skins of the boat. Moisture in the core leads to

rot, expansion of the core, and possible freezing problems. Therefore, most builders and yards will install a seacock after removing the core in an area slightly larger than the seacock.

1. Mark an area of about 2 inches around the base of the seacock for core removal.

2. Cut the interior skin only, with a Dremmel tool or other appropriate cutter or grinder. If you are tempted to try cutting the skin with a large hole saw and a drill, know that doing so is as good a way I can think of to break something, like an arm.

3. Bevel the edge of the core to allow for the layup of fiberglass over the hole and the edge of the core, thereby sealing the core.

4. It is not necessary to build the thickness of the glass back to the original thickness of the hull with core, but the replacement fabric should be the same type and at least as thick as the original inner skin.

5. Once the inner skin has been sealed to the outer skin, do the same facing procedure as outlined in the through-hull installation section above.

6. Proceed with the rest of the installation as described in steps 5 through 8 on pages 159–160 for a single-skin hull.

One final word of caution: If the resin your hull is made of is unavailable, contact the boat's manufacturer to ensure that the materials you select will be compatible with the hull laminate. This is especially important today with the use of epoxy and other materials in hulls. Adhesion of polyester resins to epoxy resins have been a problem. Interestingly enough, the reverse is not true. Epoxy resins will adhere well to cured polyester resins.

I hope I have provided enough information here to allow you to adapt to other circumstances and installations not specifically addressed. Although the specifics may need to vary with your situation, the overall process should remain the same.

Marine Heads

Marine heads come under the category of necessary evils—snorting pieces of equipment connected to mazes of hose that twist their way through lockers in ways designed to clog at the most inopportune times. We have added Y-valves, holding tanks, holding tank pumps, macerator pumps, deck pumpout plates, and bypasses to make the whole rig even more interesting.

Without question, the newer head systems are improving the environment, but the discharge requirements have made them a bit more vexing. This chapter will take a quick look at a few types of heads and head systems, consider some common problems and how to resolve them, and give an overview on how to decommission and recommission heads.

Types of Marine Heads

Increased regulation of discharge has spawned a variety of heads. The regulations, covered in detail in most yachting publications, allow for three types of systems. Types I and II allow for some treated discharge, while Type III is designed to hold discharge for pumpout or offshore disposal. A steadily growing number of places are opting for no discharge laws and, therefore, it appears that the Type III systems are the wave of the future.

Each system has a number of variations, but three types of heads, with collateral equipment, comprise what is seen on most cruising boats: manual, electric, and vacuum.

Manual heads are operated with a single lever to provide both intake water and waste discharge. The double-action pumps (waste out one way, water in the other) on these heads are mostly piston pumps of various configurations, and they are generally reliable pieces of equipment. Raw water is sucked into the pump on the same stroke that waste is discharged. Then when the handle is pushed the other way, water is discharged and waste is sucked in. A variation on the manual head is the manual/ electric head; this often is a manual head that has been modified to let a motor do the pumping for you.

A second type of head has an electric motor with specially designed discharge and suction pumps connected to the motor.

The third type, the vacuum head, is becoming more common on larger (over 40 feet) boats. (The gear required for vacuum heads is a bit too much for smaller boats.) The ease of operation and lack of odor has led many Hinckley owners to request that the SeaLand VacuFlush head be installed on their yachts.

Vacuum heads have a pump that pulls a vacuum on the discharge side and flushes waste to its destination with a big whoosh. Intake water is provided either through a pressurized water supply (often the vessel's freshwater system), or from the vacuum created in the bowl from waste removal.

A less common type of head is a recirculating head. I have never been shipmates with this type of head and, therefore, will beg off covering it here.

The manual head is, by far, the most prevalent head used today. It is the least expensive, simplest to install, and relatively easy to understand when it comes time for repairs.

Headaches

Head problems are one of the most dreaded shipboard problems. For a few folks I know, they are right up there with sinking. Proper operation of a marine head, regardless of type, requires that all seals, gaskets, check valves, and diaphragms are in good working order. Other than clogs, wear and deterioration of these internal parts cause most head problems. Head odor, of course, is another nagging concern.

Heads are not user friendly when it comes to pumping solids through them. The old rule of not putting anything into the head that has not been eaten first probably says it well, although a bit ungainly for my comfort.

Clogged Discharge

When a head seems to be bound up, it is likely that a solid clog needs to be removed, although you should consider other causes, too.

First, find out if there really is a blockage. With the complicated valve systems controlling flow direction in many boats, it may be difficult to determine which way the effluent is going. Carefully examine the valves, including the discharge seacock, to determine that they are set in a proper configuration for passage of the waste. If there is no danger of discharging sewage into protected waters, try moving the valves; this might loosen a blockage within a valve. If it is difficult to tell what is going where, remember to label the valves after the immediate problem is solved.

If the valves are all set in the correct direction, and the discharge is being sent to a holding tank, check the holding tank to see if it is full. Holding tanks are often unrealistically small because of the ever-present storage problems on boats. An enthusiastic pumper can fill a holding tank quickly.

Another problem might be the buildup of solids, including calcium deposits, in the lines and valves. Before pulling apart the hoses, though, let the blockage sit for a few hours; perhaps it will soften and allow pumping.

If the passive approach does not work, try reducing the blockage with chemicals. Of course, this will work only if you are able to pump some fluid through the system. Do not use household chemicals. They are usually bad for the rubber and other gasket materials. This includes not only toilet bowl cleaners, but most other aggressive detergents (such as Lysol and Mr. Clean) as well.

A mild muriatic acid solution (check manufacturer recommendations for the mix) may help reduce the buildup, but it must be used carefully and then thoroughly rinsed to prevent damaging the head's internal parts. Depending upon the strength of the solution, allow it to set in the bowl and bubble for a few minutes before pumping it farther down the line and waiting again. Repeat the process until the solution has worked its way through the system. Note that storing muriatic acid aboard is not recommended.

When finished, remember to pump water through the system to neutralize the acid, which would corrode metal parts. Then, add a small amount of mineral oil or head conditioning fluid to the bowl and pump it through the valves to preserve the life of the valve and gasket materials.

When all else fails, it may be necessary to remove the hoses and mechanically remove a blockage. Before taking any hoses apart, though, think through how you will capture the liquids that remain in the hoses. Spills into the bilge will stink and are tough to thoroughly clean up. Close seacocks and inlet valves. If possible, undo hose connections at the high points, such as at the vented loops, to reduce spillage. A straightened coat hanger might work as a plumbing snake, but take care not to poke through any check valves in the line.

Finally, if the head has been pumped after a blockage has formed and pressure has built up, wait to remove any fittings until the pressure has bled away. The explosion of releasing a pressurized sewage hose is beyond description. Trust me.

Leaking Valves and Siphon Breaks

Both head discharge and intake lines on heads mounted at or below the waterline should be installed with vented loops. Not all are. When a head is located below the waterline and a valve becomes stuck or is left in the open position, a siphon is likely. Even with vented loops, if a vent is plugged, the potential is there for starting a siphon. Once the siphon starts, it does not take long for the head to overflow and, if not caught, the boat sinks. I recommend owners close seacocks when leaving their boats in cases where siphoning is a potential problem. To prevent the problem, regularly service the valves in the head; also, remember to check the vented loop often. The small rubber or metal stop in the vented loop might be corroded or stuck in the closed position. Additionally, operate water intake valves (both hand and foot operated) to ensure that they are shutting off the intake water flow at the head as designed.

Head Odors

The best defense against head odors is a superclean head and high-quality hoses specifically designed for sewage use. Such hoses have smooth interiors, are ruggedly built, have good odor impermeability, and can flex into the necessary bends that most discharge hoses need. SeaLand Technology makes a good hose, as do others.

If you have a head odor problem and replacing hoses is not an option, try wrapping the hoses in thin plastic wrap such as Saran Wrap. It has excellent odor containment properties and might be an inexpensive answer to a nasty problem.

Problems with Electric Heads

With both manual/electric and fully electric heads, the electric motor can be a problem. Typi-cally, the motor has to exist in a relatively damp and inhospitable environment. The potential for corrosion is high.

If the motor is not operating correctly, first check for adequate power and then try to run the motor unloaded. Either disconnect the motor linkage to the pumps or remove the hoses to run the motor with as little load as possible. Incorrect valve settings or blockages will stop the motor as well; be sure to check the system as described on page 163.

Problems with Vacuum Heads

Vacuum heads will occasionally develop problems with the seal at the bottom of the bowl that helps create the vacuum in the discharge line. The seal may be damaged by abrasion or chemicals, or it might be plain worn out. The problem is usually signaled by increased running of the vacuum pump; replacing the seal is usually required. Removing the head base is necessary and easily done.

Another problem frequently encountered with vacuum heads is blockage as a result of too much hose or too many bends. Boat interiors do not lend themselves to straight plumbing runs, and each bend induces some resistance to the system. You may need to redesign the discharge plumbing to achieve a trouble-free system.

Rebuilding Heads

Regardless of the type of head, you should carry a full spare-parts kit aboard. Even with the best of care, most heads will require rebuilding every few years. This is one piece of preventive maintenance that is low on many owners' list of fun projects. But the process will decrease the potential for cruise disasters like those described above.

Most manufacturers have a spare-parts/rebuild kit already made up for their heads. Check for one at a chandlery or parts store. When you rebuild the head, if a piece looks good and you are tempted to *not* replace it, replace it anyway and save the old piece for an emergency. Then reorder a new parts kit for reserve.

Decommissioning Marine Heads

Winterizing a marine head is a relatively easy task. Basically, all that is required is to close the intake seacock, remove the intake hose from the seacock, and place the hose in a bucket of anti-freeze mix. Use ethylene glycol antifreeze only—other types can harm synthetic internal parts. Then, pump antifreeze through the system.

If the boat is in the water, it may not be easy to be sure that antifreeze is distributed throughout the discharge side of the plumbing. After pumping the antifreeze several strokes beyond the bowl (depending on the discharge hose length), close the discharge seacock, disconnect the discharge hose at the high end (usually the vent), and pour some antifreeze in the hose to prevent freezing.

Both the hose to the head and the line to the seacock should be treated in this fashion.

If your boat has a holding tank, see that it is pumped and treated with antifreeze.

As with all water systems, follow the plumbing and look for low spots, leaks, and other problems. Don't forget to check hoses and clamps. Reattach all hoses and tighten hose clamps when done.

Recommissioning Marine Heads

Recommissioning usually requires only opening the seacocks and/or valves and pumping the antifreeze out of the system. Run some mineral oil into the system to help lubricate the valves.

Impellers in electric heads may be stiff from the layup period. Occasionally, these will require extra work or replacement.

Finally, some sort of chant and sacrifice to the gods of marine heads is always in order.

CHAPTER 16

Steering Systems

The steering systems on most yachts are reliable, simple, and often underserviced. Some owners assume that if they have a well constructed boat the steering system will function without problems. Every steering system, however, requires periodic maintenance as well as replacement of components on a regular basis. This chapter takes a look at the components of a steering system and then considers some potential problem areas.

Because steering systems vary from one boat to another, it is difficult to write a complete overview of all the possible layouts and components. Therefore, in the interest of simplicity and at the risk of angering the experts, I will concentrate on the more common types of systems. I hope that an understanding of these basics will allow boatowners to diagnose problems and understand some preventive steps they can take for their particular system.

Steering System Components

Perhaps the most important component of any steering system is the rudder. Quite a few powerboats and an occasional sailboat may have two or more rudders. Materials used in making rudders include wood, bronze, stainless steel, mild steel, aluminum, fiberglass, carbon fiber, and foam. Most rudders are made of combinations of these materials; for example, stainless or bronze posts with fiberglass or other glass composite skins over a foam core.

The two most common rudder designs are keel-mounted, or skeg-mounted, with the rudder attached to the boat at the forward edge, and spade, where the rudder usually stands alone, separated from other appendages. There are variations of these basic types.

Every rudder has a bearing system that allows it

(opposite page) This steering pedestal is the center of a well-planned cockpit. Instrumentation and communication equipment are within reach at all times.

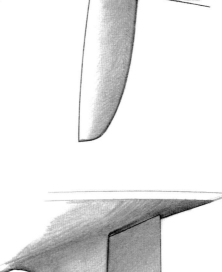

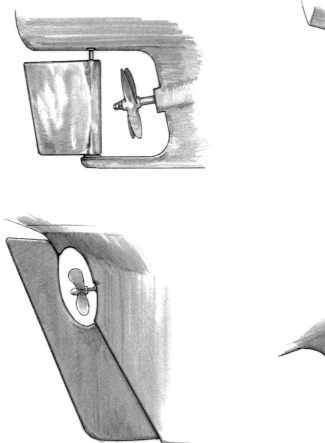

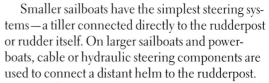

These and many other rudder styles and configurations are found on cruising yachts. Generally, the farther a rudder is from the center of effort of the boat and the more independent a rudder is, the more power it has to steer the boat. A spade or balanced rudder also typically makes steering a bit quicker. Rudders hung on skegs or on the back edge of the keel are less efficient, but they also are less touchy.

to pivot smoothly. Larger auxiliaries and powerboats typically have multiple bearings, either in the hull alone or in the hull and also down along the keel or skeg. The bearings are subject to wear and need to be maintained regularly; I will discuss maintenance procedures a little later in this chapter.

Smaller sailboats have the simplest steering systems—a tiller connected directly to the rudderpost or rudder itself. On larger sailboats and powerboats, cable or hydraulic steering components are used to connect a distant helm to the rudderpost.

Regardless, a quadrant, tiller arm, or drive wheel (such as Edson's radial drive unit) can be mounted on the rudderpost to permit connection of steering system components to the rudder. These are made of various materials that should be compatible with the rudderpost material, the loads, and the space available.

Rudder stops prevent the rudder blade from moving too far to one side or the other. These stops limit the movement of the quadrant or tiller to prevent the rudder from hitting the hull.

They are often set to allow the rudder to turn 35 degrees on either side of the centerline. Any additional swing would not add much to the performance of the boat. Rudder stops must be very carefully installed to ensure that they are rigidly mounted, and they should be inspected to determine that they have not worn to a point where they no longer limit rudder movement to the intended arc.

Cable steering is most common on sailboats

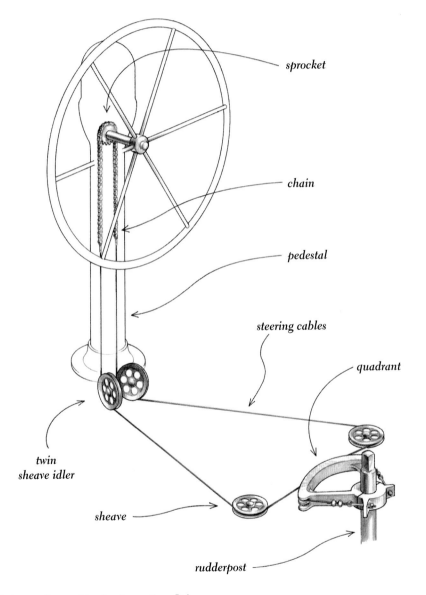

sprocket

chain

pedestal

steering cables

quadrant

twin sheave idler

sheave

rudderpost

This is a basic layout for a cable steering system. It is an easily understood and reliable system when given a modest amount of care.

less than fifty feet long, while hydraulic steering systems are normally seen on power yachts and larger sailboats. Wheel steering with a mechanical linkage to the rudderpost, or rack and pinion steering, also work well, but they are not seen as frequently as cable or hydraulic systems.

In cable steering, a pair of wires is connected to a short chain that rides over a sprocket at the helm. The wires, driven by the sprocket and chain, connect to a quadrant or drive wheel at

Hydraulic steering systems do not offer the feel that sailors prefer, but they have been used for years on power yachts and larger sail yachts with good results. An understanding of the system components is important for troubleshooting.

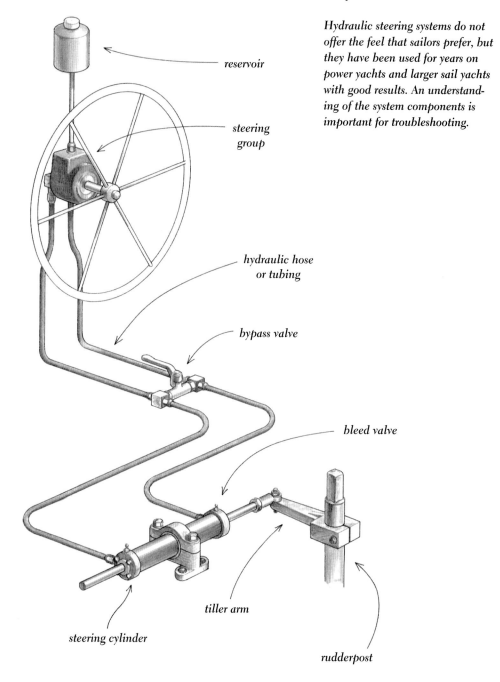

reservoir

steering group

hydraulic hose or tubing

bypass valve

bleed valve

tiller arm

steering cylinder

rudderpost

the rudderpost. Sheaves align and guide the cable through its passage.

In hydraulic steering systems, a wheel usually drives a pump located at or near the helm(s). The pump is connected via a pair of hydraulic lines to a cylinder that in turn is connected to a tiller arm on the rudderpost. The system may serve multiple steering stations, be connected to an autopilot drive, and include other equipment such as a remote fluid reservoir.

Variations on these basic design elements include modifications such as mounting the hydraulic pump at the base of a pedestal steerer with a chain drive to the pump from the wheel shaft itself.

At the control end of cable or hydraulic systems is the wheel. Sailboats tend to have large wheels to generate power through leverage and to permit the person at the helm to move outboard and see the sails more easily. Hydraulic systems often have smaller wheels because the hydraulic pump provides the necessary leverage. Either way, the wheel is attached to a pedestal, bulkhead, or steering box that contains the gearing or pump mentioned above. In addition, the steering system often contains a brake at the steering station to create drag on the system or to lock the wheel in a set position.

Rudder Problems

The most common problems with rudders are actually bearing problems, but from time to time there are problems with the rudder itself.

Inspect the rudder any time your boat is hauled out of the water. Look for straightness in the rudderpost, wear in bearings, and the condition of the rudder blade.

Rudders seem to be damaged more often by grounding than by anything else. Bent rudder blades or shafts usually require specialized repair, but here are some things you can look for. A slight bend may not be immediately apparent. However, an increase in steering effort or vibration in the steering system may indicate a bent rudder.

Check the alignment of a rudder by placing a reference stick on the ground or other stable surface with a pointed end directly under the lower end of the rudderpost at the center of rotation for the rudder. Turn the rudder. If the post or rudder is not bent, the reference point will stay directly under the end of the rudderpost. If it is bent, the runout will be apparent.

Small rudders or rudderposts can sometimes be straightened in place, but usually the job is best done off the boat by an accomplished machine shop. Occasionally, the post or blade will be so bent as to require replacement. The biggest parts of the job usually are removing the rudder from the boat and replacing it.

Particularly with metal rudders, look for signs of pitting, stress cracks, or heavy surface corrosion on both the post and the blade. If a rudderpost is pitting, it is normal to find that the underwater bearings are wearing as well.

Check the exterior shells of composite rudders. Most sailing auxiliaries have rudders with fiberglass or composite shells built around metal rudderposts. The posts have fins attached to prevent the blades from turning around the posts. There may also be foam cores inside the shells. Some rudders use carbon fiber for the post or even the blade as well. In all of these composite constructions, look very carefully for signs of wear or unusual movement that can be caused by the enormous loads generated when steering in heavy seas and when backing down hard.

One of the first signs of a rudder problem might be slackness in the rudder movement. The slack may be caused by loose steering cables, which I will deal with later. It also may be caused by a structural problem with the rudder: separation of the blade skin from the rudderpost, wear of a bearing in the rudder system, or wear of a keyway in the rudderpost, quadrant, or tiller arm.

Blade delamination from a rudderpost can be difficult to diagnose if a boat is in the water. First, check for other possible reasons the rudder blade does not respond solidly with the steering system. Are the steering cables reasonably tight? If they are not, adjust them. Does the quadrant or tiller arm move—even slightly—around the rudderpost? If yes, there's a problem with the keyway or retaining pin holding the arm.

Now check the blade itself. With some rudder and stern configurations, you can do this from in the water (perhaps in a dinghy). However, it is more easily accomplished with the boat hauled.

Check for a loose rudder blade when the boat is out of the water by locking the rudderpost and moving the blade back and forth. It is important to ensure that the rudderpost does not move as

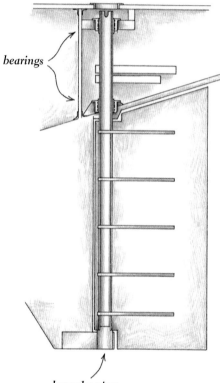

This rudder is skeg mounted and has a hollow rudderpost and three bearings. The blade stiffeners are installed through the rudderpost; they keep the blade in alignment with the quadrant. The three bearings must be carefully aligned for smooth operation, but when working correctly this rudder will have minimum bearing wear because the quadrant is attached between two securely mounted bearings, and the bottom of the rudder is held firmly in place by the skeg heel fitting.

you move the blade. If the wheel brake is on, the post still may move due to loose steering cables or a loose key in a quadrant or tiller arm. The rudderpost should hold the blade rigidly.

If the rudder blade shell is loose, there are some steps you can take that might fix it. Replacing the rudder is obviously one alternative, but first consider repairing it.

If the rudder blade is foam filled and the fins or plates attached to the rudderpost have become loose, it may be possible to inject resin to solidify the fins. Better yet, open the shell with a hole saw or other power tool and insert fiberglass laminate or choppings. When the interior has been solidified, the outer skin must be repaired as one would a hole in the hull.

It could be possible to remove the blade from the rudderpost and then replace it. To fashion a replacement, you could attach a new inner core of PVC foam and/or fiberglass panels to the post, shape it, and then glass it over. Then fair and paint the new blade.

If there are large cracks in the rudder edge or around the rudderpost, the rudder is probably taking on water, which could create problems. Rudders often have significant voids to reduce their weight; the voids can hold water that will freeze during a cold layup period. The ice can cause a wedging action within the rudder. Consequently, the skin could slowly separate from the rudderpost and could, itself, delaminate. Also, internal water could speed osmotic blistering of the rudder skins.

It is not uncommon to find very small cracks around the outside of a rudder. These are often caused by minor cosmetic cracking of the gelcoat used to patch the edge of the blade. Small cracks will not necessarily create an immediate problem; however, if left unattended for extended periods of time, they too may permit moisture to reach the inside of the rudder laminate.

One way to detect water in a suspect rudder is to use a moisture meter, available at most boatyards or through a marine surveyor. Another way to ensure there is no large quantity of moisture in a rudder is to drill a number of very small drain holes in the rudder and then patch them with an appropriate epoxy patching compound once the rudder has drained or it has been determined that there is no interior moisture.

Over the years, a fair number of rudders have been designed with vents to allow water to fill them. This is intended to provide balance in the rudder weight. These rudders often have excess moisture in their skins. If you are concerned about this problem, I highly recommended that you contact the manufacturer of the boat, a marine surveyor, or a yard technician to discuss potential solutions. These might include sealing or foam-filling the rudder or, if damage has been done, replacing the rudder blade. In most yachts, this replacement process is not beyond the capability of a talented boatowner.

After checking that the rudder blade is properly adhered to the rudderpost and stiffeners, and that excessive moisture is not in the blade, a careful inspection of the bearings is in order. Boats with a keel- or skeg-mounted rudder often have a bearing at the bottom of the rudder. In addition to a bearing at deck level, frequently there is a third bearing in these systems located near the top of the rudderpost to stiffen the rudderpost between the bottom hull connection and the deck. This enhances the rudder's ability to handle quadrant or tiller arm side loads.

Newer boat designs often have spade rudders that are not supported at the lower end of the blade. These rudders have bearings where the rudderpost exits the hull and higher, often at deck level, or they may have special, long and extra-strong hull bearings.

All of these bearing designs should be inspected regularly. The lower external bearing of a skeg- or keel-mounted rudder is often constructed in the form of a casting or weldment with a pin that inserts into the bottom of the rudderpost, or a socket into which the bottom of the rudderpost fits. These bearings are particularly subject to wear where there is shallow water and a great deal of bottom gravel, such as southern Florida. Gravel inside a bearing will abrade its surface. When moving the rudder from side to side, if there appears to be slop in the lower bearing beyond a few thousandths of an inch, it's

likely the bearing wear is increasing to the point where replacement is necessary.

This problem is reduced in systems where the lower end of the rudderpost is bored out to accept the pin on the gudgeon, because gravity helps gravel fall out of the bearing. In systems where the lower fitting is a socket and the rudderpost is turned down as a pintle, gravel tends to work into the socket and gravity, of course, keeps it there, aggravating the problem.

Rudder-bearing wear typically accelerates over time. As the bearing loosens, the space enlarges for foreign material to fit between the surfaces, thereby increasing the wear on the bearing. If you have a lower bearing with a socket, consider modifying the bearing to allow material to pass through the socket and out the bottom of the fitting. This will permit a flow of water to wash foreign materials away from the bearing surface.

Traditional bronze bearings that are located in the hull have a packing gland (or stuffing box) similar to that used on a propeller shaft. This stuffing box is tightened by turning the packing nut or by bolts that are tapped to a flange on the base of the stuffing box.

Some boats have an alternative bolt-down water seal along with an internal roller or ball bearings to reduce friction in the system. Occasionally, a rudderpost will have roller or ball bearings inside a long fiberglass tube that extends almost to the deck, negating the need for the water seal cap. If excess movement is found in this area of the bearing system, more often than not replacement of part or all of the bearing must be considered. In any case, it is important to determine whether the wear is in the rudderpost, in the bearing, or both. As in the lower bearing, increased movement in this area will allow the rudderpost to develop a misalignment with the bearing. This will increase the load on the bearing area, thereby accelerating the rate of wear.

Grit is not a big factor in bearing wear at the upper bearings. Both upper and lower bearings are, however, somewhat affected by marine growth. In the case of stainless rudderposts, the upper bearing area, if submerged, is a common area for crevice corrosion. This type of

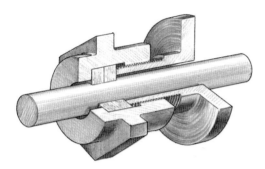

This stuffing box installation works for both a propeller shaft or a rudderpost. The packing will require periodic replacement, and the bore should be checked for marine growth, scratches, and pitting.

corrosion likes the relatively calm water inside the bearing.

Finally, industrial quality bearings such as self-aligning pillow blocks are sometimes used as upper bearings. Easily bolted to a structural member of the deck or to a bracket built under the deck, these bearings allow for self-alignment with the rudderpost and are, comparatively speaking, inexpensive. However, they are made of materials that do not hold up well in the marine environment.

High-quality UHMW (ultra-high molecular weight) plastic or ball bearing fittings similar to the ones that are used at the hull exit are available in versions that will work at the top of the rudderpost. They, of course, have the advantage of being located in an area less subject to corrosion. Slack in an upper bearing requires replacement of the bearing, along with careful inspection of the rudderpost in that area to ensure there has been no wear or scarring, which will quickly destroy a new bearing.

Bonding Problems

Look at the bonding of the rudderpost and bearing. Depending on the bearing system, both the rudderpost and rudderport may need bonding; in better installations, you will find that the bonding

has been provided. On boats with synthetic bearings and carbon fiber rudderposts and blades, there is no need to bond the rudder. On boats with no bonding system, of course there will be no bonding at the rudderpost. (See Chapter 20 for information on bonding systems.)

Bonding should be designed to permit full rotation (stop-to-stop) of the rudder. Braided cable, wire, and brushes are options that might be used to electrically connect the rudderpost to the bonding system. If the bonding has come loose or the connection has become corroded, remove the connection, clean the surfaces, and reinstall the bonding.

Quadrant and Tiller Arm Problems

Carefully examine tiller arms, quadrants, or other drive types for wear around a keyway or pin. It is not uncommon to find an undersized key that permits movement of a quadrant or tiller arm around the rudderpost. Or, you may find a sheared key, broken pin, or a key that has fallen out.

Fortunately, replacing these parts is not difficult. To remove a quadrant or tiller arm you need only remove the steering cables or cylinder and loosen and remove either two or four bolts from a split flange in the base that fits around the rudderpost. Install a new key or pin, bolt the system back together, connect the cables or cylinder, and test it.

Steering Cable Problems

In a cable steering system, the control is transmitted through a system of cables, chain, and sheaves. Check the connection of the cable to the quadrant on a regular basis. On most systems, the cable connects to the quadrant via an eyebolt that allows you to adjust the cable tension. The cable is run around a thimble in the eyebolt, through a pair of cable clamps, where it is thoroughly secured to itself. One possible problem is any loosening of the nuts holding the eyebolt to the base of the quadrant. Another is slipping of the cable clamps, allowing the cable to loosen. If the cables become slack, it is important not only to retighten them, but also to examine the cable run to ensure that the cable has not fallen out of the groove on the quadrant, nor out of any of the sheaves, where it may jam. Normally, the cables should be quite taut, although it is possible to overtighten a cable system using the nuts on the eyebolts. Excessive tightening will lead to misalignment of the rudderpost, place excess stress on the bearings, sheaves, and cables, and increase overall drag in the steering system.

Steering cable is either galvanized or stainless 7 x 19 cable. The advantage of galvanized cable is that it will bend around sheaves better than stainless. However, stainless is less likely to rust. Plan to replace steering cables every five to seven years. In a boat that is used constantly, I recommend you replace the cables every one to two years. Cable system components may fail in extreme weather conditions when it is all but impossible to replace them. An extra set of steering cables is not expensive; buy a spare set before an emergency arises. And speaking of emergencies—make sure that you have an emergency tiller that fits and is long enough to provide the leverage needed to work. Try it out.

Before replacing steering cables, carefully note and mark the positions of the wheel, rudder, and any autopilot connections that may need to be realigned when installing the new cables.

Replace the steering cable or cables by loosening one of the eyebolts on the quadrant until there is enough slack in the system to ease the tension slightly on the cable clamps. Do not loosen the eyebolt so much that it will be difficult to hold the cable clamp firmly in order to loosen its nuts. Do not remove the bolt from the quadrant unless absolutely necessary.

Remove the cable clamp, or clamps, permitting the cable to slide through the clamps around the thimble and free from the quadrant. You may wish to attach a messenger line to the ends of the cables to ease the process of releading new cables.

On many steering systems, the cables cross from either side of the quadrant. In a pedestal steerer installation, this is often accomplished between the sheaves (or idler) at the base of the pedestal and the drive sprocket at the top. In

replacing the cables, be sure to adhere to the proper path for the cable leads in this area. If you make a mistake, the steering will be backwards.

With a unit that has a pedestal-mounted wheel, the next step is to remove the compass and any other plates installed above the drive sprocket. Be sure to mark the compass orientation exactly so that it can be reinstalled with precision. Also be sure not to move any magnets mounted in the compass base; doing so would require recompensating the compass.

Lift the cable and chain assembly out of the pedestal or, in a bulkhead mounted unit, off the sprocket. Messenger lines are particularly helpful for this operation.

Remove the wires from the chain, unless replacing the whole assembly, and install the new wires. Attach the quadrant end of the new steering cable to the messenger and pull it back down through the pedestal. Place the chain back in its original position. The center of the chain should be at the top of the sprocket when the king spoke (if the wheel has one) is at the top. Lead the cable through the sheaves in the same manner as the one removed, attach it to the eyebolt, then lead it through the cable clamps and around the thimble back into the cable clamps.

When installing the new cable it may be necessary to further loosen the eyebolt so there is more play in the system when the cable clamps are tightened. Then retension the cable by tightening the eyebolt. Tighten the locknut on the eyebolt and test the system. Adjust the eyebolts as necessary to realign the wheel and rudder.

Owners of an Edson radial drive system will find that similar steps are necessary, although the layout of a quadrant is somewhat different than that of the radial drive. The cable is still tensioned by eyebolts, and attachment systems are generally the same.

Steering Sheave Problems

Steering sheaves are so simple that you would think little could go wrong. My experience with them has taught me that they are devilish devices. They have failed me in a number of ways.

First, the axles in sheaves have a nasty habit of coming loose and working their way out. They are pinned in, but I have found sheared cotter pins on several occasions. I suspect the sheave starts to bind on the axle, and the axle starts to turn in the bracket. The cotter pin is then repeatedly pushed against a barrier that shears it off and voilà, a loose axle. This problem often does not immediately cause a steering failure. For example, when a boatowner once complained about steering drag, I found that a loose axle was the cause. The sheave was bound up, but the cable evidently slipped enough in the groove to permit labored steering.

A second problem is loose cables that become bound between the sheave and the sheave housing, bringing the steering to a rapid halt. This type of pinch is hard to pull out, and the cable is often damaged, requiring replacement.

Many years ago, I sailed a 50-footer to Miami only to have the steering fail in the entrance to Government Cut. Jammed cable. If that wasn't bad enough, while we were trying to get the system loose and the emergency tiller in place, the engine quit. Time to take up farming. It all worked out, but not without some excitement.

Finally, sheaves are often placed on brackets fiberglassed to the hull in glass boats. These brackets may not be constructed heavily enough or be properly attached to the hull. When loaded, the brackets may pull away from the hull or break internally. The former happened to me on a trip to Bermuda a few years ago. The fix was to install a compression post that connected the sheaves together, reducing the load on the hull-to-bracket connection.

None of these problems is fun to deal with, and each could have been avoided by more carefully inspecting the steering system at the dock.

Sheaves that are attached to fiberglass angles or brackets on the hull often are turning the load of the rudder steering system through angles up to almost 180°. When inspecting such an installation, I find it valuable to have someone else at the helm pull the wheel all the way hard to one side and then to the other side while I carefully observe the steering brackets and bolts. On a larger boat this may be done with an individual of rea-sonable size standing on a wheel spoke transmitting as much load down the system as possible. I caution that it is possible to pull nearly any system apart, so you must set some limit on this stress.

On the other hand, sailors who have a fair amount of experience sailing offshore in heavy weather know that heavy loads can be placed on steering systems. They would not be surprised at the severity of my testing procedure.

Sheaves or brackets that do not pass the test should be replaced with stronger equipment, re-inforced, or redesigned and rebuilt to handle the loads that may be placed on them. Perhaps a boat that was originally built with a steering quadrant and sheaves may be a candidate for a system such as an Edson radial drive, eliminating sheaves mounted on the hull and the attendant problems.

Helm Equipment Problems

At the helm end of a cable steering system is a steering pedestal, bulkhead steerer, or steering box where the steering cable connects to the chain which, in turn, rides over the top of a sprocket. Within this subsystem, problems can occur with the wire-to-chain connection. This connection is subject to chafe in this restricted area. Also, it can make noise if the cables are not properly tensioned.

Wheels, shafts, and sprockets may also need attention. Wheels must be properly sized to withstand the loads anticipated and must fit on the pedestal shaft properly. These items are usually dealt with at installation. However, modifications, as well as wear and tear, may cause problems.

One additional component of many wheel systems is the wheel brake. Installed at the helm, it permits the wheel to be locked. Problems with brakes, usually related to wear of the brake lining in the clamp assembly, are rare. Relining or replacing the brake is an infrequent maintenance chore.

Hydraulic Steering Problems

Hydraulic steering systems do not have many of the cable and sheave problems of the cable steering systems; however, they have their own set of potential problems. Some of the problems can appear back at the tiller arm at the rudder.

First, the connection of the driving cylinder to the tiller arm receives a lot of torque and is subject to severe wear if it starts to move. Hydraulic cylinders are powerful and exert an enormous load on the usually short tiller arms. Check for wear on keyways or locking bolts. Ensure that clevis pins are not wearing and that any cotter pins, or the like, are in good shape.

Next, at the opposite (bracket) end of the cylinder, carefully inspect the swiveling connection. Bolts and backing plates should be tight and unbent. Look for signs of wear or bending on the cylinder end.

Further, ascertain that operation of the cylinder is smooth and that fluid is not leaking from either the seals around the shaft or from the fittings. The cylinders, and especially the fittings and piston, should be kept as clean as practical.

Carefully inspect the hydraulic hose and/or rigid tubing connecting the driven cylinder to the driving cylinder at the wheel or pump. They may leak, bulge, abrade or, perhaps in a system that has never seemed to operate properly, be the wrong size. A system with excessive resistance and otherwise good installation may have undersized tubing.

Finally, in the hydraulic system, the pump connected to the wheel needs to be carefully inspected for the same leak and seal problems that might be found at the cylinder. It is not uncommon, particularly on sailboats, to find a chain-driven pump mounted under the steering pedestal, connected to the steering wheel. In this case, the chain and both axles need to be carefully inspected. Keep the chain well tensioned.

When filling reservoirs with fluid after maintenance, use clean, compatible hydraulic fluid only. Carefully clean the fill plug before removal to prevent any dirt from getting into the fluid. Dirt in a hydraulic system is bad news. It will jam valves, score precisely machined components, and damage O-rings. These problems will allow fluid to pass by these components and the steering system will start to loose its "power."

Bleeding a hydraulic system of air is critical to proper operation. When filling a hydraulic steering system after servicing, it may be possible to remove any air from the helm pump or reservoir. With single steering-station installations, it is usually acceptable to open the bleed screw on the pump and operate the wheel from side to side. This will move the air along the line to the high point and allow it to escape. With multiple steering stations that are not connected with a common reservoir or return line, it may be necessary to start by rotating the wheel at the lowest station and work up to the highest station before all the air is bled away. Do not open a pump reservoir in a lower station if there is fluid in a system above the pump.

If the system has been emptied or hoses removed, you will need to bleed the cylinder. For a single-pump system, the process is relatively straightforward. First, ensure that bypass valve(s), if any, are closed. Then, locate and loosen slightly (do not open) the bleed valves on the steering cylinder.

With a full-helm reservoir, apply light pressure on the helm and further loosen the bleed valve on the cylinder, allowing fluid and air bubbles to escape. Continue to fill the helm reservoir as fluid is drained at the other end. When the fluid stream contains no more bubbles, close the valve and repeat the process on the other side of the cylinder by turning the wheel in the other direction. When the cylinder has no more air, rotate the wheel from side to side, working any air along the lines up through the system and out through the reservoir.

Multiple-station steering systems have check valves to ensure that each wheel drives the steering cylinder, not another wheel. Although bleeding the cylinder from the top wheel will work, you may need to bleed each steering pump to remove the air in its particular loop. It may sound a bit complicated, but it really is not when you take the time to sit down and understand the system. Here again, it makes good sense to understand the system and what kinds of service it may need before a problem arises. Read the systems manual and do not hesitate to contact the manufacturer or a yard.

PART 5

Electrical Systems

CHAPTER 17

An Overview of Marine Electrical Systems

Today's boats, both power and sail, are more reliant upon their electrical systems than their predecessors. Electronic navigation instruments, lights, stereos, and refrigeration, among other goodies, put an ever increasing strain on batteries and charging equipment. The sophistication of marine electrical systems has grown manyfold. As a result, boatowners are often not comfortable working with their electrical systems. Although some equipment definitely requires the experience of a trained service professional, there is a lot an owner can do to maintain, troubleshoot, and upgrade his or her boat's electrical system. This chapter is an introduction to the basics of batteries and chargers for those who have found the subject intimidating. Later chapters will examine in more detail the components of different systems and how to maintain, troubleshoot, and upgrade each.

Basic Systems

The accompanying drawing illustrates a basic battery system for a boat with only one battery and a minimum of accessories. This illustration shows only the main wiring. There are other circuits that relate to this system, but they have been left off for clarity.

This system's battery provides power to the main switch, which, in turn, supplies power to the engine for starting and to a panel that distributes the boat's accessories such as lights and electronics.

The engine is started by turning a key or pressing a button to activate a solenoid that closes the circuit, thereby allowing power to flow to the starter motor. Once the engine is running, the engine's alternator supplies power to the battery through the main switch.

The boat's DC equipment is supplied with power through the boat's electrical panel. These

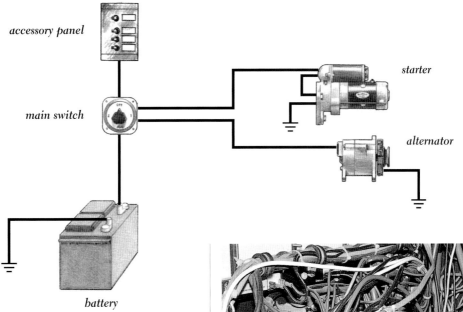

accessory panel

starter

main switch

alternator

battery

This is about as basic as it gets: a battery, an off/on switch, a starter motor, an alternator, and a distribution panel. These components, in one form or another, are found in almost every cruising boat with an engine.

This electrical panel has undergone a few too many quick-fix modifications. Following the logic of the wiring is difficult even though the panel is relatively small and simple.

appliances are commonly connected with two conductor cables. The positive supply comes from the panel, and the negative lead typically goes to a negative buss bar that is located close to the panel. In some cases, a single negative conductor will work with several positive conductors. Mast lights on a sailboat are a good example of this.

This system, although simple, can cause problems with electronics and other onboard equipment. The voltage drop caused by the engine's starting requirements can cause some devices to shut off or, in the case of navigation electronics, lose their position.

Complicating the system a bit more, but making it more comparable to most modern cruising boats, we add a second battery in the next drawing and change the type of main switch. This configuration allows the system to charge (and use, if desired) both batteries at the same time. The benefit of this system is that you can switch

from the "both" position to either of the two individual batteries. This will prevent discharging the other (reserve) battery if you run the lights or other equipment too long. You can switch to the reserve battery to start the engine if the other is too low, then switch to the parallel, or "both," position and recharge both batteries.

It is important with this type of system to avoid turning the battery switch off when the engine is running. Better marine switches have a field disconnect switch that stops the alternator from charging when the switch is disconnected. Not

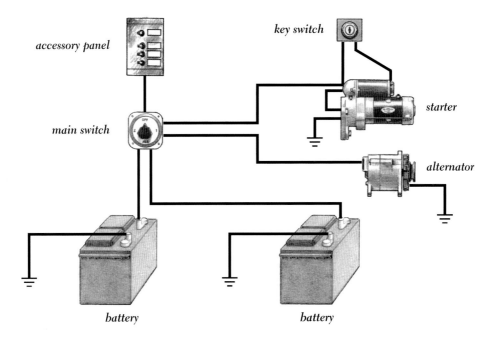

accessory panel

key switch

main switch

starter

alternator

battery

battery

(above) Adding another battery to the basic system provides a backup that will provide engine starting power if the lights or equipment drain too much power from the primary battery.

(below) This sketch shows the basic layout of a shore-power converter installation. Galvanic isolators and isolation transformers are being added to systems to help isolate the onboard system, but the basic concept starts with this type of layout.

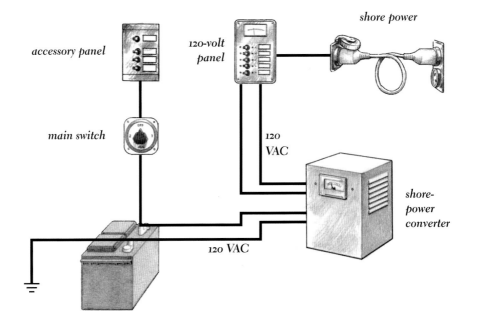

accessory panel

120-volt panel

shore power

main switch

120 VAC

shore-power converter

120 VAC

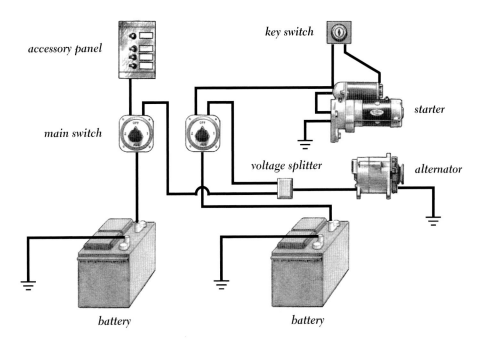

accessory panel

key switch

starter

main switch

voltage splitter

alternator

battery

battery

Adding a second switch and voltage splitter to the two battery systems allows for the isolation of the two systems (for example, the starting battery and the house battery). Now using up the house battery will not hurt the starting battery, and charging will be controlled automatically.

all switches work as designed, however, and damage to the alternator, loss of engine power (on gasoline and some small diesel engines), and possible arcing of the switch itself may result.

One final configuration that is common on Hinckley yachts is an improvement on these two systems: Add a second switch so you can isolate the two systems. Now you have dedicated batteries, switches, and wiring for each system. A variation on this system is to add a momentary switch and solenoid that will parallel the batteries to provide power to start the engine in case the starting battery won't do the job.

Hinckley now often installs a fully separate starting circuit for their customers that includes a separate key switch placed in an out-of-the-way area that uses the lighting batteries (not paralleled with the starting battery) to start

the engine. The circuit would be valuable if the starting battery was truly gone and a paralleling arrangement would not work.

momentary switch with solenoid

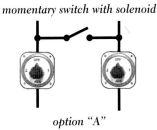

option "A"

Finally, if a momentary switch and solenoid are added to the system, the lighting system can provide emergency starting power to the starting system.

Adding a Shore-Power Converter

Now let's add another component to the system. If you are going to be tied up to a dock, you will probably want to add a shore-power converter.(I discuss the details of installation in Chapter 19.)

Isolation Transformers

Isolation transformers, which separate the wiring of the dock from the wiring aboard the boat, are not often found on domestic yachts less than 50 feet long. They transfer power magnetically through a transformer winding. With an isolation transformer, there is no ground path from the shipboard circuits to shore ground; therefore, the potential for shock and stray current flow to onboard gear is theoretically eliminated.

In their simplest form, isolation transformers have only hot (black) and neutral (white) conductor output. The American Boat and Yacht Council (ABYC) recommends a bare wire with green insulation be added to provide an onboard path for shorts in equipment or outlets to the ship's ground; doing so allows current to flow and the breaker to trip. If this path did not exist, a short from the hot line to the case would not cause current to flow because the case is isolated.

Isolation transformers are heavy and therefore are not often welcomed aboard boats. If you operate your boat overseas or in areas where shoreside power grounding is suspect, though, you should consider using one. Present changes in the standards for isolation transformers and other devices warrant a discussion with a marine wiring expert if you are thinking about upgrading 120-VAC supply equipment.

Let me now provide an overview of how a shore-power converter fits into the basic electrical system. The most common converters are 120-VAC systems; however, other voltage systems are not unusual in larger boats. This section will concentrate on 120-VAC systems.

The shore-power converter is actually only one component of a shore-power system that includes: source (dockside socket); shore-power cord; shipboard watertight socket (for connecting the shore-power cord); polarity light and/or alarm (to warn of reverse polarity); shore-power converter; and shore-power switch. Systems also frequently include a pilot light for indicating power to the system, voltage and amperage meters, a circuit breaker panel for power distribution, and other appliances.

Wiring for 120-volt systems normally consists of three conductors (as they do in shoreside installations): green is ground, white is neutral, and black is hot. The ground wire is common to the ship's ground at one location *except* if there is an isolation transformer, which eliminates the connection to shoreside ground.

Power is transmitted from a dockside outlet to the shipboard outlet via a cord. Internal wiring then connects to a polarity indicator placed between the neutral and ground lines.

If there is power on what should be the neutral line (because the hot and neutral are reversed) the light and/or alarm will be activated. Reversed polarity must be fixed immediately.

A fuse or circuit breaker is installed in the line to protect and disconnect the power from the boat's system. The protection is a double-pole breaker that disconnects both the hot and neutral lines. The wiring is then most often supplied to a circuit breaker panel which, in turn, provides power to the shore-power converter or other onboard 120-VAC appliances.

In its simplest form, the converter is a transformer that lowers the voltage, then a pair of rectifying diodes (which allow the current to flow in one direction only), changing the lower voltage to direct current. Current-limiting and voltage-regulation circuitry control the converter's output. The shore-power converter's output is provided to the batteries to charge them as required.

This overview of a basic electrical system should provide a basis for evaluating system components. Energy storage devices (batteries) and energy production equipment (alternators and chargers) are discussed elsewhere in this book, as are bonding systems and zincs. Below are some important components in electrical systems that boatowners should understand.

Fuses, Circuit Breakers, and Switches

Fuses, circuit breakers, and switches are the controls that operate and oversee the basic operation of the electrical systems on your boat. They tend to be forgotten in the overall maintenance program until something goes wrong. Here are a few things about their operation that may be of help in maintaining them and diagnosing problems.

Fuses

Fuses are seen less and less on the modern yacht. Not long ago, most production boats had panels with rows of fuse holders alongside circuit operating switches. It was incumbent upon the boat-owner to maintain a fairly large inventory of spare fuses to ensure that the proper fuse was used for replacement purposes. Today, most fuses have been replaced by circuit breakers, but in-line fuses are often still provided with electronic devices, and large, replaceable-element fuses provide protection for main lines near batteries. The proper replacement should be part of a boat's spare-parts kit. Using an improperly sized fuse may cause problems. If the fuse is too small, it might blow when the equipment is run; if it is too large, it won't protect the equipment from current damage.

Fuse holders and the fuses themselves often corrode in the marine environment. If a fuse or holder appears to have some corrosion, clean it with a mild abrasive material such as a fine-grit sandpaper or an abrasive pad.

Circuit Breakers

Circuit breakers have been a great boon to the boatowner. They typically just work. If, when you troubleshoot a problem and conclude that the circuit breaker is inoperative, try first to revitalize it by repeatedly clicking it on and off to clean the contacts. Then, if it is still not working, replace it with a comparable unit.

Switches

If you are upgrading or replacing switches, keep in mind two factors: quality and size. There is a wide spectrum of quality among switches—from the simplest toggle switch to larger, main battery switches. The best solution to picking a good-quality switch is to stick with the better-known manufacturers. Cole-Hersee and Guest both build quality marine products.

A quality switch won't do you much good, though, if you have selected the wrong one for the job. Switches have ratings, so double-check the load that you have (or will have) and be sure that the switch you are considering buying will handle the current requirements. Selecting improper components for a boat's electrical system is a common error, especially when it comes to switches and wire.

Overloaded Components

As equipment is added to a boat, electrical components that were properly designed to handle less gear become inadequate. A wire that handles the current feed to a panel that was sized for a 60-amp maximum when the boat was built might be pushed to its limit with the addition of refrigeration or extra lighting. As mentioned time and again within this section of this book, anyone working on an electrical system must be sensitive to the capacities of components and potential loads.

What are some solutions? Upgrading the components is certainly one. Make sure that main switches and breakers can handle the larger load and/or replace wiring with larger sizes. (See the tables on pages 219–220 for assistance with wire sizing.) Another approach is to divide the loads into smaller components. For example, remove the electronics from the panel and create their own panel with a separate feed from the main switch. Some components, such as anchor winches, may be best handled by having their own switch and breakers. These require so much current that they will create a negative influence on other equipment that shares the same circuitry. In extreme cases, where the load and distance are so great that wire sizing is a problem, a separate battery might be provided for such high-load items. Doing so, however, creates the need for another charging circuit.

CHAPTER 18

Batteries

Marine batteries are certainly not the most complicated part of a boat's electrical system, but for some people they are the source of the greatest headaches. Weak or dead batteries can be the bane of a good weekend cruise. We have learned to rely on the lights and navigation systems, not to mention the stereos and refrigeration, that are powered by these heavy black boxes. Most of us can not start our engines without them. It seems that we must learn to live with their limitations.

Battery Types

When designing electrical systems and selecting their components, it's often difficult to match the demands an owner will make of the batteries with the proper sizes and types of batteries. If you don't select batteries properly, you will constantly be dealing with electrical problems.

A battery is a battery is a battery, right? No! Not by a long shot. At first glance, the requirements for a marine battery may seem similar to those of an automotive battery but, in fact, most marine applications are quite different. Exceptions might be smaller craft with out-

boards and a few inboard powerboats that do not ordinarily use electrical equipment without the engine running. In these instances, electrical systems receive a constant source of power from the running engine, and batteries designed primarily for high cranking power are probably adequate.

Larger craft, however, especially sailboats, often run equipment when the engine is not supplying any power; these vessels must be able to rely on batteries as power-storage devices (unlike automotive applications). These boats need deep-cycle batteries to handle their lighting and equipment needs. Deep-cycle batteries are more heavily constructed than automotive batteries and are designed to handle longer-term power requirements and more repeated discharging.

For many years, most batteries found on boats were lead-acid storage batteries. Today, other types of batteries are gaining acceptance in the marine environment. Gel-cell batteries have become the battery of choice for many builders and owners. Although they once did not have the capability to service marine applications, that is no longer the case. Newer gel-cell batteries have increased deep-cycle capacity, are low maintenance, and often may be charged at a more rapid rate.

A new alternative to the gel-cell battery is the absorbed glass mat (AGM) battery. Like gel batteries, the AGM is a sealed battery. The AGM has a promising future; it stacks a lot of plate size in a small package, which gives it the capabilities of larger batteries.

A fourth type, nickel-cadmium batteries, are high performers but are too expensive for most boatowners.

Lead-Acid Batteries

As mentioned earlier, many boats use lead-acid batteries that undergo a chemical change as they charge or discharge. When a battery is newly charged, it might have a specific gravity of 1.280. (The specific gravity is the ratio of the density of the acid to water.) After a charging device is shut off, and the battery sits and stabilizes, that reading may drop back to around 1.265. A discharged battery might have a specific gravity of 1.135. The objective is to maintain a specific gravity of as close to 1.280 as possible.

As a charged battery discharges or provides current, the acid combines with the lead plate and creates lead sulfate. As it recharges, the sulfate is remixed with the water to produce a stronger acid. The heat created by the normal charging and discharging of a lead-acid marine battery consumes water in the electrolyte; the water then needs to be replaced—preferably with distilled water. It is important that the water in the cells covers the plates, but not be so high that it easily spills or boils out.

The condition of a battery's cells are most easily tested with a hydrometer (see ranges above), which should be standard equipment on your boat. A hydrometer will tell you the specific gravity of the acid (or electrolyte) in each cell. For accuracy, testing should be done after the battery has set without either a load or being charged for a short period to allow the battery acid to stabilize.

The acid from a cell is drawn up and into the body of a hydrometer, and a float inside indicates the specific gravity. The floats are typically marked to read at 80°F (26.7°C); you'll need to adjust the reading a bit for higher or lower temperatures. Many hydrometers have thermometers that aid this process. If you find a cell with a reading lower than 0.050 less than the highest cell reading, you should be suspicious of the condition of the lower cell. If one cell in a battery is wearing out and not accepting a full charge, it will restrict the entire battery to a lower charge.

If a lead-acid battery sits too long in a partially or fully discharged state, the plates will become sulfated, a condition that makes the battery appear (sometimes accurately) to be in poor condition. When left for an extended period, the sulfate on the plates becomes so hard that it will not easily return to the acid solution. If the sulfate is not too hard yet, you might be able to rejuvenate the battery by discharging and recharging it several times. Depending on the equipment that is available, you might turn on a resistance load, such as the lights, to discharge the battery. Do not discharge the battery by turning on the refrigeration system. DC equipment motors might be harmed as the battery voltage drops below its normal operating range. It is interesting that at least one battery manufacturer is now recommending you deep-cycle its batteries three or four times when newly installed to get full capacity from them. I think that a monthly deep-cycling is a good preventive maintenance procedure.

When recharging batteries, you must be careful of the charging rate. The batteries can become hot and the fluid in them will "gas" if too heavy a charge rate is applied. The gas is a mixture of hydrogen and oxygen, which is an explosive mixture in the wrong circumstances. A properly operating battery charging device will slow the charge rate as the battery becomes recharged, and the resulting lower rate will reduce the heat buildup. If the battery becomes dry while charging, the plates will warp and ruin the battery.

This is a good place for me to put in a pitch for careful examination of battery ventilation and installation procedures. Batteries need a clear, efficient ventilation system that allows for venting gases to the boat's exterior, and the batteries need to be securely fastened in place. These items are, unfortunately, too often not given sufficient consideration in boat construction.

Gel-Cell Batteries

Gel-cell batteries are much easier to maintain than lead-acid batteries. You do not have to add any liquid to them, nor do you need to check them with a hydrometer. Also, gel-cell batteries will sustain a deeper discharge/recharge cycle than lead-acid batteries, and with less damage. They may be installed in virtually any position and have less tendency to emit gas or corrosive acid fumes than lead-acid batteries; therefore, they can be installed in less accessible areas.

Although under normal conditions gel-cell batteries do not emit any fumes, they will build up excessive heat and release hydrogen and oxygen if they are charged too rapidly. They should be ventilated for this eventuality.

When overcharged, gel-cell batteries are less forgiving than lead-acid batteries—they might sustain permanent damage and gassing. The optimum recharge voltage indicated by one gel-cell battery supplier is 13.80 to 14.10 volts (2.30 to 2.35 volts-per-cell). They should not be charged at a rate in excess of 2.4 volts-per-cell (14.4 volts for a 12-volt battery) for a period longer than 16 hours. These voltages must be reduced considerably in warm (tropical) waters; there are tables available from manufacturers to help make this adjustment.

Because there is no practical way to test individual cells in a gel-cell battery, the inability of such a battery to accept or hold a charge is the indicator for replacement.

Battery Configurations

Marine batteries are predominantly sized or arranged to provide 12 volts of power, although both 24- and 32-volt systems are found aboard larger boats. Often, two, 6-volt batteries are used in series to create a larger capacity 12-volt battery.

Additionally, 12-volt batteries are sometimes placed in parallel to increase the system's total Ah (amp-hour) capacity. Combinations of the two methods (series and parallel) are common for lighting systems on larger cruising boats. The combination of four deep-cycle, 6-volt batteries in a series/parallel configuration creates a powerful battery system with lots of plate area that improves the recharging characteristics of the system. The accompanying illustration shows some common battery combinations.

An important point to remember when replacing or adding batteries to an existing system is to not mix battery types. If you have a lead-acid battery bank with one bad 6-volt battery, do not replace it with a gel-cell battery. The performance characteristics of the two types of batteries are not the same, and the differences will prohibit one or the other from operating properly. It is acceptable, however, to use starting batteries that are gel-cell and lighting batteries that are lead-acid, or vice versa, as long as they are used and charged by independent systems.

Starting Batteries

If you have selected the correct batteries, your starting batteries should be relatively trouble free. Take the time before a problem arises or when purchasing a new starting battery to review the design and installation of your starting system. Here a few hints for doing just that:

- Know you engine's cranking needs. You'll find the information in the engine's instruction manual.

- Compare that information with the battery specifications to be sure that the existing or new battery is up to the job. If a battery is to be used primarily as a starting battery and will not see the deep-cycle service described on page 187, a cranking battery will be adequate. Many boats, however, use the same battery for starting and lighting and therefore require a deep-cycle battery that also has the cranking capacity (cold-cranking ampere

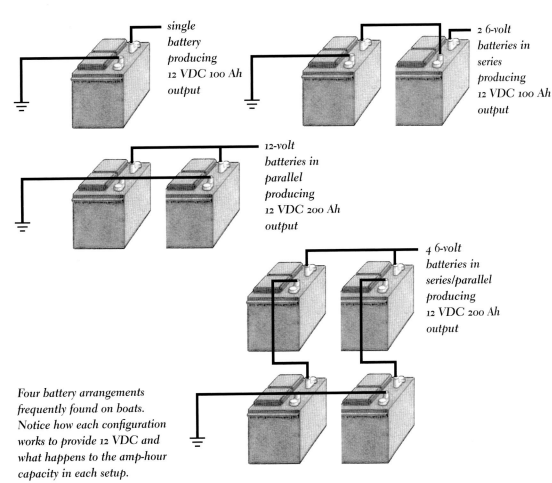

single battery producing 12 VDC 100 Ah output

2 6-volt batteries in series producing 12 VDC 100 Ah output

12-volt batteries in parallel producing 12 VDC 200 Ah output

4 6-volt batteries in series/parallel producing 12 VDC 200 Ah output

Four battery arrangements frequently found on boats. Notice how each configuration works to provide 12 VDC and what happens to the amp-hour capacity in each setup.

rating) to do the job. Such a battery will typically be larger, heavier, and costlier than the cranking battery.

- The cold-cranking amperes (CCA) of a battery is the important number to obtain — it indicates how many amperes can be delivered at a given temperature for a given time. Your battery is likely to get a workout on cold mornings. CCA assumes a temperature of 0°F (-17.8°C) and a cranking time of 30 seconds. As the temperature drops, two things are happening that affect the engine's ability to start on cold mornings: First, the engine is harder to turn over in colder temperatures; second, the battery's ability to deliver amperes to the starter is decreased in cold

weather. That is why it is so important to consider cold-cranking amperes. When in doubt, oversize.

- If the battery appears to be in good condition, is properly sized, and is still unable to do the job, make sure that all the connections are properly made and that the size of the battery cable is adequate and as short as possible. There will be a lot of current flowing through those wires and terminals when your starter calls for power. The current needs a clean, nonrestrictive conduit to the starter. If in doubt about the size of your cables, check the engine manual and/or oversize the cables. Remember that the cable size requirement increases dramatically with length. Most manuals include charts that list the required cable size for a given load and distance. It is important to remember that circuit length is measured in both directions—to and from the load.

Emergency Starting Provision

On boats with separate lighting (also sometimes called "house") and starting batteries, or two sets of batteries that can be switched separately, it is a good idea to have a provision for paralleling (connecting the batteries to provide more capacity) the starting and lighting batteries for emergency starting.

One way to do this is to install a main switch that lets you use either or both batteries by selecting "1," "2," "both," or "off" positions. This arrangement will parallel both batteries when it is turned to the "both" position. If you do not want both batteries paralleled except for starting purposes, a spring-loaded pull switch that operates a solenoid (which is needed because the current is too great for the switch), will prevent inadvertently leaving the batteries cross-connected for long periods of time.

Lighting Batteries

Lighting batteries present a slightly more difficult situation than starting batteries. They must work when the engine runs and when it's shut down; they must provide power for an extended time and supply that power at a fairly constant rate; and they must be able to accept a high rate of charge to reduce the charging time required to replace the power used.

Analyzing Lighting Battery Needs

If you have problems with your boat's lighting batteries being low on power or discharged too often, begin working on the problem by analyzing the load and their capacity. It is important that your battery or set of batteries is properly sized to service the load you require.

Calculate the Load

To calculate a battery's load, you first need to know the current rating in amp-hours (Ah) for every piece of electrical equipment on your boat. You'll find the Ah number for many appliances in their instruction manuals or on the equipment itself. For appliances whose power consumption is expressed in watts (light bulbs, for example), divide the watt rating by the voltage to obtain the amperage. For example, a 25-watt light bulb will require 25 (watts) divided by 12 (volts), or 2.08 amperes per hour (2.08Ah) of current.

After you have calculated the amp-hours used by each piece of equipment, estimate how many hours you run each appliance in a typical 24-hour period. Be generous. Build a table of this information and add up the total daily use estimates. Divide this number by 24 to find an average one-hour load.

Check the Battery Capacity

When you have figured the load in amp-hours for a given period, confirm that your battery capacity is several times greater than that load. The amp-hour rating for each battery should be on the battery specification sheet. Remember, if you have a 12-volt system with 6-volt batteries (or a 24-volt system with 6- or 12-volt batteries), batteries that are in series increase the current capacity; batteries that are in parallel increase the voltage.

Figuring the Margin

A boat with an average 24-hour load of 120 Ah should have a battery capacity of at least 300 or 400 Ah (more would be better). Manufacturers say that, by keeping batteries operating within the top 50 percent of capacity (for example, using only 100 Ah of a 200-Ah battery), their life is extended. So why is double the anticipated capacity not enough? Two reasons: First, the batteries will not likely perform right up to their specifications. Second, if you are like most boaters, you will add more equipment to the system, thereby increasing the load. If your battery capacity is substantially less than suggested, you will overwork the batteries and potentially reduce their life.

The same considerations for troubleshooting

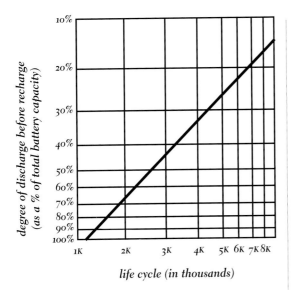

life cycle (in thousands)

Continuously using a large percentage of a battery's capacity will significantly shorten the battery's life.

a problem with a starting battery system are valid for lighting batteries. After you have examined the condition of the battery and its specifications, check the condition of the wiring and connections.

General Battery Maintenance

- Batteries and battery boxes should occasionally be cleaned with a rag and a mild solution of water and baking soda or baking powder. Be very careful not to allow any of the solution to enter the cells because it will impair the acid.

- Periodically remove the battery cables and clean the posts and cable clamps. Do not pry them off with a screwdriver. Normally, they can be removed by loosening the clamp, springing it apart, and manually wiggling the clamp back and forth. Be careful when removing cables not to allow loose cables or tools to short out. When everything is cleaned up, reinstall and cover the posts and terminals with petroleum jelly or other clean, light grease.

- If you have lead-acid batteries, keep a hydrometer aboard to check the specific gravity. If you do not have a good voltmeter, buy one. It will help you recognize a defective cell or other problems.

- Clean battery terminals or posts before they become coated with corrosion.

- If you are replacing a battery, look at the original warranty and specifications. Most battery manufacturers provide a prorated warranty which typically works something like this: If the battery was warranted for five years and lasted for four years without neglect or other charging problems, the supplier will credit 20 percent of the original price against the purchase of a new battery.

The moral of all this battery talk is: *pay attention to your batteries.* Choose batteries that meet your needs and be prepared to replace them fairly regularly if you are going to put them to strenuous use.

Battery Safety

A final word on battery safety: The gas that is emitted from batteries is explosive. Do not smoke when working on batteries. Remove any jewelry that might short on connections, and use insulated tools. Battery systems are not difficult to understand or diagnose, but they deserve a lot of respect.

CHAPTER 19

Alternators, Battery Chargers, Converters, and Inverters

Batteries are the storage portion of the power system upon which we have become so reliant, but they are not much good without a properly operating recharging system. The most common, and usually the fastest, way to recharge batteries is with an alternator. The alternator works in concert with a voltage regulator that tells it how to behave. When they are working in harmony, they are great. When they are not . . .

Alternators

Sizing the Alternator

An alternator, like batteries, needs to be matched to the job it is to perform. An alternator that is too small for the required recharging will take forever to bring batteries up to full charge. It is important to understand that a higher capacity alternator will be able to sustain a higher rate of charge over a longer period of time than will a smaller capacity unit — even though both units might be rated above the current requirement. Also, the nominal rating of an alternator is a charge rate that the alternator may never achieve in the field. As a rule of thumb, your alternator should be rated to perform at a minimum ampere level of one-third of your battery capacity. For example, a lighting system with a 400-Ah battery bank capacity should

(opposite page) Boats like this Hinckley 49 have duplicate systems for almost all electrical charging needs. To be self sufficient for long periods of cruising, it's important to have backup provisions for charging and engine starting.

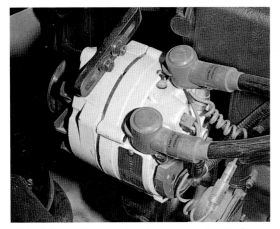

This Balmar alternator has two output circuits for charging both the starting and house systems. Internal circuitry controls the output to each system.

have a 135-amp alternator to supply reasonable recharging service. It is difficult to hold to this rule with some of the enormous battery banks used today, but not using a high-capacity alternator will extend charging time requirements. Remember: Any energy that you take out of your batteries, you need to put back in. Due to inefficiencies in the charging system, this typically requires replacing 120 percent of the energy taken out.

Basics of Diagnosing Charging Problems

It can be difficult to diagnose charging problems. Often, the first reaction is to assume that the alternator is not working when, in fact, the problem may have little to do with the alternator at all. So the first step is to do some basic detective work. Here is a plan to follow if you are having trouble with your charging system

Begin by checking the batteries. Are they healthy? Are they connected properly and are those connections well made? The answers must be "yes" before the alternator can do its job. (See Chapter 18 for more information on battery systems.) An alternator will not properly charge a damaged, dead, or badly installed battery. In some cases, it will overcharge and

cause excessive heat and gassing; in others it will undercharge or not charge at all.

If the batteries appear to be okay, next look at the alternator drive belts. Check for broken, badly worn, or loose belts. A large alternator that is being asked to provide a lot of recharging current will be a heavy load (up to several horsepower) for the engine and the belts. If the belts are not in good condition and/or properly tensioned, they can slip and provide little or none of the necessary drive for the alternator. Regularly check the condition of the belt(s) driving your alternator(s). Check the tension by firmly pushing on the belt; there should be ½-inch or less deflection. One word of caution: Overtightening the belts will induce extra wear on the belts and alternator bearings and can lead to misalignment or breakage of the alternator bracketing. If you note significant belt wear, determine the source of wear, fix it, and replace the belts. You should carry a spare set of belts aboard at all times. If improper alignment of the alternator appears to be the source of belt wear, take the time to realign the alternator bracketing. The Hinckley service department reports that alternator alignment is probably the single greatest cause of belt damage they see.

If you have a pair of belts driving your alternator, be sure to ask for a "matched pair" at the ship's store or wherever you buy your engine parts. At any rate, buy top-quality belts. They last longer and reduce friction in the system.

If neither the battery system nor belts seem to

Larger alternators require a lot of torque when they are charging hard. Two belts are commonly required, and they need to be checked regularly for tension and wear.

be causing the charging problem, test the voltage drop between the alternator output terminal and the battery positive terminal, using a multimeter. (See Appendix 1 for more information on using a multimeter). There should be less than 1 volt of voltage drop in the line. Greater voltage drop indicates some problem in the connections or cables.

The foregoing steps check the battery charging environment and, if all is in order, isolate the alternator and regulator as potential problem areas. Check the voltage regulator for correct operation and settings. With the engine running, measure the voltage across the terminals of the battery. When the engine is first started and the batteries require some charging, you should have a reading ranging from 13.8 to 14.4 volts—probably toward the higher end of the scale for lighting batteries. If your meter does not indicate this level of voltage, the problem may be either in the setting or the operation of the voltage regulator.

If the voltage is low and the regulator has an external adjustment, try changing it to attain the required voltage. If the system is not charging at all, you can eliminate the regulator for a short period by putting a jumper over it. (A trouble light with a 12-watt [or greater] bulb for resistance works well.) Disconnect the wire from the regulator to the field terminal on the alternator, at the alternator end. Connect the jumper between the positive battery wire and the alternator field terminal. If charging still doesn't occur, the alternator is probably bad. If charging starts, replace the regulator. If the alternator has an internal regulator, the alternator will need to be shop tested.

If the alternator has "seen" a voltage spike from not having a load available (switch turned off), the diodes in the alternator may be damaged. If the brushes are burned, the field coil will not be excited and the alternator will not produce current. For those who are comfortable working on alternators, replacing the brushes and diodes might not be overly difficult. The variations in alternator design and construction, however, make these repairs beyond the scope of this book. Nigel Calder's *Boatowner's Mechanical and Electrical Manual,* published by International Marine Publishing, is of great assistance in this area.

Preventive Maintenance for Alternators

What preventive maintenance should the alternator receive? Generally, not much. Good-quality marine alternators are reasonably trouble free. A light spray of CRC, WD-40, or other similar electrical coating or cleaner is a good idea to help keep the terminals and alternator casing corrosion free, and keeping the engine room dry and clean will slow the drawing of oil and grit through the alternator's fan.

Heat is a great killer of alternators. Both excessive charge rates for prolonged periods and inadequate engine room ventilation will decrease an alternator's life by breaking down the lacquered coating on coils and contributing to brush and bearing wear. Replacing the brushes in alternators every few years is a good idea. It is a lot easier to deal with the small parts in a well-lit shop or on a steady table than on a rocking boat at sea.

Carrying Spare Alternators

Many offshore boaters carry a spare alternator and voltage regulator so they can replace a worn or damaged unit and keep moving while the old part is being repaired. This is a practice I highly recommend for those who venture far from port.

If you are not able or inclined to carry complete spare units, at the very least keep a spare set of brushes aboard—and learn how to replace them.

Battery Chargers and Converters

Another method of replacing the energy taken from your batteries is to use battery chargers and converters. These units take 120-volt AC (or other high voltage) from a source, convert it to 12-, 24-, or 32-volt alternating current via a transformer, and finally convert it to direct current used in the batteries by passing it through rectifying diodes. Chargers and converters are usually dockside appliances, although they also can be used with onboard AC-generators when the main engine is not running. When the main engine is running, its alternator should charge faster than the charger or converter.

Many chargers and converters have multiple output lines. The better converters are built with voltage-regulation circuits, which work like the voltage regulators used with alternators. They have line compensation circuits that adjust for input voltage variances, and they have ignition protection that shuts the unit off if the engine is started.

Unregulated low-current battery chargers (called "trickle chargers") are occasionally used by some owners, but they are not designed for marine applications. These units work if they are closely supervised, but they do not sense a fully charged battery; that is, they do not stop charging when the battery reaches full charge. The excessive charging can result in the electrolyte being boiled off, which will wreck the battery and may cause explosive gases to build up. If you use a trickle charger, I recommend that you monitor it closely, do not leave it unattended for long periods of time (no more than a few hours), and, if you are using lead-acid batteries, regularly test them for electrolyte level and temperature.

A more sophisticated charger is the shore-power converter; the better units are automatically regulated. Some will sense potential differences between the charger and the battery and adjust output to keep the battery at the potential of the charger. Others have a constant current output that will boost the battery charge faster—but be aware that these have the potential for overcharging if they are not carefully adjusted.

Newer chargers are a combination of the potential-current–sensing and constant-current–sensing units. They hold a higher charge rate for a longer period, but when a preset voltage is achieved they switch to potential sensing mode for the final charging, which helps protect the batteries from overcharging. These units still charge at a relatively low rate and require long charging times (compared with a well-chosen alternator).

Troubleshooting a Battery Charger

There is not a great deal the average boatowner will want to tamper with in a marine charger or converter. When the charging output is too low, however, here are a few trouble-shooting tips:

1. First, check the onboard circuit breakers. Are they in the "on" position? Many boats with onboard generators or inverters have other switches to select the power source. Make sure that they are set in the right position.

2. Next, check the source of power at the dock or generator. Dockside wiring and shoreside breakers in marinas are notorious for malfunctioning. In some units, built-in compensation circuitry somewhat makes up for slightly low shoreside voltage; without that circuitry, low voltage will slow the charging rate.

3. Check any fuses or circuit breakers mounted either in the face or inside of the unit.

4. Inspect the converter's built-in fuses and/or breakers. (There are often more than one.) Larger units will have fuses in the AC line (both hot and neutral) and a fuse or breaker in the DC-output circuit. They might be accessible only from the interior of the unit. Be sure to disconnect the power before removing the cover to the converter.

5. If the 120-volt side of the system appears to be in order, inspect the low-voltage output side. Are the main battery switches in the right position? Is the wiring in place and in good order? It is possible to test the output of the converter by testing the voltage across the battery terminals, first with the converter off, and then with it on. You should see a voltage increase when the converter is on, unless the batteries' voltage is already topped off and the converter's regulator is set low.

6. If you have a multiple-battery charging output with only one sensing circuit, do you have the sensing circuit connected to a fully charged battery? If yes, the sensor would likely be telling the converter to stop charging, leaving the undercharged battery low. One way to fix this is to connect all batteries in parallel via a switch or jumper while charging. Remember, though, to remove the jumper when done.

Inverters

The inverter is the new thing in onboard conveniences. This neat device takes 12- or 24-volt DC input and converts it to 120 VAC for onboard use. Essentially, it is a transformer that works to step up the voltage, plus an electronic setup that creates alternating current from the DC output. The output of most units can be used for intermittent loads such as lights, heaters, toasters, and some motors, as well as computers and microwaves.

Some units even combine a converter and an inverter in one package. The best combination units have circuitry that senses when 120-VAC line (shore or generator power) is available, automatically disables the inverter functions, and enables the battery-charging feature. It is critical that the inverter not be putting out 120-VAC power when there is another source available.

The downside of these seemingly miraculous boxes is that they require lots of DC power to operate. Charging the batteries is inefficient (if 100 amps are drawn from a battery in an hour it may take 120 amps for an hour to replace the charge), as is the conversion to 120 VAC. This means you'll need to allow some margin for battery size and charging time.

It is also important to note that the output is not *exactly* like the power coming aboard from a shore cord or a generator. Inverter output may vary from a close approximation of the standard "sine wave" output to "modified sine wave," which may not be the best type of output for some loads. Motors may not run correctly on "modified sine wave" units.

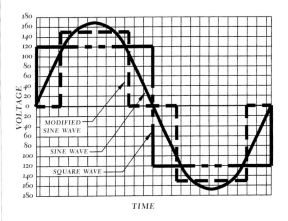

An inverter that produces as close to a sine wave output as possible is critical to the operation of many appliances. Inverters that put out square or modified sine waveforms may not work with all appliances.

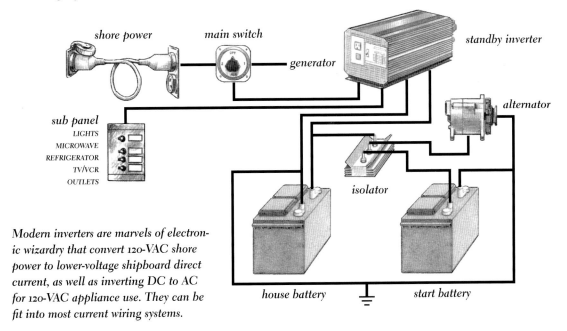

Modern inverters are marvels of electronic wizardry that convert 120-VAC shore power to lower-voltage shipboard direct current, as well as inverting DC to AC for 120-VAC appliance use. They can be fit into most current wiring systems.

CHAPTER 20

Bonding Systems

There are many opinions about the best layout of a bonding system for a vessel, including opinions as to whether a bonding system should be used at all. The idea behind a bonding system is to provide a common level of electrical potential among all the metal components of a boat that might corrode in the saltwater environment if an electrical current is passed through the water to the fittings. One group of experts believe that the bonding of boats only provides an easy path for electrical current between metal fittings in the boat, and is therefore more harmful than helpful. Another group believes that it's almost impossible to eliminate stray current and difference in electrical potential from different metals; therefore, they reason, it is important to provide a bonding system to minimize the transfer of metals between fittings due to this electrical potential difference, and to provide a sacrificial metal (zinc) to prevent more important metals (engines and seacocks) from corroding. The zinc is critical to making the system work.

Because this book is about Hinckley company techniques, and because Hinckley uses a bonding system, in this chapter I'll discuss what you should expect in a bonding system, what type of maintenance might be necessary, and how to install or upgrade a bonding system.

The typical bonding system in a Hinckley yacht consists of a network of uninsulated copper strapping. Hinckley uses strapping because it provides a large cross section of metal along with maximum surface area.

The network connects all the seacocks, fills, rigging components (including chainplates for shrouds), forestay and backstay, keel, engine (where it shares a common connection with the DC and AC [if any] grounds), electronics, and potentially a groundplate for a radio such as a single-sideband, or for improved contact with the water. The main run of the bonding system, which on a midsized auxiliary might extend from the engine to the mast, is usually malleable copper strap, 3 or 4 inches wide by about $\frac{1}{16}$ inch thick. Branches from the main run range from 1 to 4 inches wide, depending on the equipment connected. Radio gear is typically connected with larger sizes. Some other builders and electricians prefer an insulated, coarse, multistrand wire

This sketch shows the basic layout of a bonding system. The main circuit runs from at least the mast to the keel and back to the engine. Branches are installed to equipment, rigging, and other metal components.

which has been effective in many installations.

A bonding system also provides a minimum resistance path for lightning strikes by directing the current to the keel of the boat. The system is particularly effective when a boat has an external lead keel and/or heavy groundplates that permit a path of minimum resistance to the water from the rigging. However, a bonding system will not necessarily provide foolproof protection from a lightning strike. It is reasonable to expect damage to electronics and other electrical equipment connected to the bonding system because of the magnitude of the voltage surge.

Checking Out an Existing System

When checking an existing ground system, take time to examine each metal fitting that contacts salt water to ensure that the bonding system is connected to it and that the connection is not corroded, thereby increasing resistance. Additionally, make sure there is no evidence of electrolysis at the fitting. In its early stages, electrolysis may show as a greenish blue powder, particularly on the surface of bronze seacocks, or as pitting of the metal.

Connecting Equipment

If a piece of equipment or fitting is not connected to the bonding system, attachment is often best accomplished by installing a ring terminal on stranded wire or folding copper strap over on itself

This is a portion of the bonding in a Hinckley. Note that the wide conductor is connected to a chainplate. This will provide a good path for lightning as well as for more mundane bonding functions.

and then punching or drilling a hole in the strap. Insert this end over one fastener bolt for the fitting and place a second washer and nut over the strapping. Unless there is no alternative, I do not recommend you remove one of the fasteners holding the equipment or fitting in place. Some seacocks and other equipment have screws tapped into their bases to permit attachment of bonding.

Common Connections

Check the engine. It is normal to bring the bonding to the same position as the negative ground of the ship's low-voltage (12-, 24-, or 32-VDC) electrical system (on a boat that is electrically grounded). This should be the only common point between the bonding system and the boat's electrical system. It is important to note that bonding, although it makes a nice metal path, is not intended to be an electrical return line the way metal might be on a car or truck, where the chassis provides electrical (negative)

return and a single wire provides positive power to many of the accessories. This will not work on a boat.

Shaft Protection

Make sure that the bonding system's connection to the shaft is well made. Shafts are often electrically isolated because the transmission is gasketed from the block and the coupling paint is also an insulator of sorts. Consider installing brush contacts to the shaft if you are concerned about this connection.

Zincs

Finally, the system must be well connected to sacrificial zincs that are reasonably close to other metal fittings. These zincs, which may be mounted on the keel, shaft(s), rudder(s), or just to the bonding by a bolt through the hull, will corrode in lieu of the fittings as the bonding does its job. It is important to use zincs and to replace them before they are completely corroded. Make sure to check engine zincs also. Review the engine manual for locations. If they disappear, the other metals will start to corrode, starting with the least noble — which may be the engine components.

System Layout

An owner should develop a "map" of the bonding system on his or her boat. It will be an excellent tool when diagnosing corrosion problems. In the process of developing the map, the owner becomes familiar with all the branches of the bonding and is forced to examine the completeness of the layout; that is, are all the necessary components connected? The map is also an invaluable tool for an electrician or other specialist diagnosing a problem aboard.

New Options

There are a number of new instruments available that provide protection from electrolysis problems. These instruments sense electrical potential in a yacht and then set up an opposite charge of equal potential to offset the resident charge. Although they are not terribly common as yet, the instruments are reported to work well. I, however, have had little experience with them.

Hints on Retrofitting a Bonding System

Inventory and Layout

The place to start installing a bonding system on an existing boat is by making a list of the critical components and then placing them on a diagram of the boat. Critical components include the following: engines, generators, keel, rigging components, metallic tanks, deck fills, centerboard trunk fittings, maststep, electrical panel, and cases of items such as converters and through-hulls, including both seacocks and stuffing boxes. With most systems, it is also important to connect the propeller shafts and rudderpost as well, the stuffing box because they are somewhat isolated by gaskets and poor electrical connections.

Next on the drawing, determine what will be the common point of the ship's negative and the bonding system. This is normally on the engine block or mount of the main engine or one of the main engines. On a boat with an internal ballast, or on a powerboat, it's a good idea to install a groundplate to provide good contact service with the outside water. The groundplate ensures a good electrical contact with the water surrounding the boat—which is important to complete the electrical circuit. A groundplate often is an improvement over an external keel, because the water contact is better with a ground-plate than a painted keel.

Selecting Materials

When an appropriate layout is in place, it is time to select the materials you will use to create the system. The choices are pretty much standard wire and copper strapping. Most electricians will recommend you use coarse-stranded wire of number four gauge or larger; that it be colored green if insulated; and that, wherever possible, crimped fittings be used on the ends.

There are a lot of opinions about whether the crimped fittings should also be soldered. Hinckley does not solder terminals because doing so hardens the wire-to-terminal joint and does not substantially improve the contact over a well-crimped fitting.

Fitting the System

First lay out the main runs, such as the run from the engine to the keel and maststep. Then bring the branches to the main run in the shortest lengths possible. I have seen systems with individual runs from every fitting to the main, as well as systems with fittings wired in series to the main. The use of individual runs to the main run provides better protection, because a damaged wire will isolate a single fitting rather than several, but it does involve much more wire and is more complicated to install.

Connections

Ensure there are tight connections at all of the fittings and at the junctions of branches to the main, because any loose connections will defeat the purpose of the bonding system.

PART 6

Masts, Sails, and Rigging

CHAPTER 21

Sail Care and Maintenance

The evolution of sails, in both shape and material, has been fascinating to watch over the last twenty or so years. Sail design has come a long way. Sails made out of newer Kevlar and Mylar fabrics are able to hold their shape more accurately than the older sails, although for durability, the better weaves of Dacron are the best, in my opinion.

Changes in sail care have accompanied the changes in sail shape and fabric. New sails represent a huge investment for the sailboat owner, and it's important that you understand the needs of the fabric, as well as some basic maintenance techniques. What follows are a few tips for keeping your sails in good condition, including washing advice, suggestions for daily care, and some lessons in rudimentary sail repair procedures.

The stable, modern fabrics require more careful handling than the traditional synthetic fabrics whose easy care spoiled sailors of a few decades ago. The resin in the fabrics is susceptible to breaking down when roughly furled. Roller-furling main- and headsails mean that many sailors don't have to deal with the task of day-to-day sail storage. Those who don't have roller-furling gear are flaking their high-tech as well

as cruising sails to reduce wear and tear on the fabric; flaking reduces hard corners in the fabric. Additionally, sails are dried carefully to lessen the potential for mildew attacking them while they are stored.

Sails that have been exposed to lots of salt water, either from spray or from drooping overboard, should be rinsed and dried before they are stored. Roller-furling sails should be clean and dry, as should bagged or boom-furled sails.

Following, for your consideration, are some ideas on sail care.

Visual Inspection

Annual care for sails delivered to a sail loft starts with a full inspection on the loft floor. A trained sailmaker reviews the high-wear areas in great detail and makes a walk-around inspection of the entire sail, flipping it to examine the stitching on both sides. The sailmaker notes any discrepancies or problems, and if necessary the owner is called to discuss any major repairs. Finally, the sailmaker records any signs of mold or special stains that are on the sails.

Although most boatowners don't have a sail-

These wide, drooping folds are easier on the sail fabric than the tighter bends and folds of conventional sail furling.

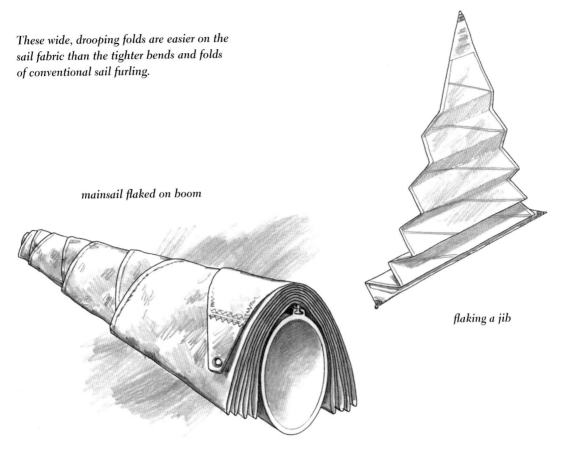

mainsail flaked on boom

flaking a jib

maker's experienced eye for detecting problems, they can perform much of the same inspection procedure during the daily use and storage of sails. A wear spot created by a spreader tip or a fraying luff slide attachment are easier to fix before the damage destroys adjacent fabric. And always keep a sharp eye out for the beginning signs of mildew.

Washing Sails

In the sail-washing area of the Fortune Sailmaker loft, sails are laid out on a large, extremely smooth concrete floor and then rinsed with cold water and a mild laundry detergent. Using a clear laundry detergent is important to prevent staining problems. The detergent is mixed with water in a large bucket before it's splashed onto the sails, to keep any concentrated detergent from touching them. Fortune washes the sails with a small hand brush and a soft, long-handled bristle brush. Dick Fortune told me that they had experimented with using a pressure washer to wash sails, but they determined that the pressure wore out the threads too rapidly—not only on sails, but also on dodgers and other canvaswork. They also found that traditional machine-washing of sails was too tough on the weave of the sails, particularly Dacron. The fabric breaks down with the excessive motion from a machine wash. Therefore, they have elected to wash sails by hand.

The objective of washing sails is to remove salt and grime. Salt acts as an abrasive and wears down the sail's surface, promoting early deterioration of the cloth and the stitching. Of course, salt also attracts and holds moisture—any sails that are stored with salt on them are ripe for developing mildew. Sails that are "put to bed" while either wet or saturated with salt crystals are likely candidates for accelerated fabric deterioration. Be careful, though, when washing your sails not to overscrub them. It's very clear that overzealous cleaning can be a serious factor in sail wear.

Treating advanced mold and mildew on sails may be a problem best left for professional sailmakers. You might try, however, using a judicious amount of a liquid bleach with a small brush on areas with mold. Use excess amounts of water to both pre-wet and rinse the bleach from the sail. If it doesn't work, sailmakers use commercial bleaches to treat mold and mildew, but they hesitate to recommend them for noncommercial use because the chemicals are potent and can damage sails if used improperly. They recommend sailors use mild forms of bleach—and that a conference with a sailmaker would be prudent prior to treating severely stained or mildewed sails.

Washing Kevlar sails is a little different from washing the more conventional Dacron sails. No soap is used when washing Kevlar sails; they are only rinsed. Further, no bleaches or detergents are allowed for spot cleaning on Kevlar sails because the chemicals can harm the fabric. Because their sandwich construction is a prime breeding ground for mildew, sails made from Mylar and Kevlar are particularly susceptible to the nasty stuff.

Here is an interesting fact that Fortune sailmakers discovered in the process of washing a J-44 spinnaker: They weighed the sail both before and after cleaning and determined that they had reduced a forty-pound sail to twenty-nine pounds—they had removed eleven pounds of salt from the sail. Considering the importance of weight aloft, serious racers should consider thoroughly rinsing their sails during their season—not just at layup time.

Keeping Sails Dry

In other sections of this book, I've discussed the problems of putting wet sheets, lines, and sails in sail lockers. Not only do the lockers become wet and moldy, so do all the parts and pieces in them. Whenever possible, I recommend that you air-dry any sails that have fallen overboard or have been used in rain. Granted, it's easier to air-dry sails when you are on a mooring or at anchor than tied to a dock. It is common to see boats flying sails from the stern when drying them at a mooring.

Sail lofts have drying rooms for hanging wet sails and fans to promote drying. Obviously, most sailors don't have access to a clean, controlled environment such as this. But if you can find a room large enough for your sails to hang, perhaps with just the clew pulled up, it makes good sense to dry them inside.

Prolonging Sail Life

What about the different treatments sailmakers offer for new and used sails? It appears that there is a significant advantage to treating sails, both for preventing seam wear and mildew.

Having a sailmaker apply a Tough Seam or seam coat (a clear coating) on seams protects the stitching from chafe and sun damage. The process is not foolproof, but it does add to the longevity of a sail.

Applying a mildew inhibitor over the entire fabric is another way to improve sail life. Discuss any treatment, though, with your sailmaker. These treatments are usually done when a sail is new; they certainly should be done in the early years of a sail's life. Sailmakers generally agree that it's not worth applying seam coating on sails older than four years, because some of the stitching is already worn and ready to be repaired or replaced.

Another way to prolong the life of roller-furling sails is to use the special sailcovers that are designed for them. The covers are actually a band of fabric applied along the foot and leech of the furling headsail. The covers are sacrificial and provide UV protection for the sail underneath. UV coating on the covers themselves helps prolong their lives. These covers work best in light colors that do not increase the heat inside the bundle, although it is not unusual to see them in dark colors. Most roller-furling

This basic stitch will hold together a ripped sail. It also works well combined with a tape repair.

covers are made in about 3.9-ounce Dacron fabric. A white, adhesive UV material that feels very similar to vinyl is also used; its weight is approximately 2 ounces per square yard.

Covers such as these are very common on furling sails and are almost always offered when sails are made. They can be added to an existing sail as well.

Shipboard Sail Repair Kit

There are times when sail repair aboard a boat at sea is unavoidable. Therefore, I recommend the following items for your repair kit:

Insignia cloth. This sticky-back Dacron tape comes in widths of 1 to 6 inches; 4 to 6 inches is probably the most valuable to have aboard. It can be used on Mylar and Kevlar sails, as well as Dacron. The sail should be clean and dry before applying insignia cloth. Apply it to both sides of the sail in the area of tears, extending it several inches beyond a cut in either direction. In a high-stress area, stitch around a tear to further reinforce the patch.

Hand sewing needles and wax thread. You will need these items to stitch sails and reinstall grommets or sail slides. The wax thread is similar to conventional #368 thread.

Stainless steel external rings. These are handy for sewing onto clews or tacks as replacements or additions to existing rings. Discuss with a sailmaker the sizes that are appropriate for your boat; the sailmaker can probably provide the rings.

Hanks and slides. If your sails have hanks or slides on the luff, you should carry spares. If the hanks or slides use shackles or vinyl chafe guards, carry spares of them as well.

Webbing material. One-inch webbing material, similar to that used in more rugged safety harness tethers, is valuable to have aboard. It can be used for reinforcing clews of sails by stitching in a radial pattern from a corner. On some boats, small webbing can be used for attaching sail slides. Webbing material has any number of other functions aboard the boat, including use as sail ties and jack lines.

CHAPTER 22

Masts and Rigging

Standing tall and majestic, most modern rigs do their job with a minimum of maintenance and fuss. Aluminum, and now carbon fiber, spars require little care compared with wooden spars of old. They do, however, need some attention and basic maintenance between the infrequent overhaul and repainting chores.

In this chapter I will look at some important inspection, troubleshooting, and maintenance methods for masts and rigging. Additionally, I will discuss adding fittings to an aluminum spar.

A thorough visual inspection is the starting point for rig maintenance. Both the spars and the rigging should be carefully checked on a regular basis. How often? For a boat that is kept in the water year-round, I suggest going aloft and looking at the sheaves, cotter pins, blocks, and other fittings twice a year.

Anytime you are about to undertake a lengthy passage, take the time to review the whole rig. If you have the rig pulled once a year, when the boat is stored, inspect it before it is reinstalled. If you do not pull the rig on a regular basis, inspection is more difficult, but even more important because some problems may be hidden inside the spar.

Inspecting the Mast

What problems should you look for with aluminum spars? Here are a few general troubleshooting spots to look for and tips for preventing or repairing them:

- Inspect the spar carefully, looking for loose fasteners, broken or missing cotter pins, chafe, cracks, and bent fittings. Try to turn the screw heads with a screwdriver; if they are loose, they may just need tightening. They also may be ready to drop out.

- Remove any tape that has been placed over fittings where a cotter pin or lock nut is located. You cannot thoroughly inspect a fitting through tape, and the tape probably should be replaced anyway. Put your hand on fittings and try to move them. Sheaves should move, cleats should not. You will be surprised by what you occasionally find in this simple inspection.

(opposite page) From the simple cotter pin to equipment such as this hydraulic furler, spars and rigging must be regularly inspected and serviced.

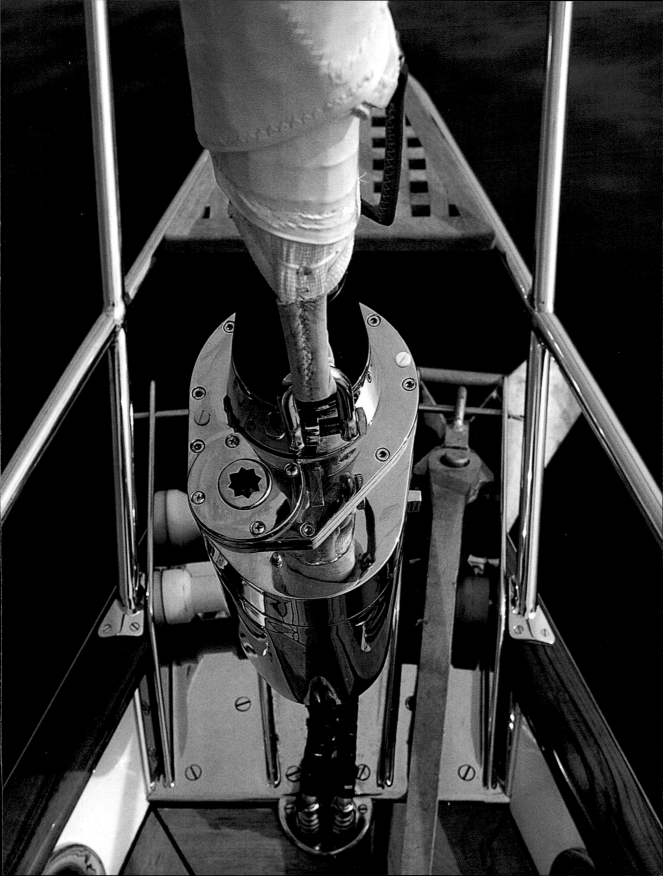

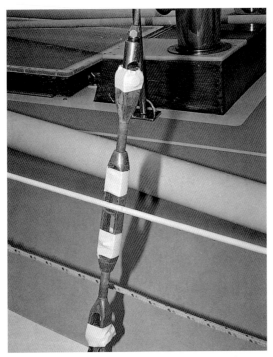

Take the time to remove the tape and inspect the cotter pins or locknuts on turnbuckles.

This mast suffers from mast corrosion. A view of the interior would reveal the same conditions, or worse. Notice the deep pitting near the base, indicating the need for serious repairs.

Mast Corrosion

Corrosion on a mast, particularly at the base or butt, can be a big problem. It is often hidden on the inside of the tube, which makes it harder to find. Corrosion first appears as a lifting of the coating on painted spars. On bare, anodized, or waxed spars, the early signs are powdering of the metal and pitting and bubbles in the surface.

The best prevention from corrosion is to keep a dry spar with a good protective coating. If the spar is painted, keep a touch-up kit aboard; sand and touch-up paint dings. If the spar is not painted, apply a coat of zinc chromate along the bottom edge and up inside the tube. Also, consider waxing the spar. Another idea is to apply a good marine grease on the butt of the spar before stepping it.

If the spar is out of the boat, inspect both the inside and outside of the tube. When the spar is in the boat it is difficult, if not impossible, to determine the condition of the tube's interior. Tap on the spar base and listen for dullness or changes in sound that indicate deterioration of the aluminum. Occasionally, holes near the base—such as those for wires—let you inspect a bit of the mast interior.

If you haven't pulled the spar for several years, the interior inspection problem should be of concern. If there is corrosion on the outside of the tube, assume there's corrosion on the inside, too—and probably more severe. Corrosion at the mast base reduces the mast wall thickness and, therefore, its strength. Uneven corrosion reduces wall thickness in a manner that concentrates stress on the other (less corroded) areas. The eventual result is collapsing of the tube and shortening of the spar with the potential of a complete failure of the spar. If you have not recently inspected the base of your spar, do it.

If you are experiencing slack rigging, don't assume that the rigging is stretching. Don't just tighten the rig. Look for deterioration of the mast base. Mast corrosion is usually caused by moisture or dissimilar metals. Water leaking down the tube will create moisture problems. Sheave boxes, gooseneck fittings, and other openings in the spar all allow small amounts of water into the interior of the spar. The base of the mast and the maststep must be designed and constructed to accommodate this fact of life.

A maststep constructed with a collar that is cast or welded to a plate is common and works well to hold the mast in position. Unfortunately, if it is not well drained, it can hold moisture. Holes should be cut at the bottom of the retaining collar to allow drainage.

Another restriction might be at the bottom of the mast itself. If the bottom of the spar is cut accurately, without allowing for drainage, the spar itself may tend to hold water. As time passes, junk accumulates in the bottom of the tube. Without a doubt, it is important to have a good bearing surface on which to spread the mast compression load, but a small drain notch or two in the bottom edge of the mast tube won't hurt. If already in place, check to see that these holes line up with the holes in the step collar. This helps if you need to pass a tool through the holes to clean out any clogs.

An alternate design for a maststep is to have it retained by a structure inside the spar; doing so reduces the problem of water being retained by a maststep collar. Even the best maststep design will not eliminate corrosion problems if the maststep is located too low in the bilge or if the bilge water level is allowed to become too high on a regular basis. The design and/or construction of the boat may make a wet maststep difficult to avoid. If so, consider installing a high-quality, reliable pumping system that keeps the water level as low as possible or isolating the step from the rest of the bilge. Raising the maststep may be an option.

Another potential cause of mast corrosion is the interaction of dissimilar metals. Although aluminum masts and stainless steel maststeps are not entirely compatible (stainless is more noble, or stable, than aluminum), they usually are not a big problem if they are kept dry. When frequently or constantly wet, however, the aluminum will corrode quite quickly. Copper wire or bonding strips connected directly to the aluminum mast can also cause a problem. Install an insulating

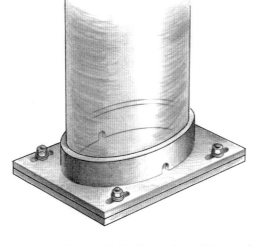

A maststep with a welded collar works well but needs good drainage to allow moisture to drain from the mast butt and collar.

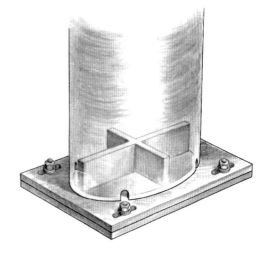

Maststeps with structures that sit inside the mast tube work well and do not retain unwanted moisture as the collar types do.

material between the copper and the aluminum to prevent rapid deterioration of the aluminum. A piece of insulating plastic with a stainless steel bolt through it would be an improvement as a bonding terminal. Depending on the step design, attaching the bonding wire or strap to the mast-step (if stainless) may suffice.

So what do you do if you have severe corrosion at the bottom of your mast? Provided that the rest of the spar is in reasonably good condition, consider sistering the tube on either the inside or outside. First, I should say that this type of work is best done by a yard with good metal-working and spar repair capabilities. It is important that the design and construction of a repair be carefully considered with either the original mast or boat manufacturer, a qualified surveyor, or other appropriate engineering assistance. This type of reinforcement involves

forming an aluminum ring that fits inside (or possibly outside) the mast tube and fastening it into place through the original tube where the material is sound. See the accompanying illustration.

For spars that are too deteriorated for this type of repair, one step you might consider (before replacing the spar) is removing the corroded section and adding a new piece on the bottom. Of course, this involves finding a new piece of the mast section that is the same as the original spar and of sufficient length to replace the damaged section. Attach the replacement piece with a splice section inserted into the remaining section of the old spar and in the new piece to provide alignment and strength. Connect with fasteners or welding. This method is the same technique used to connect two tube sections in a long spar.

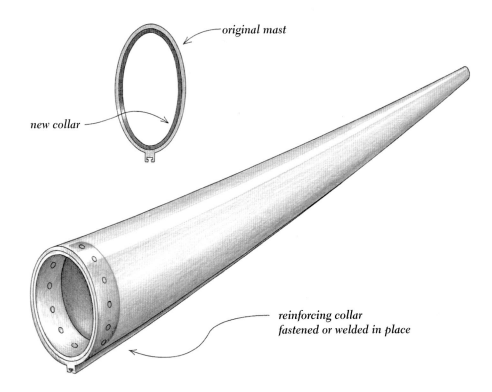

original mast

new collar

reinforcing collar
fastened or welded in place

Adding a collar inside a corroding mast butt may be
a way to repair damage to the spar.

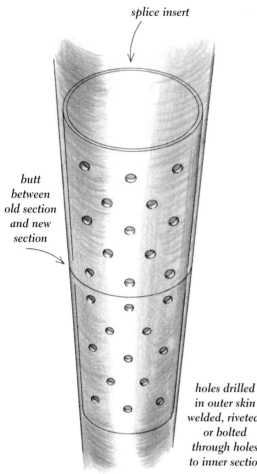

splice insert

butt
between
old section
and new
section

holes drilled
in outer skin
welded, riveted,
or bolted
through holes
to inner section

Another way to repair severe mast corrosion is to replace a piece of the mast. This requires locating another section of tube to match the existing spar, but the repair will be sound.

Wedges, Collars, and Boots

Moving up the mast, inspect the mast collar, wedges, and mast boot. Leaks in these areas are common, as are problems with wedges.

When looking for potential leaks in the mast collar area, look carefully at mast collar bolts. Even with a good mast boot preventing water from coming down the mast, pressure on the

bolts will create leaks—particularly if the mast collar side load is transmitted to the bolts only. An excellent way to reduce mast collar leaks and stress is to build the collar with a vertical flange that surrounds the mast and protrudes through the deck laminate. If the laminate is thick enough to withstand some loading and the collar is fit well or bedded in glass or epoxy, the flange will distribute lateral load to the deck over a larger area than will the bolts alone, thus reducing the tendency of the bolts to move and cause leaks.

For years, most mast wedges were made of hardwood. They seemed to work fine for a while, but eventually they cracked, and they often were lost overboard when the spar was removed. An improvement has been the use of hard rubber or neoprene wedges that wrap around the spar. If fit well, these synthetic wedges seem to hold up. A downside to the synthetic wedges is that they seem to "walk" or squeeze out of the collar. Using a large hose clamp or multiple layers of tape above them will help hold them in place.

When installing wedges around a conventional spar, place them so that the front and back of the spar are completely supported, leaving only a small section at the sides, if any, unsupported.

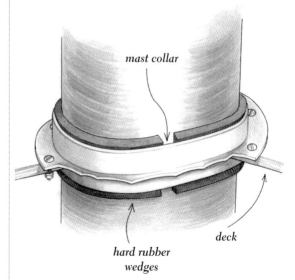

mast collar

hard rubber
wedges

deck

A good mast collar distributes load to the deck and has plenty of bearing surface for wedges.

Wedges placed on a furling mast, such as the Hood Stoway, should take into consideration the lack of strength that the spar has on the aft section. Support for this spar is critical along the sides where the sections are joined.

At least one company (Spartite) makes a pour-in-place wedge system that offers a custom fit. The mast must be properly positioned before the material is poured and must be left perfectly still for several days after pouring. This material, however, offers the ultimate in even loading and fit.

Finally, examine the mast boot. For years Hinckley has used a rubber or neoprene gasket material for the inner boot, over which is placed a canvas or Weblon cover to prevent sun exposure. This system works well and is easily repaired or replaced with the mast in place.

Alternative boots involve using a continuous loop or sleeve for a water seal. For some spars, a section of inner tube works. To install it, slide the boot, inside out and upside down, over the bottom of the spar. Then install a clamp at the top of the boot, pull the boot down over the clamp, and seal it around the mast collar.

Inspecting the Mast above the Deck

When inspecting the mast above the deck, there are several problem areas to look for. Following is a list of those areas and some troubleshooting tips.

- Corrosion of fittings and fasteners, wear on halyards and other lines from incorrect leads or sharp edges, and signs of cracking or bending in the spar or hardware are often problems anywhere above the deck.

- Inspect the gooseneck for wear and signs of movement. The gooseneck is a high-load area both for the fitting itself and for the mast around it. Immediately fix any problems you find in this area.

- Check all cleats and jammers. Are they securely attached? Do they have proper leads? These fittings, when properly installed to start with, rarely have problems, but their attach-

ment to the spar might become one if corrosion has been working at the interface between mast and fitting.

- Removing a cleat or other piece of hardware is often complicated by mast corrosion in the way of the stainless steel fasteners. Removal techniques include using a penetrating oil, an impact driver, or possibly applying heat. Reinstalling the hardware with an appropriate lubricant such as Tef-Gel and an insulator between the hardware and the spar will ease the removal process the next time it is required. A layer of Mylar, or even black electrical tape, will work as a hardware insulator.

- Look for loose connections on any hardware such as spinnaker pole tracks and internal wiring conduits. Spinnaker pole tracks and whisker pole attachment rings are, like goosenecks, high-load hardware. Catch any weakness before it causes an accident. Internal wiring conduit is great until it starts to detach itself from the mast wall. Most are connected with pop rivets and are not difficult to reattach if they have not dislocated too far. If the holes in the conduit have become too large to hold a rivet, you will need to redrill and install new rivets—but don't drill until after the wires are removed, because drilling the holes for new rivets is likely to damage wiring in the conduit. Attaching a messenger line to the wiring as you pull it out of the conduit will help pull the wires back in.

- At the spreaders, look carefully at their bases to ensure that they are well attached and have not distorted the mast tube. There may be designed-in tolerance at the spreader bases to allow them to realign with the load as the mast bends. There should be no elongation of holes, however, in the attachment of the spreader bases or any shroud tangs. The spreader bases and tips should be in good shape and provide a secure connection for the upper shroud or shrouds. Ensure that the spreader tips are adequately padded to prevent sail chafe. Additionally, make sure that all cotter pins and other sharp components are carefully taped or otherwise covered to prevent catching or abrading sails and lines. If you don't like the look of tape on spar fittings, try applying a glob of silicone or an equivalent compound over the ends of the cotter pins as chafe guard.

- Examine any lights at the spreaders as well as other equipment such as horns, radar, radar reflectors, and the like. Check for attachment, clean wire leads, and protection from and to the sails. On lights, look at the bulb sockets to ensure that they are not corroding inside.

- Examine the inner headstay, runner tangs, and all sheave boxes, again, taking care of

Silicone is an alternative to tape on cotter pins and other sharp mast fittings. Silicone holds in some areas where tape does not.

sharp areas and abraded surfaces. Try to rotate sheaves; clean, oil, or replace them as necessary. Ensure that there is not too much tolerance on the sides of sheaves—halyards can jam between the sheave and the sheave box, creating a real mess at just the wrong time. (This used to happen more when wire halyards were common because the smaller-diameter wire jammed easily. I remember going forward one night to shorten sail in the Gulf Stream. A jammed halyard made for a fun night in a stiffening breeze.)

- Examine the masthead. Look for signs of stress, including cracking or elongation of holes in brackets. The sheave operation and fit should be examined as it was on lower fittings. Check for a smooth lead and well-rounded edges on all halyard entrances into the mast. If possible, check the lead of wiring to electronics and lighting to ensure that it is not abraded by halyards as the wires pass to the top of the spar. Is it working and secure?

- Look at the masthead lights and electronics. Test the wind sensors for free operation. Look at the connectors for all electronics and check mounting bases for antennas and other bracketing. If the spar is out of the boat, test the mast lighting with a small 12-volt battery. A motorcycle battery is small and handy, but a standard automobile battery will do.

- Look at the arrangement used to hold the axles for the masthead sheaves. Examine any flag or spinnaker halyard blocks for wear and smooth operation.

When finished at the top with the spar inspection, work back down again, checking the running and standing rigging.

Inspecting the Rigging

The mast may be the tall and majestic part of the rigging, but unless your boat has an unstayed spar, it is not much good without the standing rigging—and no large spar is useful without running rigging that is in good condition. Checking out your rigging is as important as the spar inspection.

Creating a Double-Ended Mainsheet

For those boats with travelers aft of the helms and a mainsheet winch on the cabintop, sailing shorthanded can be frustrating and unnecessarily awkward. John Melchner, owner of yawl Jocar, has offered a simple solution by rigging a double-ended mainsheet. John writes,

"In place of the old lower fiddle block, I added one with a becket and a cam cleat. Now I can control the mainsheet from either end. I like to use the cam cleat since it is much closer at hand and faster. If we have more crew, or heavy air, I use the winch."

- Examine from end to end each piece of standing rigging, whether rod or wire, paying particular attention to cracks or other damage to terminals, broken or damaged strands (in wire rigging), and cuts or sharp bends (in rod rigging).

- Both swaged and hand-assembled terminals are reliable pieces of gear when well installed. They do, though, occasionally need to be replaced. Often the first sign of deterioration will be hairline cracks along the body of the terminal. Check carefully for these at each connection. Using a colored dye such as Dykem, which is a machinist's marking dye, is helpful. The dye is wiped on and highlights small cracks, as well as excess pitting.

- Water migrating into the terminals will create problems. Look carefully at wire-to-swaged terminal connections on the lower end of stays and shrouds, where water can collect, to spot any signs of rusty cable in the small voids within the terminal.

- Look for signs of strain—such as reduction of wire or rod diameter due to stretching—or slipping of the wire at the terminal.

- Standing rigging is not inexpensive but, when in doubt about a piece's condition, have an expert examine it, have it magnafluxed (to show cracks), or replace it. It is easy to replace rigging when around a yard or rigger, but it's a different story when offshore or at a remote anchorage. Consider carrying a spare piece of standing rigging wire capable of handling the highest load (even if you have rod rigging),

along with spare terminals that may be field installed. Both Norseman and Sta-Lok fittings fill the bill. Learn how to install the fitting before you face an emergency.

- Turnbuckles need to be lubricated and moved enough to know that they are operating. Ensure that pins are in place and that they are covered to protect damage to lines or ankles. A set of turnbuckle boots is a worthwhile investment for protecting these critical pieces of equipment.

- Chafing is the big problem to look for when inspecting running rigging. If you found rough areas when you inspected the spar, chances are good that you will find damage to some of the running rigging. As with the standing rigging, go over each piece, foot by foot. Where wire is used, look for dangerous wire hooks (often called "meat hooks") that break away from the main bundle and tear up everything from sails to hands. If a break is evident, replace that piece of rigging.

- Examine splices for tightness and wear. As line ages the splices may enlarge and thus not fit as well in sheave boxes, resulting in acceleration of chafe. Again, if in doubt, replace it. The old line may be fine for some other uses.

- Another small chore to undertake while examining the lines is to replace line whipping before old work comes off and the line end unravels. Some people whip the end with twine; others use heat shrink.

Once again, the rule is to catch the problem before it becomes too far gone. Preventive maintenance is the key.

Installing Hardware on Aluminum Spars

Somewhere along the line, most boatowners decide to add a cleat, jammer, winch, or block to their spar. Most of the hardware, such as cleats or jammers, will fit directly on the spar. Other equipment, such as winches or blocks, may require a mounting base to fit them to the spar shape. Here are some thoughts on mounting mast hardware.

Carefully position the hardware. Look not only at the line leads for the equipment to be mounted, but also its impact on other leads. For example, placing a flag halyard cleat above a winch to keep it clear of the lower cleats might look like a good idea at first, but it might foul another halyard lead when the winch is used for some collateral duty. Don't forget to think ahead to future upgrades—allow space for additional equipment you might add. For example, if jammers are in your future plans, leave room for them to be installed above the winches.

Avoid overloading a spar section with equipment right at the gooseneck, which takes a lot of strain. Perforating it with fasteners doesn't help its strength. The same holds true in other areas. Try not to align hardware in such a fashion that the holes create lines of weakness around the tube.

Use masking tape for layout and installation preparation work to avoid scratching the spar. Remember, after drilling and before installation, to remove the tape. Not only do you not want it left under the hardware, but most masking tape is hard to remove after it has been exposed to the elements for just a short time.

Use the appropriate drill for tapped holes. "Close enough" is not going to do it. Mast walls are relatively thin, and the threads cut by the tap must have optimum depth. If the tap calls for a letter drill, get one—don't just use the closest size you have.

Drill the holes carefully. Remember, there may be conduit, lines, or wires inside the spar. If you are concerned about controlling the drill, use a drill stop to help keep the drill bit from plunging as it pushes through the inside of the spar.

Install an insulator between the spar and the hardware. Mylar, or other plastic, as mentioned before, works well.

Install the fasteners with a good-quality anti-sieze compound such as Tef-Gel.

When you have to make a flat space on the spar to mount a winch or block, the easiest thing to do is to contact the spar manufacturer and determine if contoured castings exist for the mast section. These need, of course, to fit both the spar shape and the hardware footprint. If a preformed pad is not available, you might be able to have one custom cut from an aluminum disk. Personally, I prefer a bent stainless steel pad. The hardware can be prefit to the pad and then the pad fit to the spar. Use plenty of fasteners to hold the pad. Remember, you should at least equal the original hardware fasteners in number and size—spacing the equipment off the spar slightly, you have increased the load on the mast wall. Pads may be drilled for a winch base and the winch fasteners installed right through the pad base into the spar. Install insulation between the aluminum spar and a stainless base if using this method.

Another upgrade for a spar is making and

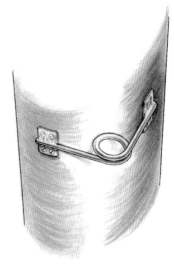

Stainless steel rod fairleads can stop halyard chafe on spars with external halyards.

installing fairleads for external halyards. Seen less and less as internal halyards have become common, stout wire fairleads served well for years and can be made in any minimally equipped shop. Use ⅛-inch-diameter stainless steel rod (preferably 316 or 304 alloy) and wrap it around a rod or small pipe to get at least one full turn and sufficient legs to hold the loop off the spar. Grind the ends of the legs flat so the edges of the fastener screws will not stick out beyond the rod and catch lines or sails.

Special Consideration for Carbon Fiber Spars

The maintenance required for the newer carbon fiber spars is basically the same as for aluminum spars—with one difference. These composite spars are well engineered and incorporate local reinforcement to allow for attachment of fittings. The application of metal fittings to the spar usually presents no particular problems, and corrosion should be much less of a concern. These reinforced areas should be carefully inspected to ensure that chafe has not weakened them and that there are no signs of cracks.

The maintenance suggestions from Goetz Marine Technology (GMT) indicate that all loaded areas, including the masthead, tangs, winch bases, and mast butt, need to be checked for cracks, crushing, or abrasion. If cracks are found, contact the manufacturer. The only exception they point out is that a small vertical crack in the filler between the aluminum and carbon is acceptable. If in doubt, call the manufacturer.

Basic Electric Principles and Procedures

The following information may be helpful for those who need some instruction on basic electrical repair procedures.

Marine Wire

Marine wire should always be multistrand cable. Solid or single-strand cable should not be used because it will not take the vibration found in marine applications. In all cases, tinned wiring is preferred for its corrosion resistance.

Conductor Sizes for 3% Drop in Voltage

Length of Conductor from Source of Current to Device and Back to Source (Feet)

TOTAL CURRENT ON CIRCUIT IN AMPS	10	15	20	25	30	40	50	60	70	80	90	100	110	120	130	140	150	160	170
12 Volts — 3% Drop Wire Sizes (gage) — Based on Minimum CM Area																			
5	18	16	14	12	12	10	10	10	8	8	8	6	6	6	6	6	6	6	6
10	14	12	10	10	10	8	6	6	6	6	4	4	4	4	2	2	2	2	2
15	12	10	10	8	8	6	6	6	4	4	2	2	2	2	2	1	1	1	1
20	10	10	8	6	6	6	4	4	2	2	2	2	1	1	1	0	0	0	2/0
25	10	8	6	6	6	4	4	2	2	2	1	1	0	0	0	2/0	2/0	2/0	3/0
30	10	8	6	6	4	4	2	2	1	1	0	0	0	2/0	2/0	3/0	3/0	3/0	3/0
40	8	6	6	4	4	2	2	1	0	0	2/0	2/0	3/0	3/0	3/0	4/0	4/0	4/0	4/0
50	6	6	4	4	2	2	1	0	2/0	2/0	3/0	3/0	4/0	4/0	4/0				
60	6	4	4	2	2	1	0	2/0	3/0	3/0	4/0	4/0	4/0						
70	6	4	2	2	1	0	2/0	3/0	3/0	4/0	4/0								
80	6	4	2	2	1	0	3/0	3/0	4/0	4/0									
90	4	2	2	1	0	2/0	3/0	4/0	4/0										
100	4	2	2	1	0	2/0	3/0	4/0											

(continued)

24 Volts—3% Drop Wire Sizes (gage)—Based on Minimum CM Area

Total Current in Amps	10	15	20	25	30	40	50	60	70	80	90	100	110	120	130	140	150	160	170
5	18	18	18	16	16	14	12	12	12	10	10	10	10	10	8	8	8	8	8
10	18	16	14	12	12	10	10	10	8	8	8	6	6	6	6	6	6	6	6
15	16	14	12	12	10	10	8	8	6	6	6	6	6	4	4	4	4	4	2
20	14	12	10	10	10	8	6	6	6	6	4	4	4	4	2	2	2	2	2
25	12	12	10	10	8	6	6	6	4	4	4	4	2	2	2	2	2	2	1
30	12	10	10	8	8	6	6	4	4	4	2	2	2	2	2	1	1	1	1
40	10	10	8	6	6	6	4	4	2	2	2	2	1	1	1	0	0	0	2/0
50	10	8	6	6	6	4	4	2	2	2	1	1	0	0	0	2/0	2/0	2/0	3/0
60	10	8	6	6	4	4	2	2	1	1	0	0	0	2/0	2/0	3/0	3/0	3/0	3/0
70	8	6	6	4	4	2	2	1	1	0	0	2/0	2/0	3/0	3/0	3/0	3/0	4/0	4/0
80	8	6	6	4	4	2	2	1	0	0	2/0	2/0	3/0	3/0	3/0	4/0	4/0	4/0	4/0
90	8	6	4	4	2	2	1	0	0	2/0	2/0	3/0	3/0	4/0	4/0	4/0	4/0	4/0	
100	6	6	4	4	2	2	1	0	2/0	2/0	3/0	3/0	4/0	4/0	4/0				

Table © 1990 American Boat and Yacht Council, Inc.

Conductor Sizes for 10% Drop in Voltage

Length of Conductor from Source of Current to Device and Back to Source (Feet)

12 Volts—10% Drop Wire Sizes (gage)—Based on Minimum CM Area

Total Current in Amps	10	15	20	25	30	40	50	60	70	80	90	100	110	120	130	140	150	160	170
5	18	18	18	18	18	16	16	14	14	14	12	12	12	12	12	10	10	10	10
10	18	18	16	16	14	14	12	12	10	10	10	10	8	8	8	8	8	8	6
15	18	16	14	14	12	12	10	10	8	8	8	8	8	6	6	6	6	6	6
20	16	14	14	12	12	10	10	8	8	8	6	6	6	6	6	6	4	4	4
25	16	14	12	12	10	10	8	8	6	6	6	6	6	4	4	4	4	4	2
30	14	12	12	10	10	8	8	6	6	6	6	4	4	4	4	2	2	2	2
40	14	12	10	10	8	8	6	6	6	4	4	4	2	2	2	2	2	2	2
50	12	10	10	8	8	6	6	4	4	4	2	2	2	2	2	1	1	1	1
60	12	10	8	8	6	6	4	4	2	2	2	2	2	1	1	1	0	0	0
70	10	8	8	6	6	6	4	2	2	2	2	1	1	1	0	0	0	2/0	2/0
80	10	8	8	6	6	4	4	2	2	2	1	1	0	0	0	2/0	2/0	2/0	2/0
90	10	8	6	6	6	4	2	2	2	1	1	0	0	0	2/0	2/0	2/0	3/0	3/0
100	10	8	6	6	4	4	2	2	1	1	0	0	0	2/0	2/0	2/0	3/0	3/0	3/0

24 Volts—10% Drop Wire Sizes (gage)—Based on Minimum CM Area

Total Current in Amps	10	15	20	25	30	40	50	60	70	80	90	100	110	120	130	140	150	160	170
5	18	18	18	18	18	18	18	18	16	16	16	16	14	14	14	14	14	14	12
10	18	18	18	18	18	16	16	14	14	14	12	12	12	12	12	10	10	10	10
15	18	18	18	16	16	14	14	12	12	12	10	10	10	10	10	8	8	8	8
20	18	18	16	16	14	14	12	12	10	10	10	10	8	8	8	8	8	8	6
25	18	16	16	14	14	12	12	10	10	10	8	8	8	8	8	6	6	6	6
30	18	16	14	14	12	12	10	10	10	8	8	8	8	6	6	6	6	6	6
40	16	14	14	12	12	10	10	8	8	8	6	6	6	6	6	4	4	4	4
50	16	14	12	12	10	10	8	8	6	6	6	6	4	4	4	4	4	2	2
60	14	12	12	10	10	8	8	6	6	6	6	4	4	4	4	2	2	2	2
70	14	12	10	10	8	8	6	6	6	4	4	4	2	2	2	2	2	2	
80	14	12	10	10	8	8	6	6	6	4	4	4	2	2	2	2	2	2	
90	12	10	10	8	8	6	6	6	4	4	4	2	2	2	2	2	1	1	
100	12	10	10	8	8	6	6	4	4	4	2	2	2	2	2	1	1	1	1

Table © 1990 American Boat and Yacht Council, Inc.

Wiring Color Codes

Color	Use
Green, or green w/yellow stripe(s)	DC Grounding Conductors
Black or Yellow	DC Negative Conductors
Red	DC Positive Conductors

Table © 1990 American Boat and Yacht Council, Inc.

Engine and Accessory Wiring Color Codes

Color	Item	Use
Yellow w/Red Stripe (YR)	Starting Circuit	Starting Switch to Solenoid
Brown/Yellow Stripe (BY) or Yellow (Y)—see note	Bilge Blowers	Fuse or Switch to Blowers
Dark Gray (Gy)	Navigation Lights	Fuse or Switch to Lights
	Tachometer	Tachometer Sender to Gauge
Brown (Br)	Generator Armature	Generator Armature to Regulator
	Alternator Charge Light	Generator Terminal/Alternator Auxiliary Terminal to Light to Regulator
	Pumps	Fuse or Switch to Pumps
Orange (O)	Accessory Feed	Ammeter to Alternator or Generator Output and Accessory Fuses or Switches
	Accessory Feeds	Distribution Panel to Accessory Switch
Purple (Pu)	Ignition	Ignition Switch to Coil and Electrical Instruments
	Instrument Feed	Distribution Panel to Electric Instruments
Dark Blue	Cabin and Instrument Lights	Fuse or Switch to Lights
Light Blue (Lt Bl)	Oil Pressure	Oil Pressure Sender to Gauge
Tan	Water Temperature	Water Temperature Sender to Gauge
Pink (Pk)	Fuel Gauge	Fuel Gauge Sender to Gauge
Green/Stripe (G/x) (Except (G/Y)	Tilt down and/or Trim in	Tilt and/or Trim Circuits
Blue/Stripe (Bl/x)	Tilt up and/or Trim out	Tilt and/or Trim Circuits

Note: *If yellow is used for DC negative, blower must be brown with a yellow stripe.*
Table © 1990 American Boat and Yacht Council, Inc.

Using a Multimeter

One of the most valuable electrical diagnostic tools you can keep aboard is a multimeter (volt-ohm meter). This common meter has the ability to measure current (amperes), voltage, and resistance (ohms). It is inexpensive and does not take up much room. I strongly urge all boatowners to keep one aboard and to become familiar with its operation. A great addition to a multimeter is a pair of extension cables or alligator clips to help hold the probes in place.

The meter comes with a useful reference book, but here are a few additional tips that I've adapted from Randy Kaeding's book *DC Electronics*, published by the Heath Company:

Measuring Current

Whenever you are measuring voltage or current with a multimeter, place the test probes carefully to avoid the possibility of shock. When measuring current, make sure that the ammeter you are using is heavy enough for the job. If in doubt about the circuit you are testing, set the meter for an amperage range above the expected range. Here is a good procedure to follow:

1. Remove power from the circuit to be tested.

2. Break the circuit at the point where the current is to be measured.

3. Connect the meter to the circuit to be measured, observing polarity.

4. Reapply the power and measure the current.

Measuring Voltage

Voltage is typically easier to measure than current because you do not need to break the circuit. Follow this procedure:

1. Set the meter to a voltage scale that is appropriate for the circuit to be measured. If in doubt, set the meter for a higher scale. Set the voltage type to AC or DC as appropriate.

2. Touch the two leads of the meter to the two points to be measured. This is often between a source and an appliance or across an appliance's terminals. Be sure to observe polarity.

3. Read the voltage rise or drop.

Measuring Resistance

When measuring resistance it is important to remove all power from the circuit being tested.

1. Remove power from the circuit and, if necessary, remove the component to be tested from the circuit.

2. Touch the two probes together and set the "o" resistance value if necessary. This is especially important if any probe extensions are being used.

3. Place the test probes at either extreme of the part to be tested—for example, the terminals of a light fixture or ends of a wire.

4. Read the resistance. Start with a low scale (little resistance) and increase as required.

You can test continuity in similar fashion to resistance. If a wire has infinite resistance, it no doubt has a break or bad connection.

The Shipboard Tool Kit

One of my memories of my father is of our trips to the store to pick out tools for his new boats. The tool salesman at the Sears store must have thought Dad was a gift from heaven. Each new boat seemed to require a new set of tools. There is no question that some of this has rubbed off on me, as tool shopping remains one of my favorite pastimes.

A well-stocked shipboard tool kit is a must. Ashore, you need only run to the store and pick up what you need. When you have a breakdown at sea, however, being without adequate tools becomes a bigger problem. It may be a long row to your local hardware store.

You must select tools carefully. Most boatowners are pressed for space. Have you ever gone aboard a boat and found almost every drawer packed full of tools and spare parts? Is your boat like this? Certainly, the owner is striving to be prepared, but having to live out of a duffel bag for cruising could wear thin on guests. Multiple-use tools and well-planned storage help keep the onboard "shop" in control.

Each boatowner has a different set of needs; different equipment has different tool requirements. For example, the growing use of metric fasteners may require obtaining both English and metric wrenches. It is incumbent upon the owner to review equipment manuals and determine what special tools are required. There are, however, some tools that are universally needed; these are listed below. Throughout this appendix, the tools that appear in italics are ones that I consider to be essential aboard a boat.

Finally, one important word of advice: Buy your tools from a reputable supplier who sells quality products and who will stand behind them.

Toolboxes

Occasionally, a boat's designer will incorporate a built-in toolbox or drawer. These are nice, but I like the flexibility of moving the toolbox with me when I work. Inevitably, when I get way into an engine room, I discover I need a smaller wrench or a different screwdriver. If my toolbox is within reach, I am ahead of the game.

Plastic toolboxes are great; the cases are noncorrosive and are less likely than metal boxes to scar the finish on your boat. If you already have a metal toolbox, glue a piece of carpet on the bottom and up the sides to protect your boat. If space is a concern, two small boxes might work better than one large one.

Another alternative is to store tools in a canvas tool bag, available in all sorts of sizes and shapes and which may even be custom made. Tool bags are lightweight, fit in oddly shaped compartments, and allow some air circulation around wet tools.

Hand Tools

Start your collection with a good complement of hand tools. Buy quality tools, and they will serve you well.

Screwdrivers

- Every boat must have a set of *straight-blade screwdrivers*. At a minimum, keep on board three or four in the following sizes: ⅛ inch, ³⁄₁₆ inch, ¼ inch, and ⅜ inch. A large screwdriver with a big blade and long shaft is helpful for big jobs as well. A short, stubby screwdriver with a medium-sized blade is a good add-on.
- *Phillips-head screwdrivers* come in several tip sizes and lengths. Two of them from size 1 to 3 would be good; a 0-sized Phillips-head is good for very small work.
- Some marine equipment requires special screwdrivers such as Torx, Robertson, and Clutch head (all of which are available from Stanley). They fit screws that have sockets on their ends and are used where there is extra torque needed or where there is danger of the screwdriver slipping.
- An offset screwdriver with one slotted end and one Phillips-head end is handy for fasteners that are difficult to access.
- If space is of paramount importance, check out screwdrivers with interchangeable tips.

Pliers

- *Slip-joint pliers* are the basic pliers that everyone knows. They are available in several sizes, but a good pair of 6- or 8-inch pliers is a must. I like the kind with the plastic grips as well. Arc-joint pliers (also known as channel-lock or waterpump pliers) are terrific for getting a hold on larger fittings.
- Vise-Grip locking pliers are a good third choice for the tool kit. They'll give you a firm grip on hard-to-hold fittings. Use Vise-Grips only when a conventional wrench of the appropriate size won't work—they tend to scratch or tear up the fitting they are attached to.
- Needlenose pliers and diagonal cutters are also good to have aboard. These tools are a bit more specialized, but they both have their uses: Needlenose pliers are great for removing cotter pins, and diagonal cutters, or "dikes," are excellent wire cutters.

Wirecutter, Crimper, and Stripper

- Following close on the heels of pliers is their cousin, the wirecutter/stripper. This tool is commonly sold with an assortment of electrical end fittings that make a good start to your electrical spare-parts kit.

Wrenches

- A good set of *combination wrenches* (box on one end and open on the other) is a must. You will use them again and again. Buy quality wrenches. As mentioned, you may need both English and metric sets. I usually keep a small set with short lengths (¹³⁄₆₄ to ⅜ inch), which commonly come in an ignition wrench set, and a regular set with sizes of ¼ or ⁵⁄₁₆ inch up to 1 inch. Owners of boats with larger engines will probably need additional larger wrenches as well.
- *Allen wrenches* are a must. The sets that fold into a metal handle are handy. This type is the only set I have owned that is not missing the most important sizes within days of purchase.
- Keep a couple of adjustable wrenches aboard. I like a small wrench (4 inches) and a medium-sized one of about 8 or 10 inches. Also, a good-sized pipe wrench of 12 inches or more is handy.
- For some boats, an additional short-handled stuffing-box wrench can come in handy. These wrenches are designed to get into small spaces and handle the locking and packing nuts on a traditional stuffing box.
- Do not forget to keep a good socket set or two aboard. I have found that a smaller set,

with a ¼-inch drive and perhaps 10 sockets ranging from ³⁄₁₆ to ⁷⁄₁₆ inch, and a larger set with a ½-inch drive and sockets from ⅜ to ¾ inch are helpful. Include in the socket kit an extension piece for both drives and perhaps a universal joint.

Taps and Dies

- A modest set of taps and dies may make a big difference in a repair job. They do not take a lot of room but will earn their way when a bolt is cross-threaded or when a stripped hole needs to be moved or drilled and tapped slightly larger.

Hammers

- A 16-ounce claw hammer can be handy, but a soft-face hammer or mallet is perhaps more important when you need to pound on a stuck fitting.

Some specialized hand tools—such as these bent reefing tools used to clean out old caulking in a teak deck—can be made from old screwdrivers.

Saws

- A hacksaw with a supply of blades can be a lifesaver. I have used one for everything from cutting bolts and rigging to cutting wood or fiberglass. A hacksaw may not be quite the right tool for most needs, but it will often save the day in an emergency.
- A keyhole saw with an assortment of blades is also handy. It can be used, for example, to start a small hole (drilled) and enlarge it to allow a hose to pass through a bulkhead.

Plane

- A wood plane may seem a bit specialized for a boat's tool kit, but it is great to have when a door or cabin sole hatch binds up. A small hand plane is all that is required.

Oil Filter Wrench

- The new spin-on filters are great—until you cannot get one off. I have tried all kinds of tricks to loosen them, including coupling my belt with a long screwdriver as a makeshift

Having the proper hand and power tools aboard is a must. A drill, preferably a battery-powered one, is probably the most important power tool to obtain.

filter wrench. Buy a filter wrench or wrenches of the appropriate size. You'll be glad you did.

Chisels

- Two types of chisels are useful aboard a boat. The common wood type is handy for adjusting hinges and getting into small corners to remove wood. You may want one with a small (¼-inch) blade and one with a larger (¾- or 1-inch) blade. Note that a cheap wood chisel will lose its sharp edge quickly. A coal chisel is handy when used with a hammer to snap off rusted bolts and to cut through fiberglass.

Files

- Files are good for sharpening chisels, scrapers, and saws. They also help when making

minor modifications to metal brackets. A small flat file and a multiple-surface file are good selections.

Wire brush

- Use a small wire brush to clean files and remove rust from metal parts. Wire brushes will rust, so be sure to store wire brushes in a dry place (such as a bag).

Paint and Varnish Brushes

- See Chapters 4 through 7 for recommendations on these tools.

Knives

- A *rigging knife* is a must. It is necessary for splicing work and should be considered a safety tool, particularly on sailboats. When at sea, keep one in your pocket at all times.
- A razor knife with a replaceable blade is handy for quick, sharp cuts. Keep a supply of blades

with the knife—but keep them in a plastic bag because they rust quickly. A razor knife will come in handy for cutting gaskets and making other precision cuts.

- A putty knife is handy to help clean up bedding compound. It can also help remove old paint if you don't have a scraper. One with a 1-inch-wide blade that is reasonably stiff is probably the handiest.

Scrapers

- A good-quality, small hand scraper is a great tool to help remove dried paint. Use it with a sharp blade for clean, easy work. Keep your file handy to maintain a sharp edge on the blade.

Awl

- An awl is great for marking metal and for help in aligning holes in hard-to-see places.

Clamps

- I have found that a couple of modest-sized clamps are wonderful assistants when you need to hold something to drill or glue. Both "C" clamps and small bar clamps will find a use aboard most boats.

Magnet

- A magnet is great to have around when you drop things into the deepest part of the bilge. Some are available on an extendable shaft. A magnet on a string will serve almost as well.

Measuring Tools

- A decent *tape measure* is the basic measuring tool needed on a boat. It need not be a deluxe model, but it should be at least 10 feet long and have some sort of coating on the steel blade.

Power Tools

Power tools will not be of much assistance offshore unless you have an inverter or generator, but when you're at a dock or hauled out they speed up the work. These may not need to

be kept aboard, but they will simplify your boat chores.

Drills

- A hand drill has always been important to have aboard. Today, battery-powered drills have taken over and, on boats with inverters, they can even be charged at sea. For sheer drilling power, though, it is hard to beat a standard electric drill. But if you are looking for simplicity and reliability, stick with a hand drill.

  When buying drill bits, buy a set that comes in a plastic case. Start with small sizes and have a selection of up to at least ½ inch. Good, high-speed steel bits are a must, and learning how to sharpen them is not a bad idea. When you have to drill metal, the bits will dull quickly.

  Along with drill bits, a screwdriver tip or two, suitable for use with your drill, is handy when disassembling equipment or cabinetry with a lot of screws.

Palm Sander

- If you intend to do your own painting and varnishing, you really need a palm sander. They are inexpensive and are available with both round and rectangular sanding pads. We have a number of Makita sanders around the shop and could not live without them.

Sabre Saw

- The sabre saw is handy for the do-it-yourselfer. Along with a selection of wood, metal, and fiberglass cutting blades, you can take care of 90 percent of the cutting chores on the boat. Lots of manufacturers make sabre saws; buy a good-quality one that feels right.

Miscellaneous

Lights

- A *flashlight* is perhaps an obvious choice of gear, but I have been aboard boats without them. Keeping several styles aboard is a good idea, as is attaching a long lanyard to a strong flashlight. You can then hook the light to a pulpit for shorthanded harbor navigation, or to a fitting in the engine room to give you an extra hand as well as extra light.

- A trouble light is a great tool. The fluorescent-wand type is great, but a standard bulb type is okay if it is well protected by a wire cage. These are mostly 110V and may not be of use at sea unless you have an inverter. For sheer illumination, though, they are hard to beat.

- A battery-powered light with a wide beam is helpful for repairs at sea. I have duct taped these lights to just about everything aboard a boat at one time or another.

- Those small, thin flashlights that operate on a couple of AA batteries are handy. I keep one in my shaving kit. It has seen lots of emergency use.

Battery Maintenance Tools

- A lifting strap for batteries and a battery terminal cleaner are worthwhile tools. Getting a heavy battery out of a deep battery box can be nearly impossible without a good lifting strap.

- Use battery terminal cleaner regularly. A small amount of corrosion on a terminal surface means a lot of resistance in the battery system.

- Owners of conventional lead-acid batteries find a hydrometer and a special battery filler useful. The hydrometer registers the battery charge by measuring the specific gravity of the acid. The filler has a special spout that automatically fills the battery to the level indicator without overflowing.

Multimeter

- The multiple meter (also voltmeter or volt-ohm meter) is the basic tool for electrical problem diagnostics. Buy a medium- to good-quality unit and learn to use it. See Appendix I for information on how to use a multimeter.

Cable Cutters (for sailboats)

- I have never lost the mast of a large sailboat at sea, but I have lost the spar in a twenty-six footer while teaching a sailing class. Luckily, everything was light enough to lift.

  A large cable cutter is very important to the dismasted sailor at sea as the rig is trying to smash through the hull. A hacksaw would be too slow, and removing the rigging clevis pins to release the mast (a system I have been told has been used with success) may be all but impossible if too much gear is in the way.

Other Bits and Pieces

- Another handy tool is a plastic spreader for fiberglass resins. It can also be used to apply wide tape and to scrape off bedding without the damage to the surface that a metal scraper will cause.

- Sailors should stock a sailor's palm, needles, and waxed thread. Basic, functional sail repairs are a must and are not difficult. If I can do them with a minimum of blood loss, anyone can. See Chapter 21 for more sail repair supplies.

- Carry a hard, wood block to use as a cushion when hammering.

- A small mirror with an extendable handle is a great aid in areas that are hard to reach and see in tight engine rooms.

- A compass is handy when laying out a rounded corner or circle for cutting.

Safety Gear

- Carry heavy nitrile gloves as well as the lightweight disposable ones available at drugstores. Use the heavy gloves when you are working with acids and bleaches. The lighter gloves make paint cleanup easier.

- Keep a good pair of safety glasses with side protection aboard and wear them around a hot engine. If something blows, they may make the difference between whether you see again or not.

Neil Rabinowitz

- Disposable dust masks are cheap and good to use when sanding.
- Many paints require the use of a properly fitted respirator, and it should be used with appropriate filters. Do not use these coatings without a respirator and the other protection called for by the manufacturer.
- The invention of the disposable paper suit has made the process of sanding and painting bottoms a lot neater. They are available with hoods and boots. I recommend keeping one aboard.

Spares and Other Materials

A complete spare-parts kit is important to the coastal cruiser as well as the offshore sailor; it's extremely important to give careful thought to building your supply of spare parts. Here are some ideas for beginning your spare parts kit. Consider this a starter list, not a definitive list.

Lubricants

- Moisture-displacing sprays such as CRC or WD-40 are wonderful to have aboard. You will use them again and again for a multitude of lubricating and cleaning jobs.
- Keep a supply of penetrating oil on board to help with hard-to-release fittings. On the other side of the coin, keep some Loctite aboard to help make a fitting less likely to release.
- Heavy grease is necessary for many pumps and windlasses.
- Special grease is available for lubricating sailboat winches.

Tape

- Everyone has a favorite duct tape story. Buy a roll, keep it on board, and use it.

- Rigging tape is important for sailors. You will use it to cover cotter pins and other rough areas that might catch sails and lines.
- Sailors also need sail repair tape. This usually-lightweight tape will slow a sail tear, and when used in conjunction with stitching will provide a passable major sail repair.
- A variety of masking tapes is good for paint and varnish touch-up chores.

Gasket Material

- Gasket material is important for replacing seals when equipment has to be taken apart and the gasket is destroyed in the process. It is impossible to stock all the gaskets that might be needed, but an offshore cruiser should carry a set for the engine(s); spare flat-gasket material and a tube of Liquid Gasket are also helpful.

Wooden plugs

- Stock up on wooden plugs, one to fit each size through-hull on the boat. It is rare that a break in a fitting can't be shut off to stop the supply of water, but if this does occur, it can be fatal. Marine stores now sell bags of assorted soft-wood plugs. They are inexpensive and well worth having aboard.

Glue

- Glue is important for fixing the occasional break or crack. Newer epoxy glues are handy and will adhere to almost everything.

Patching Epoxy

- Underwater patching epoxy is very thick and may be applied underwater. It may be the answer for small holes in a hull or deck.

Sealants

- Carrying a collection of sealants (small tubes are adequate) is a good idea. Select sealants carefully, however, because some are not for use below the waterline. Others bond so strongly that fittings need to be chiseled apart later.

Bronze Wool

- Bronze wool is great for cleaning tough areas on teak decks and does not rust like steel wool. It is very abrasive and should be used sparingly.

Varnish

- Carry varnish to touch up spots that are weathering quickly or have been damaged.

Fiberglass Polish and Wax

- Keep enough cleaner/polish and wax aboard to take care of any area that gets stained and needs to be cleaned and waxed for protection.

Rags

- Clean rags are important if you will be doing any refinishing aboard. They also help with cleanup around the engine room.

Oil Absorbers

- Disposable diapers used as oil absorbers under the engine can make cleanup of the oil drip pan much easier.

Paper Towels

- Paper towels are wonderful for just about every shipboard cleanup chore where a rag is not required.

Spare Belts

- It may be hard to find spare belts for your particular equipment in remote ports. And, of course, the belts will fail at the least convenient time. Not having a spare belt aboard often means not having an engine.

Lube Oil

- Keep enough lube oil on hand for at least one full oil change; a bit extra would be a good idea. You may find that the oil you have been using is not available at another marina, and it is generally not a good idea to mix oil types when topping off the engine oil.

Filters

- Carry spare oil and fuel filters. Like belts, specific filter elements may not be available when the filters need to be changed. Remember to obtain elements for both the primary and secondary fuel filters if you have more than one in a line.

Spare Zincs

- Carry at least one of each type of zinc that is used on your boat. Look at both the externally mounted zincs and the pencil zincs used in the engine and generator. Odd-sized zincs can be difficult to locate.

Plumbing Fittings

- You will need extra plumbing fittings (particularly when plastic fittings are used) to replace cracked fittings when trying to stop a leak.

Fastener Kit

- Build a fastener kit including screws, cotter pins, bolts, nuts, and washers. Store them in a plastic organizer of some sort. You will go to this kit again and again while making repairs.

Electrical Parts Kit

- Crimp-on wire fittings are the foundation of an electrical repair kit. Keep an assortment handy. You may wish to buy a crimp tool that comes with a fitting assortment to get your collection started.

- Include spare bulbs for both interior and exterior fixtures in the kit; keep a selection of fuses for electronics and other equipment; and stock a small amount of wire.

Winch Spares

- Sailors should consider ordering and maintaining a supply of spare parts for their winches. The pawls and springs of winches are notorious for finding their way overboard when being cleaned and greased.

Index